REPUTATION

Reputation

What It Is and Why It Matters

Gloria Origgi

Translated by Stephen Holmes
and Noga Arikha

PRINCETON UNIVERSITY PRESS
PRINCETON AND OXFORD

Published by Princeton University Press,
41 William Street, Princeton, New Jersey 08540

In the United Kingdom: Princeton University Press, 6 Oxford Street, Woodstock, Oxfordshire OX20 1TR

press.princeton.edu

Jacket design by Michael Boland for thebolanddesignco.com

ISBN 978-0-691-17535-5
Library of Congress Control Number 2017953503

British Library Cataloging-in-Publication Data is available

This book has been composed in Adobe Text Pro and Gotham

Printed on acid-free paper. ∞

Printed in the United States of America

10 9 8 7 6 5 4 3 2 1

CONTENTS

PREFACE TO THE ENGLISH EDITION

> Reputation, reputation, reputation! Oh, I have lost my reputation! I have lost the immortal part of myself, and what remains is bestial.
>
> —*OTHELLO*, ACT 2, SCENE 3

Dismayed at having lost Othello's favor, Cassio repeats the word "reputation" three times. Reputations spread uncontrollably, are echoed back and forth, and reproduce themselves in the voices of others. This is why "the immortal part" of ourselves is also the most fragile and elusive. Iago, who secretly manipulates Cassio's reputation in order to destroy him, answers cynically that we should not worry about our reputations because they do not depend on us. Although we are constantly seeking to assure ourselves of the favorable opinion of others, our personal merit often has nothing to do with why we gain or lose our coveted good name.

Reputation is shrouded in mystery. The reasons it waxes or wanes and the criteria that define it as good or bad often appear fortuitous and arbitrary. Yet reputation is also ubiquitous. On the one hand, we care intensely about the opinion of others, sometimes to the point of committing irrational acts in a bootless effort to determine how others see us. On the other hand, we rely on reputation to guide our choice of doctors, newspapers, websites, and even ideas. It seems to insinuate itself into the most intimate recesses of our existence.

This book tries to explain why reputation is so important, personally and socially, as well as how it circulates, how it is transformed and distorted, and how it affects what others say about us. The book raises two fundamental philosophical questions about reputation. First: Can reputation be considered a rational motivation for action? What drives us to defend or improve or repair our reputation? And second: Can reputation be considered a rational justification in the acquisition of information? When, on the basis of reputation, we choose a doctor or a bottle of wine or adopt a point of view are we acting in a rational way?

In searching for answers to these theoretical questions, I have immersed myself in a variety of heterogeneous literatures, spanning virtually all the social sciences. The result is a distinctly "kaleidoscopic," not to say eclectic, approach to the topic. By piecing together the fragmentary and partial treatments of reputation that I have discovered in various social science disciplines (sociology, economics, anthropology, cognitive science, linguistics, and so forth), I have tried to give shape and substance to a highly elusive concept. The result is not a full-scale theory of reputation of the sort philosophers might ideally aspire to produce. It is something more modest, namely a theoretical analysis of the concept of reputation that I have anatomized and reconstructed with an eye on the various mechanisms that govern its functioning. In this sense, the book remains eminently philosophical. I have endeavored to make the conceptual analysis it contains somewhat less sterile by incorporating the findings of social science, as is proper in my own philosophical subdiscipline, social epistemology. Nor have I hesitated to make my theoretical arguments more vivid and comprehensible by the frequent resort to concrete examples drawn from imaginative literature and everyday life.

Admittedly, the methodological eclecticism of the following pages may try the patience of readers who feel more comfortable with theorizing that keeps within well-demarcated disciplinary boundaries. Moving from Proust to economic sociology or from Jane Austen to signaling theory may seem like an unnecessary form of mental gymnastics. It makes your head spin, but does it really take you anywhere?

Readers will judge. But I am convinced that the interdisciplinary approach taken in this book is an effective way of making philosophy into a fruitful discipline, in touch with the burning issues of our times and capable of contributing to the understanding and interpretation of the present by using all the conceptual tools that other sciences (as well as art and literature) make available.

This freedom to roam freely among various fields of knowledge, it should probably be said, is to some extent the result of my personal trajectory. An Italian who immigrated to France where I became immersed in Anglo-Saxon philosophy, I have spent my life straying across intellectual and disciplinary boundaries, often erected and defended by local prejudice and snobbery. My interest in reputation is also a side effect of this passion for trespassing.

It is also worth mentioning that the book before you is replete with quotes from a heterogeneous array of disciplinary cultures and countries. This deliberate pluralism of cited sources reflects my conviction that there is no one objective "ranking" of intellectual quality. It is only by accepting the cognitive diversity and cultural complexity of our world that we can come to see old problems with new eyes.

Chapter 1 introduces the idea of reputation as our social ego, a second self that guides our actions sometimes even against our interests. The management of our social self is a fundamental social and cognitive competence whose functioning I analyze and attempt to explain.

Chapter 2 is devoted to the theoretical approaches to reputation developed in the different branches of social science that adopt the theory of rational choice. The principal questions addressed are: Can reputation be seen as a rational strategy? And is it a means to other ends or an end in itself?

Chapter 3 deals with the communicative aspect of reputation, that is, how it circulates and through which social and linguistic mechanisms it can be stabilized. This is an important question because sometimes a reputation can be ephemeral while at other times it seems set in stone. Gossip, rumors, and informational cascades contribute to the background noise that characterizes the universal human discussion of who did what to whom.

Chapter 4 introduces a set of tools from the social sciences, including social capital theory, the theory of networks, and the sociology of hierarchies, to understand how the mechanisms designed to evaluate reputations function and what makes them reliable.

Chapter 5 contains a critical analysis of our faith in experts and a presentation of the many biases that influence and distort our perception of the reputation of others.

Chapter 6 is the most philosophical chapter in the book. It proposes replacing the idea of *homo economicus* as the ontologically fundamental unit of social science with the idea of *homo comparativus*. This involves the claim that reality can be perceived only through evaluative comparisons, eroding the traditional distinction between description and evaluation. In the course of the chapter I discuss and criticize other philosophical approaches that put symbolic values similar to reputation at the center of the analysis of human action, including the economy of esteem defended by Geoffrey Brennan and Philip Pettit and Anthony Appiah's theory of honor.

Chapters 7, 8, and 9 contain case studies of the way reputations are built in three special areas: the Web, the wine market, and the university. They examine the different systems for establishing and measuring reputations in these three areas and the unintended effects and distortions peculiar to each. An early draft of chapter 7 appeared in *Questions of Taste*, edited by Barry Smith (Oxford University Press, 2007), and an initial version of part of chapter 8 appeared in *Collective Wisdom*, edited by Hélène Landermore and Jon Elster (Cambridge University Press, 2012).

Finally, chapter 10 contains an attempt to understand the implications of my conception of reputation for our epistemic life and public decisions. If what is said about us and about the things around us is decisively important as I argue in this book, then the way we think about ourselves and our role as informed citizens must adapt to this transformation. In that case, we also need to develop new tools to govern our actions and the circulation of our opinions. This is one of the foremost challenges we face as we try, perhaps against the odds, to ensure the proper functioning of our fragile democracies in the years ahead.

ACKNOWLEDGMENTS

Like many books, this one condenses into a few pages hundreds of conversations, exchanges, debates about ideas, and life experiences. It is the cumulative result of a collective and collaborative process of reflection in which I have been passionately involved for more than seven years. I cannot thank here all those who played a role in this intellectual adventure, because the list would be too long. But I would like to retrace a few of the important stages leading up to this work and to thank those who have helped me make my way through them.

Thanks go first to Pasquale Pasquino, who, in 2007, organized a conference on reputation at the Olivetti Foundation in Rome. It was at this conference that a small group of philosophers, sociologists, and psychologists began a collective reflection on the issue. Barbara Carnevali, Jon Elster, Sandro Pizzorno, Dan Sperber, Diego Gambetta, and obviously Pasquale Pasquino himself have, in the intervening years, been constant partners in developing the ideas presented this book.

In 2011, I devoted my seminar at the Ecole des Hautes Etudes en Sciences Sociales in Paris to the question of reputation. My students as well as several colleagues invited to present their work greatly enriched my thinking. I would like especially to thank Pierre-Marie Chauvin, Lucien Karpik, Gianluca Manzo, Pierre-Michel Menger, André Orléan, and Philippe Rochat. A special thanks also goes to Ariel Colonomos for his ideas, advice, patience, and intelligence. Some of the contributions to the seminar appeared in *Communications*, no. 7 (2013), published by Seuil, of which I was the guest editor. I thank Nicole Lapierre and in particular Jocelyne Obama for supporting this project.

My stay at the Italian Academy for Advanced Studies at Columbia University in New York in 2013 allowed me to work under optimal conditions and to draft the first part of this book. I thank the director, David Freedberg, and colleagues and friends across the Atlantic who have taken the time to listen to my ideas, discuss them, correct them, and offer suggestions. This book would have been very different in the absence of many stimulating discussions with Philip Kitcher, Souleymane Bachir Diagne, Philip Pettit, Achille Varzi, Nadia Urbinati, Nassim Nicholas Taleb, and my eternal friend Martino Boffa, who initiated me into the mysteries of financial reputation, an exciting subject that I do not treat in this book but that I plan to focus on in the future.

Emanuele Coccia allowed me to discuss my ideas on reputation at the Ecole des Hautes Etudes en Sciences Sociales in a workshop titled "Celebrités, prestige, réputation: Grandeurs sociales en débat," which gathered together many researchers whose work has inspired me greatly, including Nathalie Heinich, Antoine Lilti, and, once again, Barbara Carnevali.

Animated exchanges with my friends, colleagues, and students around these issues and many others have allowed me to combine pleasure with work during all these years. I thank here, in no particular order, Astrid von Busekist, Alessandra Facchi, Judith Simon, Steven Shapin, Barry Smith, Julia Oskian, Carlo Invernizzi Accetti, Ophelia Deroy, Noga Arikha, Sandra Vial, Roberto Casati, Paul Egre, Amélie Faucheux, Hady Ba, Erik Olsson, Adélaïde de Lastic, Patrick Pharo, Michele di Francesco, Nicola Canessa, Giulia Piredda, Pascal

Engel, Andrei Poama, Simona Morini, Caroline Ibos, Nilufer Gole, Bruno Karsenti, Giovanni Ramello, Najib Hamadi, Valeria Pizzini-Gambetta, Serena Ciranna, Aalam Wassef, Alain Touraine, and especially Simonetta Tabboni, my unique and unforgettable friend who left us far too soon.

Anne-Marie Varigault helped me with the French edition of this book, improving my still rudimentary French after more than twenty years in Paris and giving me many superb suggestions.

I also thank Stephen Holmes for the patience and love with which he helped me produce the English edition of this book, translated from the French together with Noga Arikha.

More than twenty years ago, I left Milan with a book in my pocket: *Rethinking Symbolism* by Dan Sperber. I wanted to study in Paris in order to meet the author. When we met, he told me that being an intellectual means being part of a conversation. It is my conversation with him, even today and every day, that gives meaning to my work.

This book is dedicated to my father, Giancarlo Origgi, *primo maestro*.

REPUTATION

1

How I See Myself Seen

> Fear of losing his loved ones but also of losing himself, of discovering that behind his social façade he was nothing.
>
> —E. CARRÈRE, *THE ADVERSARY*

> He smiled understandingly, much more than understandingly. It was one of those rare smiles with a quality of eternal reassurance in it that you may come across four or five times in life. It faced—or seemed to face—the whole external world for an instant, and then concentrated on you with an irresistible prejudice in your favor. It understood you just as far as you wanted to be understood, believed in you as you would like to believe in yourself.
>
> —F. SCOTT FITZGERALD, *THE GREAT GATSBY*

On January 9, 1993, in his house in the region of Gex, located between Switzerland and Jura, Jean-Claude Romand murdered his wife, his two children (ages five and seven), his parents, and their dog. He then tried to kill his mistress in the forest of Fontainebleau, where he had brought her for dinner, supposedly at the house of Bernard Kouchner, whom he did not know and who owns no house in Fontainebleau. Lastly, he set his house on fire, swallowed sleeping pills, and fell asleep, hoping never to wake up. Contrary to his plan, however, he regained consciousness, awakening unexpectedly from the coma induced by barbiturates and burns, and he survived. Charged with having committed these atrocious acts, he was subsequently convicted and imprisoned. According to the French prosecutor who argued the case, the motive for the crime was "the impostor's fear of being unmasked."[1]

But how could confessing to having told a lie, even an extravagantly outrageous lie, ever become more difficult than exterminating one's entire family? How could Jean-Claude Romand's reputation have meant more to him than the life of his children? This book represents an attempt to answer these questions.

Romand's gruesome story was made famous by Emmanuel Carrère's book *L'Adversaire* (2000). The author tells the tale of a man who constructed for himself a bogus reputation as a successful doctor working at the World Health Organization (WHO) in Geneva. He was purportedly a friend of important politicians and internationally renowned researchers. But the picture was fabricated from top to bottom. It was an enormous lie. In truth, Romand had never completed his medical studies and, for ten long years, rather than working as the doctor he pretended to be, he had been frittering away whole days inside his car in the WHO parking lot in Geneva or loitering in the woods or loafing in cafés until it was time to go home. He had

1. Carrère 2000, 12.

meticulously cultivated his false identity, taking home fliers and brochures he had picked up at the WHO library that was open to the public on the ground floor of the organization's headquarters. When he claimed that he was away on "business trips," he instead stayed at a modest hotel near his home where he would watch TV and peruse guidebooks describing whatever country he was supposed to be visiting. He never neglected to call his family every day to tell them what time it was in Tokyo or Brazil, and he always returned from these absences with gifts that seemed to come from the countries where he had allegedly been. He carefully tended and honed his make-believe existence, his spurious reputation, as if it were the love of his life. He clung so implacably to his fictional identity that when the façade began to crumble due to money problems, his frantic urge to defend his palace of lies led him to murder his entire family lest they discover the scandalous truth.

Romand's story raises a paradoxical question: Which was his real life? The one that his family thought he lived, full of success, trips, and international recognition, or the one that he alone knew about, the insipid existence spent reading in his car or killing time in the squalid cafés of Bourg-en-Bresse or aimlessly hiking the Jura mountains? This second life existed only for Romand himself. So how real was it? Since no one else knew about it, it was socially invisible. Moreover, he apparently experienced it exclusively as a means to an end. It was significant only as a way for him to keep up his elaborate charade, to maintain the pretense of the dream life that his family imagined he was living. When, after the murders, friends from his village realized that Jean-Claude's entire life had been a fraud, he ceased to exist for them. He was no longer the man they thought they had known: "When they spoke of him, late at night, they couldn't manage to call him Jean-Claude any more. They didn't call him Romand either. He was somewhere outside life, outside death, where he no longer had a name."[2]

All of us have two egos, two selves. These parallel and distinguishable identities make up who we are and profoundly affect how we behave. One is our subjectivity, consisting of our proprioceptive experiences, the physical sensations registered in our body. The other is our *reputation*, a reflection of ourselves that constitutes our social identity and makes *how we see ourselves seen* integral to our self-awareness. At the beginning of the twentieth century, American sociologist Charles Horton Cooley[3] called this second ego *the looking-glass self*. This second ego is woven over time from multiple strands, incorporating how we think the people around us perceive and judge us. In fact, our understanding of this second self is not created simply by *reflection* but rather by the *refraction* of our image that is warped, amplified, redacted, and multiplied in the eyes of others. This social self controls our lives to a surprising extent and can even drive us to commit extreme acts. It does not really belong to us but is rather the part of us that lives in and through others. Yet the feelings that it provokes—shame, embarrassment, self-esteem, guilt, pride—are both very real and very deeply rooted in our emotional experience.[4] Biology demonstrates that our body responds to shame as if it were a

2. Carrère 2000, 18.

3. Cooley (1864–1929) is considered one of the founders of social psychology. His idea was to root the study of society in the mental processes of individuals. In his view, the concept of the individual was an empty abstraction, meaningless if separated from society; but he believed that the concept of society was equally empty if the mental states of the individuals who made it up were not taken into account. The idea of the looking-glass self is developed in Cooley 1902.

4. These are the emotions that psychologists call "self-aware," reflexive emotions that depend on social interaction. See Elster 1999.

physical wound, releasing chemical substances that provoke inflammation and a rise in the level of cortisol.[5] A slap in the face does more harm to our self-esteem than to our stinging and reddened cheek.

In his work on the *culture of honor*, psychologist Richard Nisbett and his collaborators measured the level of cortisol in experimental participants before and after an experience where they felt their honor had been besmirched. The study was conducted as follows. A group of eighty-three students selected from southern and northern regions of the United States were invited to participate in a psychological study. Before the experiment, the subjects were asked to fill out a form with their personal information and to return it to an experimenter who, rather than being located in the room where the study itself was conducted, was instead stationed at the end of an adjoining hallway. It was only when they left the room to hand in their forms that the "true" experiment actually began. An experimenter pretending to be an employee of the university was organizing files in a rolling filing cabinet placed awkwardly in the middle of the hallway. To allow the students to pass, this fake employee had to heave the cabinet to one side. Once the students reached the end of the hallway and submitted their forms, they turned around to come back, and the fake employee was again forced to shove aside the heavy cabinet to allow them to squeeze by. He did this while expressing irritation and murmuring "asshole." Unlike the students who grew up in the North, students from the South felt that being called an asshole was a serious affront, that it had inflicted palpable damage to their reputation (and their virility). At the end of

5. See Lewis and Ramsay 2002; Gruenewald et al. 2004.

the experiment, their levels of cortisol were much higher than at the beginning.[6] The perception that their public image had been smeared had provoked a measurable chemical transformation, a much-studied hormonal reaction that frequently signals a disposition to lash out and commit acts of physical violence.

What I Think You Think about Me

More than a third of the homicides committed in the United States have surprisingly trivial causes such as verbal altercations, wanton insults, or even disputes about who is first in line to occupy a just-vacated parking space. Among the most convincing sociological explanations for crimes without weighty motives are honor, pride, and reputation.[7] Many such crimes, moreover, are committed by people without psychopathic psychological profiles. What apparently drives them to murderous extremes are frivolous social slights and niggling questions of precedence.

Indeed, all of us can react angrily to discourteous or insulting encounters, to the rude waiter who abuses his little "power" over us or to the woman in the car ahead who refuses to move five centimeters forward to let us turn left. Such visceral reactions are frequently triggered by the wounds that we think others have inflicted on the respect that we think we are "owed." They are genuine and deeply felt emotional injuries that are provoked by the conceit that we have not received appropriate respect and consideration. That was not the way we should have been treated!

6. See Nisbett and Cohen 1996.

7. See Gould 2003.

But why would an imagined injury to a flattering image of ourselves that we wish others would accept provoke a physically violent response? How can a chimerical "me," imagined but nonexistent, which is nothing but a trace, a shadow[8] of myself inhabiting the minds of others, have such precisely measurable psychophysical effects? The paradox of reputation resides in the apparent disproportionality between the enormous psychological and social value that we assign to our reputation and its merely symbolic nature. Being honorable is nothing more than being recognized as honorable by someone else. Why do we value so highly the image that others entertain of us, a representation that exists only in their minds, especially since, in the end, we are the only ones obsessively concerned with our own reputation (excepting of course those celebrities whose reputation fascinates the entire world)?

Mark Leary, a social psychologist at Duke University, has advanced the hypothesis that humans have an internal *sociometer*, a psychological mechanism or a motivational apparatus that works as an indicator of the "social temperature" around us, a kind of built-in thermometer that registers social acceptance or rejection, using the resulting *degree of self-esteem* as a unit of measurement.[9] Our social emotions, according to this theory, provide a way to keep track of the part of ourselves that inhabits the minds of others. Even if our reputation is only a reflection, from this perspective, the emotions accompanying it have a physical and psychological expression that helps us keep track of how others see us.

8. I will return to the idea of reputation as a shadow: a *shadow of the past* in classical game theory, and a *shadow of the future* in the evolutionary explanations of cooperation. See Miller 2012 and Axelrod 1984.

9. Leary 2005. That self-esteem is directly linked to social approval is controversial. For example, Elster (2013) argues that concern for a good reputation can be independent of a desire for social acceptance.

The principal problem with psychological explanations of this sort is their underlying assumption that the hypothesized sociometer is properly adjusted, that the emotions that it provokes within us and the external social temperature covary in a coordinated fashion. Unfortunately, as George Elliot wisely remarked, "the last thing we learn in life is our effect on others." How we think we are seen seldom reflects how we are actually seen.

As actors, in any case, we normally proceed by trial and error, experimenting with different selves, erecting a series of façades that turn out to be nothing but provisional drafts. When we see the effects that these invented selves have on others, we go back to the drawing board and try to fashion a different social image. Either that, or we give up and acquiesce in the picture that others have of us when we realize that we can't control it anymore. The bitterness that accompanies a ruined reputation, the Proustian anxiety about our always uncertain social standing, and the deep ambivalence that these feelings evoke are due to our fundamental incapacity to keep our double on a tight leash. Indeed, the shadowy reflection of ourselves that exists solely in the minds of others is ultimately impossible to control.

Our second ego is not the opinion that others entertain of us, however. It is rather what we think others think of us, or sometimes even what we would like to imagine that others think of us. In the epigraph from Fitzgerald that opens this chapter, Gatsby's smile reassures the young Nick Carraway, giving him the feeling that he is finally seen as he would like to be seen, no more, no less. A smile of approval evokes a feeling of emotional comfort permitting him to let himself go since he has finally been seen by someone as he would like to be seen. The mysterious Gatsby with his sulfurous reputation is the only one in a position to give Carraway the supposedly correct assessment of himself, to provide him the profound satisfaction of being seen at last as he truly is or wants to be. And Gatsby gives him the rarest and most beautiful gift: to feel for an instant that his two egos are reunited—to overcome at last the eternally ambivalent relation between being and seeming. Carraway is also Gatsby's accomplice since he understands the latter's profound need to fashion a dream-self, a parallel persona that is not merely a flimsy social façade but that represents what he would like others to think of him: "So he invented just the sort of Jay Gatsby that a seventeen-year-old boy would be likely to invent, and to this conception he was faithful to the end." Nick Carraway also upholds his own second self when he says: "Every one suspects himself of at least one of the cardinal virtues, and this is mine: I am one of the few honest people that I have ever known." And it is this cardinal virtue that Gatsby acknowledges and reinforces by his smile.[10]

Our social image is both familiar and strange. The reactions it provokes in us are largely involuntary, such as blushing before an intimidating audience. Although the way we see how others see us can occasionally cause us to lose control, it is, at the same time, the part of ourselves we prize most highly and on which we lavish the tenderest care. If we fail to distinguish between our two egos, our actions will often make no sense and we can find ourselves plunged into a state of profound confusion where we can no longer understand why we act the way we do.

This book explores the hidden logic of our double ego. Reputation itself is strikingly enigmatic. How a good name is gained or lost is often inexplicable. Why some reputations are

10. Fitzgerald 2004, 98, 59.

considered good and others bad can be equally obscure. It is a perfect topic, in other words, for proverbs and works of creative literature rich with insights drawn from concrete life experience and that vividly depict what social scientists have a hard time analyzing in abstract terms, much less explaining. A pertinent example appears in this maxim of Rochefoucauld: "Self-love is cleverer than the cleverest man in the world" (L'amour-propre est plus habile que le plus habile homme du monde).[11] The idea of a double intentionality that guides action is obviously implicit here, even if it isn't very precisely conveyed in the evocative ambiguity of the proverb.

Much of the mystery enveloping and obscuring the idea of reputation derives from the concept having been neglected, for various reasons, by serious social scientists. For starters, the concept of reputation suffers from a very bad reputation. It is commonly considered a vestige of a premodern and anti-individualistic society. *Fama*, honor, and the effort to win and maintain prestige in a social hierarchy are often dismissed as the trappings of a bygone aristocratic world that our disenchanted modernity has thankfully left behind. Studying them is sometimes said to have "merely historical interest" for another reason as well: none of these phenomena actually exists. They are dismissed as phantoms that, in earlier ages, haunted a purely symbolic world. There was apparently never anything real or worthy of study underlying them in the first place. Attempting social scientific research on reputation, from this allegedly illusion-free perspective, would be like undertaking a rigorous inquiry into the nimbus of saints, the *aura* and *luminosity* that surround supernatural beings and people touched

11. See Rochefoucauld 1678/2006, maxim 4.

by divinity that we find in Christian and Muslim iconography. Such phenomena can doubtless be examined from a historical-cultural point of view, looking, for example, at their evolution in the history of art or poetry. (*Aura* is often mentioned in medieval poetry and religious literature.) These phenomena, studied by such authors as Leon Daudet and Walter Benjamin, and that even attracted the attention of Charcot, nevertheless remain unexplained and resemble more an aesthetic concept than a genuinely scientific one.[12] Choosing to investigate *aura* in a "scientific" manner is thus something we would expect only from tabloid hacks or pseudo-investigators of the paranormal, not from natural or social scientists. Reputation sometimes seems to have acquired a similarly unfavorable notoriety, as if it were an apparition that can be taken seriously only by cultural historians. Since it is held to be nonexistent as a social or psychological reality, it is thought to defy systematic testing and analysis. From this viewpoint, elevating reputation to the

12. In 1928, Leon Daudet published his essay "Melancholia," where he tried to provide a scientific explanation of aura as the manifestation of an atmosphere around human beings that emanates from a combination of their personal condition and the influences of their environment. Jean-Martin Charcot (1892–93, 2:389) used the term "hysterical aura" to specify a series of symptoms that could allegedly predict an epileptic attack. Charcot conceived aura as a mixture of the organic and the psychological, a luminous atmosphere surrounding a patient that determines the patient's relationship with his or her environment and that, although impossible to observe, can be "felt." In his 1936 essay titled "The Work of Art in the Age of Mechanical Reproduction," Walter Benjamin defined aura "as the unique appearance of a distance, regardless of proximity" (*als einmalige Erscheinung einer Ferne, so nah sie sein mag*). The history of the concept of aura is masterfully reconstructed by Carnevali (2006). Cf. Benjamin: "To perceive the aura of an object we look at means to invest it with the ability to look at us in return. This experience corresponds to the data of the memoire involontaire. (These data, incidentally, are unique: they are lost to the memory that seeks to retain them. Thus they lend support to a concept of the aura that comprises the 'unique manifestation of a distance.')" (1968, 188).

status of a worthy object of social science research would be as frivolous as believing that ghostly presences inhabit the ruins of medieval castles.

Those who dismiss reputation along these lines see it as a psychological *illusion*. We react to it as if it existed, as if it mattered to us, but, in reality, there is nothing there. Admittedly, the belief that reputation is something real can be fatal (as in the tragic destiny of Jean-Claude Romand). But if it is to be studied psychologically, according to such skeptics, reputation should be grouped alongside the *cognitive biases* that cloud and warp our judgment.

Illusory or not, our understanding of how others see us can have extreme consequences. Concern for our reputation is so thoroughly intertwined with our behavioral dispositions that it can motivate acts that seem inconsistent with a person's ordinary conduct and that cannot be otherwise explained. Take the notorious case of Orlando Figes, a rich and famous British historian who used to spend his nights on Amazon.co.uk anonymously savaging his colleagues' books and writing fulsome eulogies of his own works, only to end up being denounced to the police and deprived of the last drop of that precious elixir he had hoped to distill online: his scholarly reputation.[13]

Image management is serious business and cannot be reduced to putting on makeup that can easily be wiped off. Far from being superficial or cosmetic, it involves the deep strategic matter of *social cognition*. We try to manipulate how other people see us, taking our idea of how they see us now as a point of departure. Reputation management is an arms race, an es-

13. On the sad follies of Orlando Figes in 2010, see http://www.telegraph.co.uk/culture/books/booknews/7601662/Leading-academics-in-bitter-row-over-anonymous-poison-book-reviews.html and my article: http://gloriaoriggi.blogspot.com/2012/01/reputazione-sirena-del-presente.html.

calation game of believing and make-believing, of manipulating other people's ideas and being manipulated by them in turn. We all know the feeling of triumph that we experience when we think we have been appreciated for what we are really worth. Previous humiliations are erased; the world recognizes us at last as we always knew we deserved. And all of us, alas, have also experienced the opposite feeling of letdown and defeat when we capitulate before the disdain of others—when we are humiliated and belittled but nevertheless accede to their unfavorable way of measuring our worth. The shame that Vinteuil cannot hide about his homosexual daughter in Proust's *Remembrance* is of this kind:

> But when M. Vinteuil thought about his daughter and himself from the point of view of society, from the point of view of their reputation, when he attempted to place himself with her in the rank which they occupied in the general esteem, then he made this social judgment exactly as it would have been made by the most hostile inhabitant of Combray, he saw himself and his daughter in the lowest depths. (2003–4, 151–52)

The results of our serial attempts to manage how others see us are highly uncertain; yet they can sometimes be quite spectacular. The uncertainty of the outcome, in fact, is what makes the reputation game so endlessly fascinating. The words and the images we employ to manage our reputation, to cite George Santayana, are "like shells, no less integral parts of nature than are the substances they cover, but better addressed to the eye and more open to observation" (1922, 131). Our second nature acquires its reality only thanks to the social environment that surrounds us. It exists only by reflection. With this in mind, I now turn to a deeper look at our social nature, this second self that lives only as refracted through the thoughts and words of others.

The Presentation of Self

Like snails leaving trails as they slither across the ground, our social interactions deposit in the minds of others a telling *informational trace* that cannot be subsequently erased. This imprint is simultaneously indelible and fragile. We control it only partly and cannot avoid leaving it behind. How is it composed and recomposed? How does it become stable and public? How is it registered and diffused through ever-expanding circles of communication?

The social contexts in which we regularly deposit such traces of ourselves range from face-to-face interactions through rumors diffused behind our backs to mass media and the Internet. Such varying mediations of what we call *social information* generate distortions and amplification effects that have been studied from many different and sometimes opposing disciplinary perspectives.

Erving Goffman's[14] many contributions to the study of reputation management in face-to-face interaction have been immensely influential. Indeed, it is fair to regard Goffman as the father of what we today call "impression management," meaning the bundle of techniques that individuals or enterprises adopt to improve how they are seen and judged. In his subtle analyses of the way in which people cultivate and embellish the presentation of self in social interactions, Goffman develops a strategic theory of the quotidian. Face-to-face interaction is the arena in which we negotiate our social image, the place

14. Goffman 1956, 1967.

where our second ego comes into play as a protagonist. This staging of self can be more or less cynical. We can believe in the personage that we want to project in a given social situation or not, even if our emotional identification with our mask is, according to Goffman, difficult or impossible to resist. It is not by chance that the Latin word "persona" means precisely "mask." For Goffman's social self, the line separating being from seeming is inherently blurry and elusive. He borrowed this insight from Robert Ezra Park, one of the pioneers of American sociology who, in his classic work *Race and Culture*, wrote that:

> in so far as the mask represents the conception we have formed of ourselves—the role we are striving to live up to—this mask is our truer self, the self we would like to be. In the end, our conception of our role becomes second nature and an integral part of our personality. We come into the world as individuals, achieve character, and become persons. (1950, 149–50)

A fascinating dramatization of this "moral transformation," by which the mask remakes the man, can be found in a little-known film of Roberto Rossellini, *General della Rovere*, released in 1959. The movie tells the wartime story of Emmanuel Bardone, a small-time crook who in 1943 Genoa impersonated a general in the Italian army. Having begun his career arranging shady transactions on the black market, Bardone ends up, with the complicity of a German officer, extorting money from the families of Italians who have been imprisoned by the Nazis, promising to help them get their loved ones released. After he too is arrested by the Germans, he agrees to collaborate with the enemy in exchange for a reduced sentence. His jailers propose that he assume the identity of General della Rovere, a recently executed leader of the resistance. Jailed in the San Vittorio prison in Milan under this assumed identity, Bardone is tasked with discovering other leaders of the resistance hiding among the ordinary prisoners. Once inside, however, he is overwhelmed and exhilarated by the esteem and gratitude of General della Rovere's admirers. As a result, Bardone becomes so thoroughly identified with his role that he "becomes" General della Rovere. His false reputation becomes his dominant and even his sole identity. The thoroughness of this transformation becomes dazzlingly clear when the fascists decide, in retaliation for the assassination of one of their own, to execute some members of the antifascist underground. At this point, Bardone willingly faces the firing squad alongside the genuine members of the resistance. He even dies shouting, "Long live Italy! Long live the king!" The impostor sacrifices his physical self on the altar of his public reputation. His death even has something heroic about it, although he was obviously not what he ultimately wished he had been.

The possibility of transforming a "natural" identity into a fabricated and artificial social identity is nicely summarized by the Italian phrase "Ci sei o ci fai?" which can be roughly translated as "Are you really what you are pretending to be or are you just faking it?" Human action, to the extent that it is embedded in social interaction, is always haunted by an unsettled or ambivalent relation between being and seeming, between who we privately are and who we publicly profess to be. It is never perfectly clear where one ends and the other begins. In fact, the developing and molting of "social skins" is an unending activity that permits us not only to negotiate our social identity along with others but also to affirm it, to construct it in our own eyes.

Along with his brilliantly perceptive descriptions of human behavior, Goffman espouses a "moral" principle that organizes social interaction and that explains why, in the end, even Bardone/Della Rovere is a moral figure. A "Goffmanian" society is organized according to the following principle: every individual who possesses and displays social characteristics has the moral right to demand that others recognize and accept him or her for just these socially defined traits.

In his 1956 book *The Presentation of Self in Everyday Life*, Goffman details the strategies that "actors" adopt to manage their image and influence the impression they make on others in social situations. He conceives social life as a theater where our entrance onto the stage elicits in the audience a cluster of expectations that lend meaning to our behavior. How we dress, our accent, our physical appearance, the fact of finding ourselves in that situation at that precise moment, all of this locates us socially and reveals who we are. Everyone, we might say, is a protagonist in their own play, or at least everyone scripts the opening scene that conditions how they will later be perceived. According to Goffman, this projection of self builds upon and consolidates a tacit agreement that the public is obliged to respect lest the actor lose face. Our social image is based on this implicit pact. To seal it, however, we have to modulate our self-presentation. We have to take account of what others are willing to accept.

First impressions are so important and also so difficult to revise because they define the storyline that actors and their audiences implicitly agree to follow. To be sure, interactions that discredit the way we have initially presented ourselves sometimes occur, casting doubt on our projected self-image and even contradicting it. In this case, the actor will feel embarrassed by the situation but, given the implicit accord, will be able to count on the fact that his public will not abandon him immediately. There are moments, however, when contradictory evidence mounts so high that it can no longer be explained away, releasing observers from their implicit obligation to accept the actor's self-presentation. At this point, the situation cracks and communicative complicity breaks down.

Here is an example. When requesting a loan from the bank, I arrive well-dressed and consummately presentable. If I am always late in making payments, I disarmingly explain, it is not from lack of funds but merely because I am so inordinately busy and have many other irons in the fire. I smile courteously. Yet if I break out in a cold sweat and begin to respond vaguely and evasively to the pressing demands of the bank official about how I plan to repay the interest on the loan, there is a point at which he will no doubt decide to drop the pretenses and pull away my mask. Scenes like this are common in both theater and cinema. They are sometimes comic, sometimes tragic. They epitomize social situations where an image of self is projected and then disavowed, often because of an egregious misstep by the one who was struggling to keep it up.

Gaffes, too, exemplify the way social interactions can undergo sudden reversals of tone. The *gaffeur* reveals something of himself or of others that is incompatible with the initial implicit agreement. The situation degrades to the point that actor and observer can no longer play the roles negotiated at the beginning and someone necessarily loses face. Both the moral resonance of reputation and the painful feelings that its subversion or undoing arouses—such as shame or humiliation—become evident when such ruptures occur in the management of social interaction. Such a breakdown implies a kind of betrayal. The moral pact that in Goffman's theory is the foundation of most everyday interactions is no longer respected and we feel ourselves betrayed, humiliated, put in a position where we are obliged to disown our social ego, to let our projected double (the best of ourselves) fall to pieces. The broken pact opens a moral wound and foments resentment at not being respected as we should have been, even in situations where it is clear that our performance was partly disingenuous and that we were playing a role, that we were inventing a reputation for ourselves.

Needless to say, we cannot play just any role or put on just any mask. In a given social context, credible self-images, ones that we can successfully project, will conform to a series of values endorsed by society. According to Cooley, moreover, this is part of the social learning process to which we are all exposed. The revised and improved image we propose to ourselves must reflect what we think others would expect to see in someone like us. As Cooley argued more than a century ago: "If we never tried to seem a little better than we are, how could we improve or 'train ourselves from the outside inward'?" (1902, 352). One way to pressure ourselves into becoming the kind of person that others admire is to make them believe that we already have the characteristics that they would like to see in us. This circle is not only virtuous, it is also immensely consequential. Trying "to seem a little better than we are" leads us to act in a more appropriate way and the very feigning ends up helping us integrate into our motivational makeup social values that we would ideally like to exemplify. Admittedly, such a circle can also become vicious if it does nothing but reinforce social conformism. All of us care about our reputation. But some of us worry about it much too much.

How we internalize social rules, it should be said, can often be awkward and ridiculous. In Molière's *The Bourgeois Gentle-*

man, the comic effect aroused by Monsieur Jourdain depends entirely on his wanting desperately to display the manners of "high society" but succeeding only in making his wife and servants laugh and in maintaining a court of opportunists interested more in his wallet than in his genteel manners. Equally painful consequences ensue when the impulse is to go beyond, or escape from, what others see in us. Vitangelo Moscarda, the tragic hero of Luigi Pirandello's 1926 novel, *One, No One and One Hundred Thousand*, decides to change his life by fleeing desperately from his "social ego." One morning his wife observes that his nose has become a little more crooked. His ensuing attempt to escape the embarrassing way he sees himself seen drives him into a futile search for his "true identity" that eventually plunges him into madness.

Similarly illuminating examples of the painful gap between how we wish to be seen and how we are actually seen are ubiquitous in imaginative literature. Take Madame Verdurin, the wannabe "mondaine" of Proust's *Remembrance of Things Past*. She is wracked by envy of the Parisian salons of the Faubourg Saint Germain where she has no entrée. She thus gives carte blanche to the Baron of Charlus so that he will organize an evening with his friends and thereby include her in the glamorously exclusive milieu registered in his private address book. But the evening that ensues is a rude slap in the face to her self-love. None of Charlus's friends even deigns to greet her: "Nobody would have thought of asking to be introduced to Mme. Verdurin any more than to the attendant in a theatre to which some great lady has for one evening brought the whole aristocracy."[15]

15. Marcel Proust, *The Prisoner*, vol. 5 of *In Search of Lost Time*. Cf. the French text: "Personne n'eût plus pensé à se faire presenter à Mme Verdurin qu'à l'ouvreuse

The social norms that we internalize, it should also be said, can change radically from place to place, making it additionally tricky to align how we are actually seen with how we wish to be seen. For example, Madame de Bargeton's clothes, which seemed to Lucien Chardon, the protagonist of *Lost Illusions*, one of Balzac's cruelest novels, to be the *non plus ultra* of elegance when they met in Angoulême, seem to him embarrassing and provincial when the two of them arrive in Paris:

> The proximity of several beautiful Parisian women, so elegantly and so daintily attired, made him aware that Madame de Bargeton's *toilette*, though passably ambitious, was behind the times: neither the material, nor the way it was cut, nor the colors were in fashion. The hair-style he had found so seductive in Angoulême struck him as being in deplorable taste compared with the delicate inventiveness which lent distinction to the other women present. (2004, 161)

The apparent lesson, once again, is the inherent fragility and even futility of our most determined endeavors to control how we are seen.

On the other hand, the reciprocal influence between our social image and our ideal self, the progressive adjustment between how others see us and what we would like them to recognize in us, can be an immensely creative part of our social apprenticeship. In this to-and-fro, at times, we are able to go beyond conformity or embarrassment, throwing ourselves into a game much more complex and seductive: the gambit of representing a character who we consciously know ourselves not to be. Simone de Beauvoir describes this subtle ploy very

d'un théâtre où une grande dame a, pour un soir, amené toute l'aristocratie." *La Prisonnière* (Paris: La Pléiade, 1983–84), book 3, p. 266.

well when she writes about women's fashion. Beyond the social codes, "as soon as she is 'dressed up,' the least sophisticated woman is not concerned with perception: she is like a painting, a statue, like an actor on stage, an analogon through which is suggested an absent subject who is her character but is not she" (2009, 575).

Goffman's impression management, to return again to that theme, is a refined analysis of face-to-face interactions. The encounters on which he focuses occur directly before our eyes. They involve the relation between "appearance" and "manner," that is, between the presence of our physical person and our mastery of certain social codes. To manage impressions requires hiding certain motivations and emphasizing others to maintain a measure of coherence between appearance and manner, and so forth. Goffman's analysis, therefore, classifies "face" as a property of social interaction rather than as a trait of individuals. This brings us to an important difference between impressions and reputations. In managing impressions, everything that happens is onstage, in the glare of the klieg lights. By contrast, reputation accumulates behind the actor's back and spreads via social communication beyond his or her capacity for control. Goffman's subtle techniques for managing social impressions, as a consequence, can prove wholly useless for controlling one's social reputation.

Moreover, the social emotions of shame, resentment, pride, and glory do not seem to be generated solely by social interaction. Although they are essentially *relational* and *comparative*, the social conditions capable of arousing them may be minimal. Experiments in social psychology have shown that a mere silhouette with two eyes, which abstractly represents the social gaze, suffices to change people's performance in tasks hinging on social approval or disapproval. And, as we saw in the dismaying stories of Jean-Claude Romand and Orlando Figes, pressures weighing upon the social ego can be nonexistent or purely imaginary. We can collapse under the weight of expectations that we believe others entertain about us, even if these others have never given us a moment's thought. We should occasionally remember to tell the young, laboring under the weight of what they imagine to be their teachers' and parents' expectations, that we too are struggling to live up to what the world expects from us and that we don't actually have that much time to impose crushing expectations on our children or students. The fear of disappointing others is often little more than a self-induced phantasm.

Social emotions, in any case, are by no means limited to face-to-face interactions. The "social interactions" that precipitate them are not necessarily real. They may well be fictional exchanges that we have imaginatively pieced together out of the thousands of real encounters that have left variable residues in our minds.

How Do Children Acquire a Sense of Reputation?

Psychologist Philippe Rochat claims that reputation is what makes us human. What most clearly sets human beings apart from other species is the internalized gaze of others that permanently haunts us.[16] Instead of seeing reputation as a typical preoccupation of modern times, therefore, Rochat locates its emergence in ontogenesis, showing that anxiety about how we see ourselves seen exists in all cultures and manifests itself at a very early stage of child development. Hyperattention to our social image (amour propre) is not therefore a "mark of

16. Rochat 2009. The title of an article by Rochat in Origgi 2013a was the inspiration for the subtitle of this section.

modernity," as some have claimed, but rather a characteristic feature of human psychology. Already at the age of two, according to Rochat, children have a "co-consciousness" of self that is linked to the famous mirror stage studied by psychologists and psychoanalysts.[17] This is the stage at which the child recognizes itself in its reflection. The *identity* of these two images forms the basis of our *personal identity*. Recognizing our double in the mirror makes us discover that we are precisely ourselves. According to Lacan, when children first recognize themselves in a mirror, they experience a kind of jubilation produced by their finally perceiving their body as a unified whole.

But what makes the mirror stage even more interesting is that it constitutes a measurable threshold in childhood development. Putting a visible mark on the child's face without its knowledge makes it possible to establish whether the child recognizes itself or not. Children normally pass this test at twenty-one months. But the experience is not associated with the kind of jubilation alleged by Lacan. On the contrary, children feel a sense of malaise and shame when spotting a blemish on their faces of which they were unaware. This first experience of the ego is precocious and painful at the same time. Self-consciousness, according to Rochat, results not only from an ability to reflect on ourselves but also from the integration of the gaze of others into our personal identity. The precocity of this sense of identity, of socially refracted existence, may depend on one of the most fundamental cognitive competences of the newborn, a capacity for *shared attention* that develops during the first year of life. The survival of a newborn depends on its ability to attract the attention of the adults who

17. Studied for the first time by Henri Wallon, the mirror stage was taken up by René Zazzo, Jacques Lacan, D. W. Winnicott, and Françoise Dolto, among others.

care for it. The child's ability to experience objects and events in its environment jointly with its mother, for example, facilitates learning, reassures the newborn of its existence, and allows it to explore the world through a social filter, thus minimizing risks. The child who starts acting up to get the attention of a busy mom who is on the phone or is distracted by a sidewalk conversation does not require attention for sentimental reasons alone. Thinking *with* its mother, experiencing the world by sharing its mother's attention to their common surroundings, is a profound cognitive requirement without which childhood development would be impossible.

The social side of cognition, it turns out, is extraordinarily precocious. The child comes into the world "equipped" with cognitive mechanisms that allow it to monitor its social environment and that predispose it to care about its mirror image, its double in the eyes of others, as if the cocktail of self-awareness and social cognition makes human beings into a unique species, one perennially obsessed by the judgment of others. Thinking with and through others soon becomes seeing oneself as seen and evaluated from what one believes to be the other's point of view.

The incorporation or internalization of the social world into human self-understanding is nicely illustrated by the difference between two basic social emotions: shame and guilt. If shame depends on the social gaze, real or imagined, the sense of guilt, which is another eminently social emotion, can exist without the presence of others. The measure of their judgment is, in the second case, so internalized that we can come to expose our physical self to condemnation and punishment merely to "save" our social image.

In sum, the relation between how we appear and who we really are is highly complex and ambivalent.

Edmond Rostand's character Cyrano de Bergerac is a romantic hero of authenticity, as opposed to false appearances. He fights valiantly against hypocrisy, pride, and false consciousness. In one of his famous monologues, he issues his *Manifesto of Authenticity*:

> To work without one thought of gain or fame
> Never to pen a line that has not sprung
> Straight from the heart within. Embracing then
> Modesty, say to oneself, "Good my friend,
> Be thou content with flowers,—fruit,—nay, leaves,
> But pluck them from no garden but thine own!"
> And then, if glory come by chance your way,
> To pay no tribute unto Caesar, none,
> But keep the merit all your own! In short,
> Disdaining tendrils of the parasite,
> To be content, if neither oak nor elm—
> Not to mount high, perchance, but mount alone![18]

Yet even Cyrano, while dying before the love of his life, wounded by his cowardly enemies, and expecting to ascend uncelebrated to heaven, "without laurels and without roses" as

18. Travailler sans souci de gloire ou de fortune,

> À tel voyage, auquel on pense, dans la lune!
> N'écrire jamais rien qui de soi ne sortît,
> Et modeste d'ailleurs, se dire: mon petit,
> Sois satisfait des fleurs, des fruits, même des feuilles,
> Si c'est dans ton jardin à toi que tu les cueilles!
> Puis, s'il advient d'un peu triompher, par hasard,
> Ne pas être obligé d'en rien rendre à César,
> Vis-à-vis de soi-même en garder le mérite,
> Bref, dédaignant d'être le lierre parasite,
> Lors même qu'on n'est pas le chêne ou le tilleul,
> Ne pas monter bien haut, peut-être, mais tout seul!

Edmond Rostand, *Cyrano de Bergerac*, Act 2, scene 8

he concludes his final monologue—even Cyrano will die accompanied by something immortal: his "panache," that is, his signature plume of feathers, his famously big nose, and his flamboyant manners, all socially recognized endowments by which he was widely acknowledged to be the unique person he deeply and truly was.

2

Is Reputation a Means or an End?

Somebody told me they thought he killed a man once.

—F. SCOTT FITZGERALD, *THE GREAT GATSBY*

Dear Madame de Volanges, I am sure you will be more than pleased to hear of an action by Monsieur de Valmont which seems in stark contrast to everything else that other people have told you about him. . . . Monsieur de Valmont, discovering that in the village of —— an unfortunate family was about to be dispossessed for non-payment of taxes, not only immediately settled those poor people's debts but even gave them quite a considerable sum of money. This most charitable act was witnessed by my servant. . . . This is not just a casual act of pity, resulting from chance, but a deeply charitable concern, a deliberate intention to do good, that most noble quality of noble souls. . . . Merely hearing about it moved me to tears.

—PIERRE CHODERLOS DE LACLOS, *LES LIAISONS DANGEREUSES*

Reputation and Rationality

The fraught quest for reputability can propel some individuals into committing extreme, senseless, and absurdly risky acts. The violent emotions associated with such destructive and self-destructive behavior might suggest that reputation—assuming it refers to something real rather than imaginary—is a fundamentally nonrational or subrational driver of human behavior. If Jean-Claude Romand had undertaken even a cursory cost-benefit analysis to determine what to do, would he not have concluded that slaughtering his entire family was more costly than suffering the embarrassment of confessing the phoniness of his public reputation?

Up to this point, admittedly, I have focused on a few particularly disturbing cases where devotion to reputation verges on delirium. In these cases, a compulsive fixation on how others view us became so blindingly irrational that it precipitated a personal catastrophe. But it is obvious that there is nothing particularly irrational about the need to gain, uphold, or embellish one's reputation. A judicious investment in the management of one's public image is almost sure to have beneficial results. Knowing how to make others speak approvingly about us, for instance, is a valuable social skill. The ability to come across as reliable and caring, too, is almost sure to be rewarded.

In order to explore the various ways in which cultivating one's reputation, given the costs it imposes and the benefits it confers, can be a rational strategy, we need to make some preliminary remarks about rationality. In this mostly methodological chapter, I examine how several of today's most prominent social scientists approach the question. As my analysis proceeds, I will be employing the term "rationality" in a strictly minimal sense. Actions can be considered rational, as I am using the term, if they conform to the elementary constraint of maximizing utility (however defined) by reducing costs compared to benefits. This is a very simple and parsimonious principle that permits us to make predictions about the behavior not only of human beings but also of animals, robots, large companies, and so forth—in short, of every entity that can plausibly be treated as a decision-making agent. Any rational actor, able to make decisions about how to behave in the future, will respect this constraint. For example, if I observe someone who has decided to buy a vacuum cleaner on the Internet and who has two sites open before him or her, one where the product in question is selling for $200 and another where an identical product can be purchased for only $150, I can predict, without knowing anything about this person, that he or she will prefer to buy a new vacuum cleaner on the second site instead of the first. Similarly, if, on spotting a goldfish foraging for food in a pond, I toss it two pieces of bread, one near where it is swimming and the other farther away, I can predict that the fish will pounce on the morsel that is closer. Understood in this way, rationality is not a cognitive capacity belonging to agents, or at least not necessarily. It is better understood as a constraint placed on theories or models that aspire to explain and predict the behavior of agents. This is why we can apply it fruitfully to so many different kinds of choosers and decision-making contexts.

Most contemporary social and natural sciences impose this minimal rationality constraint on their models of decision making. Understanding the behavior of agents (individuals, governments, corporations, businesses, animals, and so forth) requires us to postulate that their decision-making systems operate under the constraint of rationality in the indicated minimal sense. An agent decides to undertake an action in order to maximize utility. Its utility, in turn, depends on a hierarchy of preferences that can, in turn, be of various types. We may prefer children to career, nation to the family, and so forth. The order of preferences organizes the space within which options are laid out and choices are made. Crucial for modeling (and making sense of) agents and their actions is that the agents' preference orderings work according to certain logical rules, such as transitivity. If I prefer an apple to a banana and a strawberry to an apple, then minimal rationality dictates that I will prefer a strawberry to a banana. Unless we assume the existence of such constraints, we won't be able to predict what agents will do, even if we know the structure of their preferences. But for the purposes of this chapter, further elaboration on the theory of rational choice would be a distraction. It suffices to be clear that when we speak of rationality, we are simply posing a minimal set of restrictions on the kinds of explanation that can be plausibly given of human actions. These constraints emphatically preclude explanations such as "He picked up the fork because a mysterious force compelled him to do it" and favor instead explanations such as "He picked up the fork because he was hungry."

This distinction between permissible and impermissible explanations leads us back to our central question: When we attempt to explain the decisions of minimally rational agents by citing their desire to improve or repair their social reputation, are we offering an explanation of the first or second type?

How Does a Social Trait Emerge?

Considering reputation as a potential spring of action means treating it as a fundamental social trait. As a result, we first have to understand social traits—or characteristic behaviors that distinguish a specific social group or species from others—and explain how they emerge in a specific society. Understanding society through rational models means "decomposing" it into a collection of social traits or characteristics and observing how these traits or characteristics interact. That, at least, is the ambition of the naturalistic theories of social behavior to which I now turn.

A synthesis of the neo-Darwinian theory of evolution with the economic theory of rational choice produced one of the most significant paradigm shifts in twentieth-century social science. This "new synthesis" made it possible to apply models of human motivation and action not only at the individual level but also at the level of populations ("population thinking"). Explanations using these models presuppose "rational" agents in the minimal sense sketched above. They permit us to examine the dynamics of group interaction and thereby to understand how a specific social trait or characteristic originally emerged in a given society. The study of such dynamics involves formal models, computer simulations, and observations of populations. One of these approaches, sociobiology,[1] was at first heavily criticized for its allegedly reductionist implications. But sociobiology is today experiencing a kind of rehabilitation in the fields of experimental economics and evolutionary game theory. Researchers in these fields study, through analytically simple and elegant models, conditions for the emergence of crucial social traits such as cooperation. Admittedly, disputes continue to rage about the viability of such models. And crudely reductionist sociobiological versions which, following Wilson, treated social traits such as exchange,

1. E. O. Wilson's 1975 book, *Sociobiology*, is usually considered the foundational text of the discipline, although a series of influential articles by Robert Trivers on altruism were published a few years earlier. See Trivers 1971.

altruism, or cooperation as "organs" whose evolution can be compared to that of bodily organs are no longer taken very seriously by researchers in the field.

For the purposes of this chapter, I will treat explanations that synthesize evolutionary theory with rational-choice theory only as "theoretical models" useful for illuminating the conditions for the possibility of the emergence of a social trait (such as reputation). I will not treat them as if they claimed to present true and proper "descriptions" of social reality. This form of scientific theorizing turns up today in many disciplines, from biology to economics, from evolutionary psychology to sociology, from political science to artificial intelligence and the study of multi-agent systems. Given its ubiquity in social science research, such an approach is difficult to ignore. In my reading, it is best understood as an updated version of classic thought experiments in political philosophy, particularly in the modern social-contract tradition, which delighted in postulating the existence of a "state of nature," that is, a set of initial conditions where individual-level behaviors eventually generated a politically organized social life. As deployed by writers such as Hobbes and Rousseau, the philosophical fiction of a presocial state of nature (which human beings manage to rise above thanks to a social contract that lays down the rules of mutually beneficial coexistence) has exactly the same narrative purpose as the just mentioned contemporary social science models. Both investigate conditions for the possibility—logically necessary and sufficient—of society emerging from a presocial condition. In the fictions of the fathers of political philosophy, too, the possible actions of agents who enter the social contract must be subjected to a rationality constraint. This parallel with social-contract theory implies that the viability and fertility of the social-science models discussed above do not depend on their furnishing an account of the *nature* of society, as do models in the natural sciences. Their claim is more modest: to provide a plausible account of the *logic* of society.

Much of the debate surrounding the Darwinian model of human nature is organized around an opposition between "natural" and "cultural" explanations. But this dichotomy is highly misleading and has been brilliantly and devastatingly criticized as such by twentieth-century sociology. There is nothing eternal or universal in nature; it is only a matter of one's time horizons. Stars gutter out and dinosaurs have long since vanished from the face of the earth. True, the life cycles of biological and social phenomena unfold on very different time scales, but they are not essentially different. Norbert Elias describes this complex "relation between the rate of change of social figurations to that of biological phenomena" with admirable concision:

> Seen from the standpoint of the former, the latter change so slowly that evolution seems to be standing still. We have here, therefore, an image of mankind as a river with three currents running at different speeds. Seen in isolation, the phenomena in each of these streams are unique and unrepeatable. But in the context of the differing rates of change, phenomena in a slower current are apt, from the position of a faster current, to seem immutable, eternally recurrent. (1983, 14)

Only a superficial theory would seek to erase the differences between psychological, sociological, and biological phenomena, ignoring the peculiarities of each. Individuals are constantly confronted with the flux of personally lived experience, societies manage the creation and dissolution of transient ways of organization and have to deal, over time, with the systematic loss of socially gained knowledge and experience; and biological nature, too, is in constant evolutionary movement, is a ceaseless process of coming into and going out of existence, of simultaneous gain and loss. Yet, for any satisfactory explanatory theory, the actions of "agents" at all three levels must adhere to the constraints of rationality described above. This is what allows for a formal modeling of their behavior including, for instance, actions aimed at establishing the actor's reputable standing in the community.

Altruism and Reputation

How to explain *altruism* is one of the classical challenges to rational-choice theory. Is altruism a fundamental social trait? And if it isn't, how can it emerge from the behavior of rational and self-interested agents? Why should rational agents, seeking to maximize benefits, waste time helping others? Why should a rational maximizer favor others at his or her own expense? Sociobiologists claim to have found an explanation for the empirically observable but puzzling existence of altruism in the theory of kin selection. If natural selection acts at the level of genes rather than at the level of individuals, agents will act altruistically toward those to whom they are genetically related—parents or children—or toward the entire group in the case of species where all individuals share the same genetic heritage, as, for example, bees.[2] The problem with this sociobiological hypothesis is that the human species goes far beyond such simple forms of kin-based altruism. Humans regu-

2. See Haldane 1955; Nowak and Sigmund 2005.

larly display a readiness to cooperate that seems to reflect a capacity for goodwill independent of bloodline and for engaging in mutually beneficial exchanges with entirely unrelated and even unknown individuals.

The career of Robert Trivers, a flamboyant biologist with a sulfurous reputation, has oscillated between moments of glory and periods of academic oblivion. In an article published in 1971, Trivers claimed that the theoretical solution to the paradox of human altruism hinged on the idea of reputation. Having grown up as a child prodigy, Trivers failed to finish his law degree owing to a series of nervous breakdowns. He subsequently decided to pursue a doctorate in evolutionary biology under the direction of Ernst Mayr, even though he had never taken a biology course in his life. His breakthrough article of 1971 was destined to become a milestone in the discipline. The prestige he acquired through this single article earned him a teaching position at Harvard for several years. He then vanished again, some saying that he moved to Jamaica, others that he had joined the Black Panthers. Then, at the turn of the new millennium, he suddenly reappeared, publishing several other highly influential articles.

Trivers is today considered the greatest living evolutionary biologist. In his celebrated 1971 article, "The Evolution of Reciprocal Altruism," he shows that natural selection can explain altruism in a way compatible with the selfish rationality of agents. An altruistic gesture, such as saving someone from drowning, allows the agent to accumulate a positive *reputation* and thereby creates in the beneficiary of the altruistic act a moral-emotional pressure to reciprocate in the future.[3] In

3. The work of Axelrod (1984) on the evolution of cooperation are based on this principle.

other words, altruists expose themselves to momentary risks contrary to their short-term interests because they are anticipating future gains. The pervasiveness of this hope to obtain future benefits from acts of seemingly self-denying generosity has been amply confirmed by experimental economics, which conducts laboratory studies on the behavior of agents asked to follow simple rules of interaction and transaction. In the dictator game, for instance, one experimental subject receives a sum of money that he can divide however he wishes with a second participant. The two subjects do not know each other. Yet the dictator, that is, the individual who can unilaterally decide how to distribute the money, seldom acts in a wholly self-interested way. On average, he gives at least 20 percent of the original sum to the other participant. This shows, according to the conductors of such experiments, that human beings expect to be able to draw some benefit from behaving at least "somewhat" generously.[4] The principal benefit they anticipate receiving is *a good reputation.*

But how likely is it that a perfect stranger we will never see again will show us the same selfless generosity that we at one point exhibited toward him in a brief laboratory game? And how likely is it that a poor fellow we fished from the Seine will show up, in the future, exactly at the moment we need him? It turns out that human beings worry about their reputations much more than is warranted *either* by a simple calculation of immediate interest *or* by the hope of receiving a future benefit from someone who remembers their selfless gestures in the past. So how can this remarkable "surplus" of altruism be explained?

4. See Henrich, Boyd, et al. 2004.

Indirect Reciprocity: The Advantages of a Good Reputation

Contrary to those who insist that mankind's assiduous cultivation of reputation depends on a selection mechanism identical to that which exists in other species (especially species that exhibit symbiotic behavior), the human species is not content with bookkeeper-style altruism of the "I'll scratch your back, you scratch mine" variety. We often behave altruistically toward total strangers. We can cooperate with people we will never see again. And we are frequently caring not only toward those who treated us caringly but also toward those who were generous toward others, including toward people we do not know and will never meet. The idea of *indirect reciprocity* provides a possible explanation for the existence of such unrequited altruism, for why rational agents with little chance ever to reencounter their benefactor or beneficiary can nevertheless be observed behaving toward each other with seemingly selfless generosity.[5] Indirect reciprocity describes a situation where agent A's act of altruism toward B inspires a second act of altruism but not of B toward A. (Thus the original pair need never meet again for an initial act of altruism to inspire a subsequent act of altruism.) Generosity can *indirectly* generate generosity in two different ways. On the one hand, the beneficiary of an act of altruism can be inspired to act altruistically toward a third party: if A helps B, then B will be more willing to help C. On the other hand, A's altruistic act toward B can dispose C to help A. This second form of indirect reciprocity presupposes and illustrates the social power of reputation since C's selfless generosity toward A is evidently inspired by A's *social image* as an altruistic and generous person.

5. See Alexander 1987; Nowak and Sigmund 2005.

In the passage from Pierre Choderlos de Laclos's famous epistolary novel *Les Liaisons dangereuses*, cited as an epigraph to this chapter, la Présidente de Tourvel attempts to embellish the reputation of her nephew, the treacherous Vicomte de Valmont, in the eyes of Madame de Volanges by relaying word of an act of generosity on Valmont's part about which everyone is talking. The letter in which la Présidente de Tourvel informs Madame de Volanges of Valmont's caring gesture is the result of Valmont's calculated act of generosity aimed at changing the attitude of the haughty and austere lady toward the Viscount, preparing her to show herself "altruistic" toward him in turn. The positive assessment conveyed by la Présidente de Tourvel, we might say, alters the "valence" of Valmont's reputation and as a consequence changes how Madame de Volanges sees and judges him.

So what would social science say about such an example? According to Evolutionary Game Theory, the emergence of reputation (including a reputation for altruism) can be explained by its role in facilitating indirect cooperation. Social cooperation is possible only because people speak to each other about each other and are thereby constantly making, remaking, and unmaking the social image of everyone involved in the process. Reputation is no ethereal or ghostly apparition, therefore. Rather, reputations embody and communicate collectively gathered information and collectively shared evaluations. This is why reputation plays such an indispensable role in the processes by which groups develop and enforce their most fundamental norms.

For many authors writing in this tradition,[6] social emotions such as shame, indignation, guilt, and moral disapproval are

6. See, for example, the work on emotions by American economist and psychologist Robert Frank (1988).

the result of a uniquely human proclivity to take an interest not only in interactions in which we personally participate but also in those that do not concern us directly.[7] Indirect reciprocity is specific to human society and, on this theory, provides the basis for the evolution of moral norms. As biologist Richard Alexander, who coined the expression "indirect reciprocity," writes:

> Indirect reciprocity is the foundation of moral, ethical, and legal systems. Its existence and pervasiveness in human social life, I believe, are the most important factors to consider in an analysis of the nature and complexity of the human psyche. I think they account for human interest in theater in all of its guises, from soap operas to Shakespeare, poetry to sociology, neighborhood parties to the Olympic games. (1987, 107)

That which principally preoccupies our minds, according to Alexander, and which represents the uniqueness of the human species, is our ceaseless evaluating of the actions of others, evaluations undertaken partly in an effort to understand how the people we observe are likely to interact with each other in the future, that is, to answer the questions: Who is going to help whom? And who is going to abuse whom? Literary narratives are very suggestive here, for most of them contain variations on an answer to one and the same question, namely: Who did what to whom?

All morality, arguably, depends on reputation. Social and moral norms emerge and gain their binding power only through complex processes whereby social actors transmit characterizations and evaluations of each other to each other.

7. See Alexander 1987.

This process also plays an essential role in the social evolution of reciprocity.

Reputation Seen by Others and by Ourselves

It is sometimes difficult to distinguish a genuinely moral motivation from a strategic interest in cultivating a good reputation in the eyes of others. Some theorists have even argued that all altruism is inevitably hypocritical, implying that every apparently altruistic act is in reality a ruse calculated to elicit a positive response from others. But such a cynical view of altruism is not necessarily realistic. For a counterexample, we need only consider the behavior of individuals who challenge their society and its shared hierarchy of values at the cost of their own lives and in defense of moral values that the world in which they live is not yet ready to recognize.

Why does Hester Prynne, the heroine of Nathaniel Hawthorne's *The Scarlet Letter*, refuse to reveal the identity of her daughter's father, preferring the stigmatization of the community and the shame of having to embroider a red letter A on her clothes signifying adulteress? What "advantage" does she draw from adhering to an inner (and what we may consider a "higher" and "more just") morality, when her silence leads inevitably to an ineradicable defiling of her social reputation?

In a recent article, Nicolas Baumard and Dan Sperber discuss the similarly telling example of the hero in the German film *Das Leben der Anderen* (The Lives of Others, 2006):

> Wiesler is an agent of the secret police of East Germany, the Stasi, in charge of spying on a pair of intellectuals suspected, wrongly, of dissidence while actually being the victims of a corrupt minister. Investigating their lives, Wiesler grows

> emotionally closer and closer to the two objects of his covert surveillance to the point where he chooses to protect them when they eventually decide to become the dissidents they were once falsely suspected of being. He chooses to shield them even though he knows the great risks he will be running. In the end, he loses everything, including his job and his reputation, and he never even meets the pair he managed to protect. He thoroughly sacrificed his public reputation, in other words, in order to perform an unrequited moral act.[8]

According to Baumard and Sperber, who adopt an evolutionary perspective, natural selection may favor such genuinely moral sentiments at the individual level so that the species can benefit collectively from indirect reciprocity. This is why an individual can have a truly moral disposition and genuinely worry about others even if such altruistic proclivities are incorporated into our cognitive makeup only because of the contribution of indirect reciprocity to the survival of the species. In this way, nature acts strategically at the group level, which allows us, as individuals, to retain our freedom to act morally and nonstrategically, that is, without any ulterior motives.

According to Jon Elster, who devoted a two-volume work to the question of the possibility of sincerely disinterested acts,[9] it can be perfectly rational to prioritize the interests of others without calculating how such altruism will enhance our reputation in their eyes or the eyes of third parties. Personal morality and concern for one's social reputation, in his view, have distinct genealogies. Wiesler's care for others, in other words, is not necessarily the product of group selection pre-

8. Baumard and Sperber 2013, 12, my translation.
9. See Elster 2009, 2013.

disposing him to feel genuinely moral sentiments, as in Baumard and Sperber's model. From Elster's perspective, Wiesler is an individual and, as such, may have perfectly rational preferences for the well-being of strangers based on nothing more than his rational desire for self-esteem.

To understand Elster's thesis, we need to distinguish between two aspects of rationality: the internal consistency of our decisions and the maximization of interests.[10] According to utilitarian economists and evolutionary theories, the two go together, naturally and necessarily. Elster disagrees, arguing that human beings can be rational and coherent on the one hand and wholly disinterested on the other. Being rational in this minimal sense simply means acting according to one's own beliefs and desires. If the moral image I have of myself—the conviction that I am a good, honest, and virtuous person—is the most important thing for me, then I will refuse to behave in a way that endangers this self-image, regardless of what others think. After surreptitiously observing the lives of his surveillance targets, on this account, Wiesler finally comes face-to-face with his deepest personal preferences. He can thereafter freely renounce his social standing for the sake of an inner moral consistency. He understands who he is (that is, who he sincerely wants to be), and he willingly sacrifices his public reputation to that self-understanding. To the morally upright Wiesler, recognition by the Stasi leadership no longer counts for anything. He has finally figured out who he deeply is and he wants, above all, to remain true to himself.

One can sacrifice one's public reputation, like Wiesler or Hester Prynne, for the sake of a higher morality or to maintain

10. This distinction was the subject of Elster's inaugural lecture at the Collège de France: "Raison et Raisons," July 1, 2006 (published in English under the title *Reason and Rationality* [Princeton: Princeton University Press, 2008]).

one's inner coherence. But one can also do so to comply with an authoritative norm that impels us to act in a certain way even when that norm is outdated and morally dubious and does not represent anything for anyone else, only for us. Thus Mr. Stevens, the impeccable butler of Kazuo Ishiguro's novel *The Remains of the Day*, has spent his life serving others loyally and proudly on an aristocratic English estate. Although times have changed and all the "gentlemen" for whom he has worked his whole life have proved to be cowardly, corrupt, and compromised by underhanded deals struck with the Nazis, he refuses to betray his fond self-image as an irreproachable majordomo, an image he keeps up to honor his father's memory and that, in his eyes, is worth more than a happy life, something he renounced long ago after having glimpsed it ever so briefly. His example reminds us that self-denying loyalty to one's self-image, far from exemplifying moral nobility, can be wholly conventional and habitual and can even suggest a willful blindness to the changing world around one. It does not necessarily have anything to do with higher morality at war with conformist social pressures.

The image we cultivate of ourselves can matter so much to us, in any case, that we are sometimes driven to act against our tangible interests in order to defend it. As Elster remarks, "For many, the two things that matter most are first our interests and second *especially* that aspect of our self-image that is not shaped purely by self-interest" (2013, 32). On the other hand, to paraphrase Tolstoy, all self-interested individuals may be alike, but everyone is disinterested in his own way. Multiple mechanisms that drive us to act altruistically, according to Elster, come into play when we are defending our self-understanding or self-image: the need to demonstrate character, concern for morality, the continuity of our identity ("being ourselves"), and the feeling of belonging to a community or a tradition, even if it is only imaginary. This last mechanism is emphasized by philosopher and historian Pasquale Pasquino (2007) in his commentary on the vicissitudes of Eléazar, the protagonist of the opera *La Juive* by Jacques Fromental Halévy:

> Persecuted as a Jew, Eléazar—who had narrowly escaped death several times already and had been forced to leave Rome after seeing his children executed as heretics by Christian fanatics—finds himself condemned to being burnt at the stake in 1414 by the Council of Constance, the small town where he has sought refuge. The President of the Council, Cardinal Brogni, comes to visit him in prison and offers him a deal: Brogni will save the lives of Eléazar and his daughter Rachel if Eléazar abjures his Jewish faith and converts to Christianity. Here is how Eléazar responds to the Cardinal's offer:
>
> Did I hear right?
> What do you propose?
> Renounce the faith of my fathers!
> For foreigners' idols!
> Bow my head and degrade myself!
> Never! Better to die![11]

The loss of his real or imagined reputation as someone unbendingly loyal to the faith of his fathers would be a worse

11. L'ai-je bien entendu? . . .

> que me proposes-tu?
> renier la foi de mes pères!
> vers des idoles étrangères
> courber mon front et l'avilir,
> non, jamais plutôt mourir!
>
> *La Juive*, Act 4, scene 18

form of death for Eléazar than death by fire. His second self, the most precious part of himself, matters more to him than his physical survival. He is therefore behaving perfectly rationally when he chooses to die an excruciating death as a martyr, along with his adopted daughter, rather than to consign his reputation as a faithful member of his religious community to the flames.

As these examples suggest, the *rationality* of one's concern for one's reputation is more complex than a simple calculation of interests. Indeed, our disinterestedness can be perfectly rational if it helps to preserve an image of ourselves that is precious in our own eyes. In this sense, to answer the question posed by the title of this chapter, reputation sometimes is an end in itself rather than a mere means to obtain subsequent benefits. We can spend our lives building an image of ourselves and trying our best to conform our actions to it. This ideal self is our most intimate creation and the one most difficult to actualize with any finality. It is an unfinished masterpiece that can never be brought to perfection. Would it really be rational to throw precipitously away something so precious for a merely ephemeral benefit?

Sometimes, admittedly, our carefully cultivated reputation weighs all too heavily on our shoulders. The expectations we have aroused in others and in ourselves can become too great to be satisfied, turning our ideal self into a captious scold who torments us unforgivingly. In such cases, it would be more rational to abandon our fabricated reputation and to become someone else, to escape into a different social circle where we can solicit recognition from new sets of eyes unaware of the overly demanding idea of ourselves that we had previously cultivated and communicated to others. At times, in other words, it makes sense to sacrifice our ideal self in order to salvage our biological self. Galileo Galilei is a telling example. Accused of heresy and threatened with torture by the Holy Office, Galileo yielded and publicly abjured his theories in 1633. His life was saved and he escaped torture. He was obliged to live in Florence, at his villa d'Arcetri, where he could see his family and disciples and where he continued his research until his death.

He purchased his physical survival at the price of his freedom to publish his discoveries as well as his precious reputation as a fearless Copernican savant. In this case, his action was both rational and self-interested. But it would have been equally rational for him to have given up his life and freedom to defend his reputation and his ideas.

A Methodological Caveat: Evolution, Genealogies, and Philosophical Fictions

When the instinct of self-preservation gains the upper hand, it is often accompanied by a strong sense of discomfort, even humiliation, a feeling of being "obliged" to sacrifice one's reputation to save one's life or merely to improve one's life conditions. We do not always have the wherewithal to live up to our ideal expectations for ourselves. Sometimes we have to come to terms with reality and discard our dream self in favor of our really existing self. But the regret we feel in such cases is real and testifies to the power of nonstrategic moral considerations as movers of human action.

This "noble" vision of human beings involves a number of difficulties, however. If both maintaining consistency with one's ideal self-image, as Elster argues, and selfless identification with a moral community or tradition, as Pasquino suggests, are rational motivations, then the question remains how such motives for action originally emerged in a specific social group. In the previous chapter, we briefly summarized several psychological theories that treat reputation as a cognitive trait, consolidated at key stages of ontogenesis. In this chapter, we have been discussing theories that focus on phylogeny, or the evolution of a social trait at the level of the population. In this context, to explain the presence of a characteristic way of acting, we need a theory about how the *reasons* that lead people to act this way emerge. Theories of emergent properties exert a particular fascination on contemporary social sciences, to the point of suggesting that we cannot understand the function of a social trait such as reputation without carefully examining its origins.

The history of philosophy is replete with genealogies that purport to explain the emergence of human society. In his *Discourse on the Origin and Basis of Inequality among Men* (1754), for instance, Jean-Jacques Rousseau reconstructs the history of humanity on the basis of the motivations and needs that, he contends, drove human beings to join together in a social contract.

After satisfying their needs for subsistence and survival, after learning to hunt together, live in families, and build shelters to protect themselves, human beings, Rousseau writes, begin to examine each other. And in the course of evenings spent in front of their primitive dwellings, exposing themselves to the gaze of others, both self-love and the desire to be seen emerge:

> They grew accustomed to assemble in front of their huts or around a large tree. Song and dance, true children of love and leisure, became the amusement or rather the occupation of idle men and women gathered together. Each began to look at the others and to want to be looked at himself, and public esteem had a value. The one who sang or danced

> the best, the most beautiful, the strongest, the most clever, or the most eloquent became the most highly considered—and this, then, was the first step toward inequality and at the same time toward vice. From these first preferences arose vanity and contempt, on the one hand, and shame and envy, on the other. And the fermentation caused by these new leavens eventually produced compounds fatal to happiness and innocence. As soon as men had begun to make assessments of one another and the idea of esteem was formed in their minds, each claimed a right to it, and it was no longer possible for anyone to deprive anyone of it with impunity. (2012, 95–96)

Like evolutionary explanations, genealogical fictions about how society originally emerged from the state of nature help us reconcile sociological explanations of how subconscious drivers of action (such as amour propre) originally emerged with an individual's conscious reasons and motives for acting, thus avoiding a vicious circle. Both genres combine a strictly philosophical exploration of the conditions for the possibility of the emergence of a social trait with ordinary historical and causal inquiry.

As a result, contemporary evolutionary explanations of the emergence of society have exactly the same merits and defects as traditional fables about the state of nature. Their status is extremely dubious from an epistemological point of view. To see why, it suffices to recall the criticisms leveled by Michel Foucault against all theories of origins. His archaeological and genealogical method was formulated in opposition to "the meta-historical unfolding of ideal meanings and indefinite teleologies" and against every "search for origins" (1977, 140). The all-inclusive explanations he condemned seem to confuse the conditions for the possibility of a concept with the conditions for its actual emergence, thus reintroducing a historical teleology that we might have thought superseded at least since Nietzsche's critique of history. These grand narratives treat the concepts they study as if they were fixed metaphysical universals whose history could be traced in a linear fashion.

Foucault's genealogical method was supposed to be an antidote to such grand narratives: "A genealogy of values, morality, asceticism, and knowledge will never confuse itself with a quest for their 'origins,' will never neglect as inaccessible the vicissitudes of history. On the contrary, it will cultivate the details and accidents that accompany every beginning" (1977, 144). Reading these lines in light of our leading question helps us see that care for one's reputation is distributed very unequally in different eras and societies. It is a fundamental value in certain historical periods, while in others it is condemned as aristocratic vanity and pretentiousness. In the Middle Ages, *fama* was a publicly recognized value, which possessed a precise legal function,[12] while the quest for "fifteen minutes of fame," to recall Andy Warhol's popular gag, is now considered perfectly frivolous and futile. The work of the sociologist Norbert Elias reinforces this point. Elias shows how the emergence of court society in Europe, that is to say, a society in which consumption habits were a function of social status and had nothing to do with expected gains, is historically situated and therefore highly contingent. Elias cites a telling example of the aristocratic ethos specific to seventeenth-century European courtier society, citing a gesture of the Duc de Richelieu narrated by Hippolyte Taine in his history of the ancien régime in France:

12. It was possible to invoke one's fame or reputation as proof of honesty in a legal process. See Fenster and Smail 2003.

> He gives his son a purse full of money so that he can learn to spend it like a *grand seigneur*, and when the young man brings the money back his father throws the purse out the window before his eyes. This socialization is in keeping with a social tradition that imprints on the individual the duty imposed on him by his rank to be prodigal. (1983, 67)

A pivotal moment in the education (*Bildung*) of a young gentleman at the time was when he learned to consume not for material satisfaction but to display his illustrious social rank!

That such impulses can persist into the present time has been stressed by one of the most astute commentators on the behavioral style of Donald Trump before he became the U.S. president:

> Trump has thumped around Manhattan for an epoch like a dinosaur that survived extinction, anachronistic proof of Veblen's late 19th-century *Theory of the Leisure Class*, an anthropological examination of the robber barons, published in 1899. Veblen described the tycoons flaunting their conspicuous consumption, their atavistic appropriation of feudal symbols suggesting pre-industrial rank, and their treatment of women as "trophies"—an "archaic trait" that "begins in the lower barbarian stages of culture." The key to understanding these displays was that they established social status as based on the moguls' distance from actual productive work.[13]

Yet this sort of snobbish disdain for "bourgeois" thrift and productive work cannot be observed in all historical periods. Although it played an important role in the formation of Euro-

13. Blumenthal 2017.

pean consciousness during the apogee of courtier civilization, it is usually considered a lapse of rationality in most developed societies today. We can also criticize ahistorical accounts of reputation's social function by pointing out that there are strong differences in the way reputations are managed depending on social class and geographical location. Preoccupation with reputation is an aristocratic obsession taken up later by certain members of the middle classes obsessed with ascending the social ladder. But such a preoccupation was despised by both the poorest classes and the commercial bourgeoisie. True, *fare bella figura* or presenting the best of oneself remains a powerful motivation for Italians and Japanese today. But it is largely absent from cultures such as those of northern Europe and the United States. In Japan, a culture of honor remains alive today, presumably a legacy of the chivalrous culture of the samurai. It is linked to manners, to social distinction, and to an essentially *comparative* vision of moral value. The culture of honor in the American South or in southern Italy, by contrast, is linked more explicitly to masculinity and violence.[14] President Donald Trump's seemingly insatiable need to soak up the limelight and his obsession with how he is portrayed in the media presumably have more to do with wanting to look like a macho "winner" than with any Japanese-style reluctance to appear indecorous or disreputable.

Could a genealogical reconstruction, in the style of Foucault, of the "epistemological breaks" or contingent historical discontinuities in the evolution of the concept of reputation help us understand reputation's role in contemporary social epistemology? I doubt it for several reasons. First of all, gene-

14. On the culture of honor in the American South, see Nisbett and Cohen 1996; on the culture of honor in Japan, see Ikegami 1995.

alogy à la Foucault, an epistemologically praiseworthy project aimed at doing away with all grand great narratives, has become today, especially in those postmodern approaches fashionable in American departments of cultural studies, another form of all-encompassing narrative: a search for the unclean origins of moral and social concepts by revealing the indecent relations of power and abuse of power that underlie them. Second, it seems to me that both epistemological approaches—evolutionary and genealogical—can be criticized by raising the same methodological objection, namely that both fall victim to a genetic fallacy, or the lack of a demonstrable causal link between the history of a concept and the concept itself. Thus, just as ontogeny does not recapitulate phylogeny, so ontology does not recapitulate philology. What a concept explains does not necessarily have anything to do with its history.[15] The centrality of reputation in furnishing the everyday knowledge we need to navigate a complex modern society, for example, cannot be understood through a genealogical reconstruction of reputation's beginnings.

Neither the search for the "conditions of emergence" typical of evolutionary theories nor the search for "epistemological breaks" characteristic of genealogical approaches is very helpful for understanding the complexity of a phenomenon such as reputation, because their common aim—to give an ahistorical account of the emergence of the *hidden motives* of our actions—is overly ambitious.

In the rest of this book, I adopt neither of these two epistemologies. I prefer a much more modest intellectual approach: the conceptual analysis of the idea of reputation as it exists in

15. The phrase "ontology recapitulates philology," cited here in the negative, is borrowed from the American philosopher W. V. O. Quine. See Quine 1960.

the language of everyday life and as it is studied by social scientists. I want to understand the trajectory of its meanings, put them in the context of existing theories, and see if they satisfy the minimal rationality constraints on explanation that I presented at the beginning of this chapter, while always keeping in mind the highly contingent historical and social dimensions of reputation as a complex and changing phenomenon. The social epistemology or "situated epistemology" that I follow is largely inspired by the theory of knowledge advocated by authors such as Ian Hacking, Lorraine Daston, and Steve Shapin. For these authors, philosophy is the history of the present or a kind of *historical epistemology*. To maintain the requirements of the rationality of explanations, they adopt a situated and contextual perspective in their philosophical study of concepts. To write a history of the present is to analyze how a concept is structured and stabilized at a certain historical moment, around specific values and practices, in order to understand its contemporary significance. Historical epistemology requires accepting a "minimal nominalism" about the ontology of concepts and concentrating, among all the possible worlds that a concept could have helped create, on those that it actually contributed to creating. This, I argue, is a form of conceptual analysis that makes eminent sense. To examine concepts apart from (and even against the grain of) all grand historical narratives does not mean deconstructing them or revealing that they are "socially constructed." It is neither hermeneutic exegesis nor paranoid genealogy. This is why our students do not need much exegesis to profit from reading a text by Hobbes or Rousseau. Understanding the context that gives reality to an idea does not mean deconstructing it historically. And this is why conceptual abstraction, empirical analysis, and historical interpretation can proceed together and collaborate to give a concept such as "reputation" sufficient theoretical richness, lucidity, and fertility. To pursue such a historically sensitive and analytically revealing examination of the evolving reality of reputation as a crucial factor in social life, we must not, of course, neglect literary works, an inexhaustible source of examples and counterfactual situations that enliven conceptual analysis thanks to marvelous journeys on which they take us through possible worlds that are very close to our own, even if they never become reality.

But before proceeding in the next chapter to the heart of my argument, I need to introduce one more analytical tool, which, like the rational-actor theory presented at the beginning of the chapter, helps us understand how a reputation can be formed and maintained. I now turn briefly to signaling theory.

Tell Me What You Do and I'll Tell You Who You Are: Reputation as a Signal

The story of Gaius Mucius Scaevola is recounted by several ancient authors, including Livy, Plutarch, and Dionysius of Halicarnassus. In 507 BC, this young hero of the Roman Republic thrust his right hand into the fire in front of the Etruscan king Porsenna, looking him straight in the eye and saying, "Watch, so that you know how cheap the mere human body is to men who have set their eye on great glory!" By this gesture, Mucius signaled his undying dedication to the republic and his commitment to defend it against a renewed attack by the Etruscans. Released by Porsenna, who was impressed by the young Roman's steely determination, Mucius then revealed that there were at least another three hundred Roman soldiers ready to sacrifice themselves in an attempt to kill the

Etruscan king. Frightened by the revelation, Porsenna beat a retreat.

Holding one's hand steadily in a fire without wincing from pain is a credible signal of one's valor as a tenacious and unflinching warrior devoted to his country. Indeed, it is virtually impossible to let your hand burn while gazing silently into the eyes of your enemy unless you actually *are* a tenacious and devoted warrior. Mucius created his own reputation and proved its veracity on the spot.

In trying to make sense of the strategic use of reputation, and not only to intimidate one's enemies, many studies invoke *signaling theory*. Sociologist Diego Gambetta (2009) describes this theory in an original way by weaving together disparate strands of research ranging from the work of Thorstein Veblen on conspicuous consumption to that of Bourdieu on the signs of social distinction, from the writings of Goffman to those of Thomas Schelling and Robert Jervis on strategic interactions between states. He brings in evolutionary biology and the study of signals exchanged between animals as well.

Unlike strategic theories of reputation based on rational calculation, signaling theory has the advantage of combining rationality constraints on strategic behavior with an understanding of reputation as a fundamentally communicative phenomenon. As we will see even more clearly, the hallmark of reputation is that it can be communicated: Who says what about whom? Signaling theory also helps explain how we can strategically exploit the fact that our behavior always tells others something about us.

The main problem afflicting the communication of signals is as follows: I want to convey a quality *k* to someone, for example, that I am filthy rich or fiercely vindictive or secretly well connected or amazingly clever. There are a number of actions that I can take to communicate the quality in question to the receptor of my signals. If the receptor acknowledges that I possess this quality on the basis of my signal, then I benefit. But beware: I benefit whether or not I actually possess the quality *k*. If I successfully convey to my bank that I am very reliable by always arriving punctually and well-dressed for my appointments with the loan officer, I can receive a low-interest loan, whether I am a low-risk borrower or not. But the receptor, in this case the bank, will benefit only if I really possess the quality *k*. If I am not reliable but the loan officer believes I am, the bank will be left with a client who has trouble paying her monthly installments. Signaling theory is built on this fundamental asymmetry between what the transmitter of a signal knows and what the signal's receptor knows.

Most of what it is important to know about others—honesty, reliability, efficiency, wealth, intelligence—is empirically unobservable. We must infer these invisible traits from signs. But these signs can be more or less honest. Signaling theory, therefore, draws a basic distinction between honest and dishonest signals, based on the classical distinction between signs and signals.[16] A signal is produced *intentionally*, as when I deliberately communicate to others my possession of an unobservable quality *k*. A sign, by contrast, is not produced intentionally. Speaking a foreign language with an accent provides others with information about my origins, but I do not usually adopt such an accent intentionally. A sign is simply everything that can be perceived in the environment and that modifies our beliefs about people or things. Nevertheless, signs, while unintended, are not always "natural." Their informational value depends on what receptors are able to perceive and interpret. A

16. See Grice 1957.

hairstyle can be a sign of adhering to a particular social class in one social milieu and not in another. I was once in a London pub with a friend who told me to order white wine and not beer because, at the time, a woman drinking beer in a pub signaled a lack of class. Signs are not intentional, therefore, but neither are they "natural." Wrinkles are an unintentional and involuntary sign of aging, but the fact that people perceive wrinkles as a sign of aging and pay attention to them in certain situations depends precisely on the context and the social and cultural norms that shape the sensibilities of the receptor and interpreter of this particular sign.

For analytical purposes we need to distinguish signs from signals. But signs can become signals when we flaunt them in an ostentatious manner. I can decide to reveal in a provocative way a scar or a tattoo by deliberately exposing to public view the part of my body where it appears. Although most of our traits do not become purposely conveyed signals, some do. These constitute our "reputation," that is, the subset of signs that we purposely emit and that subsequently escape our control by falling into the hands of those who observe us. I can be more or less conscious of the way others interpret a number of my traits and actions as "signifying" certain of my hidden qualities, and I can therefore try to manipulate these signs by making them more or less visible, or showing them only to those people capable of extracting especially gratifying and positive information about me.

Conversely, past signals can become signs today: I first get a tattoo to indicate that I am a free-living girl with no inhibitions, but when I subsequently become a serious academic, that tattoo embarrasses me. It remains there, a trace of the reputation I once strove to convey but that I now wish to conceal. The "signals" studied by biologists—apart from a few exceptions—are not intentional. They are chosen by natural selection, that is, for their value in promoting fitness. The splendid peacock's tail when fully extended is a sign of beauty. The male peacock can "decide" to open and shake his tail to seduce a female, but he does not decide the length of his feathers, even if the female peacock will interpret long feathers as an indicator of her suitor's power and prowess.

For Veblen and Bourdieu, individuals produce signals no more intentionally than do peacocks. What individuals falsely believe to be their voluntary signals are, seen realistically, nothing but expressions of their place in the social hierarchy. The way an individual displays his relative social status is, in reality, a function of his social class and, ultimately, of the master class's drive to consolidate its power. In his seminal 1899 book, *The Theory of the Leisure Class*, a sociological classic describing the lifestyle of the new class of wealthy Americans, Veblen argues that leisure is a way for a dominant social class to signal its wealth. Highly developed athletic skills or mastery of ancient languages is a sign that its possessors have plenty of time on their hands. These are luxuries that only the wealthy can afford. Just so, the long fingernails of well-groomed ladies are signs of a life of leisure. Just try having a nice manicure if you have to cook and do the dishes every evening!

One of the thorniest problems of signaling theory, in any case, is the possibility of misrepresentation. I can sometimes convey a signal that indicates my possession of a quality that I lack. The risks of strategic misrepresentation are therefore very high. This is why game theory speaks of semi-sorting equilibria. Although a signal s will be emitted by anyone who wants to signal their quality k, s can also be emitted by some who does not have the quality k.

So how do honest transmitters and receivers guard themselves against the menace posed by imposters? Formulated differently, what is the perfect signal? The answer is: a perfect signal would be a signal that could never be successfully feigned. The theory of honest signals, that is, signals that are not wholly fake proof but are nevertheless designed to be very difficult to fake, helps explain phenomena ranging from animal behavior to interaction between states. We have already encountered the example of Mucius. Another good example of an honest signal, unlikely to be mimicked by an impostor, would be the decision of an architect to move to the top floor of a skyscraper he designed. Such a move provides credible evidence that the building is in no imminent danger of collapsing. But in daily life, most of the signals we emit are the semi-sorting or imperfect type. They convey credible but not completely credible information. Honest signals are believable to the extent that few can afford to imitate them. Faking such a signal would normally cost too much.

Yet some perfidious signalers seem willing to pay any price. Take the example of suicide terrorists. Being ready to die for a cause is a very expensive signal. Yet today we see a virtual cascade of "martyrs" who in reality have no particular desire to attack the West, no precise ideology, no zealous devotion, and no special predisposition to violence. They are often casually recruited (or self-recruited) on the Internet and are willing to emit a highly costly signal without knowing why. Some want to go to paradise, apparently. Others have nothing better to do. But whoever observes such signals will tend to project onto the self-sacrificing suicide terrorist a strong commitment to a cause, although in many cases such a commitment does not in fact exist. Indeed, reading heroic commitment into costly signals, as we are tempted to do, can lead to ill-formulated deradicalization policies in cases where such a heroic commitment is actually nonexistent and is indeed nothing but a figment of the receptors' imagination produced by misinterpreting a high-cost signal. Signaling theory, of course, does not maintain that formally "honest signals" are invariably reliable. What makes the signal relatively reliable is the difference between the low cost of producing it honestly (if I have the quality *k*) and the high cost of producing it dishonestly (if I do not have the quality *k*). But although extremely high costs deter dishonest signaling most of the time, they do not make dishonest signaling impossible.

Signaling theory, as we shall see, helps us understand strategies for honestly or dishonestly fashioning and communicating one's reputation in the expectation of subsequent benefits in the context of more general systems for exchanging social information. But it assumes a very simple form of reputation, linked to the presence or absence of a quality *k*, without taking into account a basic social component of reputation: its complex and variable *distribution* within a population.

With these preliminary methodological reflections behind us, we can now turn to the next chapter, dedicated to examining the essentially communicative dimension of reputation: its existence not only in the eyes of others but within the cascade of communicated words and speeches that others share among themselves as well as with us.

3

"Somebody Told Me," or How Reputations Spread

> I think that both candidates, Crooked Hillary and myself, should release detailed medical records. I have no problem in doing so! Hillary?
>
> —@REALDONALDTRUMP, AUGUST 20, 2016

> Reputations of this sort, even if true, are created out of other people's ideas.
>
> —MARCEL PROUST, *SWANN IN LOVE*

A reputation is composed of the opinions of others. References to "opinion" are inevitably incorporated in lexical definitions of the word. In the *OED*, for instance, reputation is defined as "1. The condition or fact of being highly regarded or esteemed" and "2. The general opinion or estimate of a person's character, behavior, etc.; the relative esteem in which a person or thing is held." In the *Larousse*, similarly, reputation is defined as "the favorable or unfavorable opinion that the public holds of someone or something." But such definitions, while accurate enough, fail to account for an essential aspect of reputation, one brought into focus by the prefix "re" indicating repetition. A reputation is no mere opinion. It is an opinion that is verbalized, spoken, repeated, and disseminated and that is therefore essentially communicative in nature. Shakespeare was fully aware of the essentially communicative nature of reputation when he had Cassio, who was sinking into despair after having tarnished his own reputation in Othello's eyes, reiterate the term three times: "Reputation, reputation, reputation! Oh, I have lost my reputation! I have lost the immortal part of myself, and what remains is bestial." Incurably wounded, Cassio knows that his immortal self lies not only in Othello's view of him but also in the assessments that the wider world entertains and that are echoed back and forth from one person to another. These socially resonating opinions contain whatever signs of prestige and recognition that others are willing to bestow. They circulate by hearsay as well as by other means for spreading information that are more susceptible to control, including, for example, the written word.

Reputation is a cloud of opinions that circulates according to its own laws, operating independently of the individual beliefs and intentions of those who hold and communicate the opinions in question. The strategic uses of reputation, described in chapter 2, show that reputations can occasionally be consciously and successfully manipulated. But this does little to reduce the general anxiety and uncertainty stemming from an ungovernable transmission and propagation of reputations, the risks of defamation, and the difficulty of restoring a reputation once it has been blackened by rumors and gossip.

The essentially communicative nature of reputation is often disregarded in studies of the phenomenon. Yet reputation, far from being a simple opinion, is a public representation of what we believe to be the opinions of others. We may find ourselves expressing and conveying this *opinion about opinions* for all sorts of reasons, out of conformism or to appear to be in sync with the opinions of everyone else. There is a fundamental difference between a mere opinion and what we believe we *should* think of someone on the basis of the opinion of those we consider more or less authoritative. For instance, I can have an opinion about my prime minister yet still be susceptible to what a newspaper I regularly read and trust has to say about him. In this case, I may well end up uncritically absorbing, as if by osmosis, the views espoused by my favorite editorialist. Most of our opinions about the people and things around us depend on the *weight* we ascribe to the opinions voiced by others. Both the essentially communicative nature of reputation and its centrality to social order become clear once we see it as *an opinion we have of the more or less authoritative opinions formed by others*—that is to say, as a second-order opinion, as something we believe we must believe.

To explore the various ways in which reputations spread, we need first to distinguish between two basic categories: (1) informal reputations and (2) formal or "objectivized" reputations. The first category contains all the sociocognitive phenomena connected to the circulation of opinions: rumors, gossip, innuendo, indiscretions, informational cascades, and so forth. The second includes all of the official schemes for putting reputations into an "objective" format, such as rating and ranking systems, product labels, and informational hierarchies established by algorithms on the basis of Internet searches. I shall return to formal reputations later in the book. In this chapter, I will be focusing primarily on reputations that spread informally.

Informal reputations have a terrible reputation. Idle gossip and scandalmongering are blamed for many of our wholly baseless and erroneous opinions. The social world is crisscrossed by informal communication pathways—secondary routes through which information steals anonymously, trails that appear on no map and that are beaten flat only by the repeated passage of travelers. These surreptitious and unofficial channels from which we draw many of our beliefs are said to nourish and exacerbate collective ignorance, mass irrationality, and uncritical credulity. But is this really the case?

The continuous warnings we hear about the risks inherent in informal communication are to some extent justified. But they may also conceal a drive for authoritarian control of the sources of our beliefs about the world. Alternatively, they may reflect a kind of primitive anxiety aroused by the clandestine pathways through which disparaging or embarrassing opinions freely and invisibly circulate. This chapter attempts to map these pathways in an effort to show that they are not always so dangerous and that they may, on the contrary, make a positive contribution to the circulation of ideas and the construction of opinions. We simply need to understand the structure and form they episodically assume and learn how to control them.

Opinions that circulate are reputations, that is, the viewpoints of other people to which we feel in some manner obliged to subscribe. This is why, as Robert Darnton (2010) has demonstrated, calumny in pre-Revolutionary France was deemed a literary genre in its own right. It was deployed at the time as an effective tool for combating the alleged abuses of sovereign authority. Libertine writers, polemicists, and pen pushers were arrested and tortured for using illegal publications to attack the reputations of France's elite, that is, for their defamatory and rapidly diffused writings against court and king.

A counterexample can illustrate the positive cognitive role that, contrary to their ill repute, informal channels for challenging undeserved reputations can play. *Pluralistic ignorance* is well known to social scientists. People are sometimes induced by social circumstances to subscribe publicly to a certain opinion, such as a preference for a political party or a positive appreciation of a work of art, only to discover belatedly that, contrary to what they thought, no one they know actually shares that opinion. Turkish American sociologist Timur Kuran (1997) argues that one reason why political changes, such as revolutions, are so hard to predict is because there is a divergence between the preferences people feel compelled to express publicly and those they really have. The extent and intensity of public discontent are revealed only when the old system begins to crumble. Subjects of a dictatorial regime, for instance, are typically wary of open dissent against their government. For safety's sake, they aim to keep their heads down by giving lip service to whatever they take to be the majority opinion. In so doing, they enable the circulation of pro-regime opinions that they do not share but that they falsely believe to be widely held. The phenomenon of pluralistic ignorance thus illustrates the essentially communicative aspect of reputation. Reputations are maintained by a circulation of true or false opinions about opinions. They can be destroyed, subversively, in the same way. The point to stress here is that reputation is always an opinion about an opinion, that is, a "meta-representation" that dictates what opinions we *should* hold about other people. In short, it is an idea about ideas that guides us in selecting what we ought to think, or pretend to think, of other people.[1]

Pluralistic ignorance is not a new phenomenon. Psychologists Daniel Katz and Floyd Henry Allport introduced the concept in 1931 to explain the attitude of students who pretend that the material explained in class is perfectly clear and who ask no questions because they are convinced that others have understood everything perfectly and do not want to lose face before their peers. We often adopt an attitude or opinion because we believe we must. We attribute a good reputation to an idea, person, artwork, or organization out of fear of acquiring a bad reputation ourselves if we do not second the collective verdict. But sometimes this collective verdict *does not really exist.* It is simply a matter of everyone being erroneously convinced that everyone else has endorsed it. What we have here is, first, an individual belief that is strong enough to induce us to act as if we believed something which in fact we do not believe and, second, a collective consensus that is extremely fragile because, as soon as a few dissenters dare reveal their true preferences, others may quickly follow suit, tumbling like dominoes, as the phony collective verdict unravels.

Pluralistic ignorance is not the only vehicle by which "information clouds" form reputations. Other vehicles include informational cascades, rumors, and gossip. Each depends on the essentially meta-representational properties of reputation. What we think is what we believe we are obliged to think, in a delicate oscillation between a preoccupation with our own reputation (which impels us to adopt the beliefs that will enable us to show our best side to others) and our simultaneous

1. On the concept of meta-representation and in general on second-order opinions, see Sperber 1996, 2000.

participation in the diffusion of the reputation of others. This is how an individual psychological attitude can turn into the collective diffusion of ideas. The macroscopic effects of the phenomenon are very distinct from the microscopic causes that gave rise to it. It is important to understand this difference in order to avoid drawing overly pessimistic conclusions about human irrationality and credulity. We are neither particularly gullible nor incurably stupid. Information that circulates, be it of the "lowest" order, such as gossip or rumor, will always have some sort of informational content. It is entirely reasonable and understandable to endorse a publicly agreed-upon viewpoint when the price we would have to pay for rejecting it would be too high, or when we simply have no idea about what to believe about a particular question. We often believe what we read in the paper because, we tell ourselves, if the truth were otherwise, we would have heard about it. We pay attention to gossip because, in a particular circumstance and at a particular moment, it may be the only way to obtain a piece of information about a topic we care about, however partial or imprecise that information may prove to be. Yet when such phenomena multiply, one ends up with collective irrationality, where we express opinions in which we do not believe, convinced that others genuinely believe what they say, and where we participate in the circulation of a piece of gossip because of the impact it would have *if it were true* ("can you believe it!"), regardless of its actual veracity.

Informational Cascades

Informational cascades are common in the media and online. They occur when a group of people accepts an opinion—or behaves as if it did—without proof of that opinion's truth.

When other individuals, who have given no thought to the matter, parrot the opinion of that group, as sociologist Fabrice Clément remarks in his preface to the French edition of Cass Sunstein's book on rumors,

> they become in turn the "heralds" of that opinion. They don't even have to believe in it. It suffices that they don't question it publicly (for instance, from fear of losing the respect of their fellow group members) for other people who have been exposed to that rumor to believe it should be given credit. Ricocheting through social networks, the belief will spread to more and more people, who will tell themselves that it is impossible for so many people to be mistaken. In this way the cascade is set in motion, and the diffusion of the rumor risks becoming massive.[2]

Cascades develop because people "buy" opinions with their eyes closed, without checking what they are buying, just because everyone else has apparently made the same purchase. They make no effort to look into the matter themselves, trusting instead in a form of "collective intelligence" that selects for them the "right" opinions. If everyone shares that opinion, there must be good reasons to believe it, even if we ignore what these reasons are.

All of us have the experience of adopting opinions because of such cascade effects, after making little effort to double-check their validity. I remember how, after the first debate between Barack Obama and Mitt Romney during the 2012 U.S. presidential campaign, most of my liberal American friends reported that Obama had revealed himself to be a terrible speaker. I started repeating this secondhand assessment, out

2. See Clément 2012, 18, 19.

of inertia, because I hadn't had the time to watch the debate in full and because, during those weeks, when everyone was talking about it, I was constantly being pressed to say what I thought about it. I was inadvertently feeding an informational cascade according to which Obama had "lost" the first debate. But when I finally took the time to watch it in full, I realized that I had been spreading a highly dubious judgment. Obama had been more skillful and precise than Romney, and he had avoided playing the game, into which Romney had tried to drag him, of "bullshit escalation," typical of such television debates, with their litany of inaccurate data, questionable numbers, and made-up statistics. The question this raises is why it is so easy to internalize and echo the viewpoint of others, unthinkingly, even when important issues are at stake.

When caught up in an informational cascade, we have difficulty maintaining critical distance on the situation or person in question: we are operating "under the influence." And it is fatefully easy to succumb to the influence of others. Indeed, believing something because everyone else believes it, without bothering to verify the accuracy of the belief, should be understood not only as a cognitive failing but also as a well-tested cognitive strategy, advantageous enough in most circumstances to have become one of the most common means for diffusing information. Indeed, the considerable risks associated with rumors and opinions that spread uncontrollably result from two main factors. One is our cognitive facility for *social learning*, that is, for employing cognitive heuristics or shortcuts that lead us, like apprentices copying their masters, to espouse the beliefs of others in order to acquire information and learn faster. The second factor is the social constellation that permits the diffusion of this information and that depends, in large part, on who is the first to put this information into circulation and on their desire to acquire prestige by inducing others to adopt their point of view.

Here are a few examples. Companies like Christian Dior and Nestlé spend millions of dollars for the "face" of such celebrities as Monica Bellucci and George Clooney. Marketing experts know how to exploit our disposition to learning by imitation, which translates into our easy acceptance of various heuristics. One such easily exploitable rule of thumb is the imperative to "follow the leader." According to evolutionary psychologists Joseph Henrich and Francisco Gil-White, this heuristic corresponds to an actual *prestige bias*, whose stability within our evolutionary history is due to its huge advantages for helping apprentices learn. Some of the most desirable skills are highly difficult to acquire. One doesn't know exactly what determines the success of a good tennis player or a great chef. It is virtually impossible to disentangle all the elements that contribute to their greatest achievement into a series of discrete actions that apprentices could imitate one at a time. Learners are therefore better-off imitating their model in its entirety, thereby copying not only the elements that contribute to the master's success but also those that have nothing to do with it.

To adopt a model is not to be uncritical, however. It is simply to be strategic. No one knows what special combination of qualities and propensities made Ludwig Wittgenstein one of the most captivating and famous philosophers of the twentieth century. This is why so many young and aspiring philosophers tacitly adopt Wittgenstein's physical demeanor, including his tics, faults, accent, and dress, in a kind of magical attempt to acquire their model's exemplary stature. I remember an Australian philosopher friend in Oxford who could not resist the temptation to wear tweed jackets in the style of

Wittgenstein in an attempt to replicate the master's style—never mind that, with his surfer's shoulders, the result was not exactly convincing.

Needless to say, this young Australian philosopher had not been encouraged in his mimetic homage by Wittgenstein himself. He had spontaneously adopted it in his search for borrowed prestige and recognition. But we cannot speak of voluntary imitation when those who coax and cajole us into copying a model have a strategic interest in our doing so that is not our own. This is the case with advertising. Here the background advantages of social learning disappear and we end up following models offered to us for entirely spurious reasons.

Sociocognitive phenomena such as informational cascades, gossip, and pluralistic ignorance arise out of a combination of cognitive mechanisms on the one hand and, on the other hand, from ecological factors that favor the diffusion of information within a social, natural, or virtual environment. What drives us to espouse the judgment of others is well studied in psychological terms, as is the case with the psychology of influence, and more recently with experimental economics, in particular the study of heuristics used in drawing probabilistic inferences.[3] Heuristics are inferences that guide our reasoning in the absence of information. According to the approach of what economist and psychologist Herbert Simon has called *situated cognition*, we do not necessarily use such heuristics only in the absence of anything better, thereby lapsing into tendentious judgments. "Less is more" is one such heuristic and, far from being a faute de mieux rule of thumb, it is at times and in certain contexts the very best way to resolve a complex problem.

3. See Cialdini 1984; Gigerenzer, Hertwig, and Pachur 2011; Richerson and Boyd 2005.

Paradoxically, less information and less precise inferences can lead us to arrive at more solid conclusions. According to Gerd Gigerenzer, one of the contemporary psychologists who study these matters, the heuristic that guides us in the case of informational cascades is "follow the majority!" In many circumstances, it is better to take into consideration the beliefs of the majority that prevails within our reference group, in order to adopt the "right" opinion or make the right decision. The presence of these heuristics is thus not a phenomenon of mass irrationality that inexorably drags us toward a *credulous society* of people who will believe just about anything, to use the phrase of Gérald Bronner, who, along with Cass Sunstein, depicts society in exactly these bleak and disparaging terms.[4] Informational cascades are due to ecologically infelicitous conditions in the application of perfectly legitimate heuristics. Think for a moment about the origins of most of our beliefs. It is thanks to these heuristics that we are able to believe what we believe. And it would be rather dismaying to conclude that all our beliefs are baseless and irrational.

"Women's Speech": Rumor and Tittle-Tattle

Gossipmongers ruin reputations. They are curious, ignorant, prattling people (often assumed to be female) who talk nonstop about what is everyone's favorite topic of conversation: other people. They adore scandals and they enjoy provoking them. They eagerly circulate false information about people just to smear their reputations. In his novel *Béatrix*, Balzac wrote that it is typical for women to "prefer the celebrity of a scandal to tranquil happiness; they fly in the face of society to

4. See Sunstein 2009 and Bronner 2013.

obtain the fatal alms of a rebuke; they desire to be talked about at any cost" (1999, 108).

Slanderous rumors, malicious small talk, scuttlebutt, back-fence chatter, and belittling insinuation—all such ways of talking about the absent fall under the category of gossip. They are evaluative assessments of people in their absence. Usually attributed to women, this type of talk is actually the background noise of all societies, where reputations are made and unmade. As soon as a rumor begins to circulate, regardless of whether it is true or false, it can ruin the reputation of the person it targets. Hebrew law forbids talking behind people's backs, whether truthfully or not: *lashon harah* (which literally means "evil tongue"), that is, to speak about someone out of their hearing, is prohibited. To say that someone eats like a pig, even if it is true, or that someone has betrayed his wife can create serious problems by corroding structured and established social relations. Malicious gossip is therefore seen as a force that is potentially destructive of social order. It is commonly condemned for this reason.

Anthropologist Niko Besnier has studied the chatter of women on Nukulaelae, one of the Fiji Islands, which typically occurs around an open-air hut—an *umu* in the local language—where they cook for the whole village. The *umu* is neither a public nor a private space; it connects village and beach. Although it is a "domestic" space, it is open to everyone. This is where women congregate to cook and talk about others. This small atoll has the reputation of being an "island of gossip." While they fan sleeping children with large palm leaves or prepare lunch, the women laugh, joke, make alliances, and lean close to each other to tell a story so that others won't listen in, always wary of the danger of acquiring an unseemly reputation as a "gossip." When Besnier (2009) interviewed the men about the island's reputation, they unhesitatingly condemned gossip, which to them was women's talk fraught with risk because it swirled around uncontrollably and ruined people's reputations irreparably.

This taken-for-granted association between women and gossip is connected to society's power structures. It is largely based on prejudice. Statistics show that over 60 percent of adult conversations concern people who are absent, regardless of the interlocutors' gender.[5] Upon those who lack official power, to be sure, gossip bestows the informal power of influencing the reputations of others. This is how gossip functions as an alternative "political discourse" that can destabilize or upend social hierarchies. But gossip can also strengthen social ties and help forge alliances, thereby allowing the gossiper to manipulate social relations strategically. In her eloquently titled book *You Just Don't Understand*, sociolinguist Deborah Tannen compares female and male talk, and tries to make sense of the prejudice that gossipy talk is more widespread among women than among men. Men, she suggests, are more likely than women to compare their own performances with each other and to hide their weaknesses. According to Tannen, men and women manage networks of social relations differently. Women, apparently, are more at ease than men with the informal side of social relations. Their role in seventeenth- and eighteenth-century salons, and generally in court society, frequently involved deploying those most dangerous weapons, defamation and malicious gossip, arrows that, once shot, could not be recalled.

Beyond its social function, gossip has a very particular pragmatics that distinguishes it from other types of speech

5. See Dunbar 1996.

acts. It is often introduced with the clause "It seems that," "They say that," and so forth, as if the speaker wants to avoid being identified as the source of the gossip and prefers to be a simple *transmitter*. Gossip is reported talk, *hearsay* that one delivers to others at their own risk and peril, without taking on the illocutionary responsibility of the act, that is, without using the direct indicative form that would imply that the speaker takes responsibility for what he or she says: "I am saying this." However, this epistemic uncertainty has no bearing on the likelihood that the piece of gossip will spread. In the terminology of linguistics, expressions such as "It seems that" and "They say that" are called *evidential constructions. Evidentiality* is a property of language, present in all tongues, that indicates the degree of control that the speaker exercises over the events he or she is talking about. It differs from *epistemic modality*, which, by contrast, indicates the degree of epistemic certainty of a fact's reality, with expressions of the type "It is possible that." In linguistics, these expressions are seen as a way to weaken the "realist" stamp typical of indicative speech. Such modal discourse becomes imbued with a sense of likelihood, allowing one to talk about things that could not happen or do not exist at all. But these epistemic nuances do not stop gossip from circulating. Why is that? Where does the authority of these expressions come from, devoid as they are of the authority of a speaker who assumes even a bare minimum of responsibility for them? Evidential constructions have a different sort of authority. They convey the authority of the social world concerning what one should and should not think of other people. The less certain their factual content, the stronger their social content. Others *are* what society or our reference group thinks of them. As a result, if I transmit that which I have learned from others, I affirm my membership in the group that thinks in the same way. I defer to the same social authority and I thereby reinforce my membership in the group. It is more likely that I will share hearsay gossip from a source that has authority for me, who comes from a social milieu to which I would like to belong, for instance, or in which I recognize myself. If I am a newcomer to a milieu that I deem prestigious, I will attempt to transmit the gossip it generates in order to demonstrate how integrated I am or wish to be. This will also help me learn its codes, norms, and language more quickly. The evidential constructions that are typical of such forms of communication, despite any residual doubts they may convey regarding the truth of the reports in question, are not therefore devoid of epistemic authority. Their epistemic authority simply operates at a different level: it is not a *factual authority* but a *social authority*. The reputation of the circle of reference is what confers authority on a piece of gossip, and my need to acquire the reputation as someone who belongs to that circle is what will induce me to participate in the circulation of that information.

Mastery of gossip can indeed be a sign of social distinction. It is typical of worldly socialites, of those who are at ease in navigating society. They are masters of small talk; they know how to spread indiscretions at will among those they want to influence discreetly:

> "I never repeat things." That is the ritual phrase of society, from which the slanderer always derives a false reassurance. . . . "If you don't wish it to be repeated, why do you say it?" That is the answer of the unsociable, of the quarrelsome.[6]

6. Proust 2003–4, vol. 2, *Within a Budding Grove*, Kindle edition, loc. 2524.

In this passage from *In Search of Lost Time*, Marcel Proust reveals the secrets of socialites who manage social information with discretion. They avoid taking complete responsibility for it and even beg that it not be disseminated further in order, presumably, to make it more attractive to those who will end up transmitting it anyway. Proust writes:

> That thing which is universally decried, which no one would dream of defending—gossip—has itself, whether it be aimed at ourselves and thus becomes especially disagreeable to us, or whether it tells us something about a third person of which we were unaware, a certain psychological value. It prevents the mind from falling asleep over the fictitious idea that it has of what it imagines things to be and that is actually no more than their outward appearance. It turns this appearance inside out with the magic dexterity of an idealist philosopher and rapidly presents to our gaze an unsuspected corner of the reverse side of the fabric.[7]

Gossip therefore has a double social function: to transmit informal and unauthorized information that nevertheless permits the questioning of received ideas and to reinforce membership in the circle of recognition of those who accept the authority of the "social evidence" that is transmitted by gossip.

Anthropologists and psychologists have also studied the social function of gossip. A few of them have argued, from a functionalist perspective, that gossip serves as social glue, reinforcing a group's shared norms. In 1963, Max Gluckman, a South African anthropologist and anti-Apartheid political activist, wrote one of his first essays on the virtues of gossip and

7. Proust 2003–4, vol. 4, part 2, chap. 3, Kindle edition, loc. 7856.

scandal in primitive societies, where he argued that they helped cement unity within the group. By constructing a story about a person, scandals served as "founding myths" of a group within a society. To know nothing about, or be uninterested in, the scandals pertaining to a society's distinguished members is to be an outsider. What makes social cohesion virtuous is the preservation of an informal community, one that recognizes itself within norms and values that can deviate from those of the official community. This is why Gluckman took an interest in the unofficial byways of communication in 1960s South Africa, a time of strong social segregation.

More recently, psychologist and primatologist Robin Dunbar took a step beyond the bounds of cultural anthropology by anchoring the benefits of gossip in evolution. According to his hypothesis, the practice of gossip in human societies replaced that of grooming in primate societies—those communal sessions of reciprocal cleaning by which primates map out social relations. For Dunbar, gossip functions in a similar way, serving to delineate a map of social relations, of who does what in society. Within our species, language is what makes it possible to go beyond the interaction between two people and to develop a pattern of "virtual" relations based on mutual knowledge of each other's reputations.

Over two-thirds of spontaneous conversations are about matters of social import: Who did what? Why? Was it allowed? For Dunbar (1996), the real function of language, and that which explains why it has evolved in our species, is not to produce an Einstein or a Shakespeare but rather to spread an endless blabla, a *basso continuo* akin to the buzzing of bees, which maintains social cohesion by helping identify a group's *free-riders*, that is, those who take advantage of the altruism of others without giving anything back in return.

It has always been condemned by authorities, experts, and governments. But gossip is neither frivolous palaver nor fake news. It is a form of *social information* that plays a crucial role in establishing—and sometimes subverting—a cognitive order. Otherwise, why would dictatorships fear whispering campaigns as much as they do, while democracies tolerate sleazy tabloids and have turned gossip into a virtual media industry?

In 1941, in the Soviet Union, Nina Vatolina produced a famous poster denouncing the risks of gossip. It depicts a menacing woman entreating the viewer to be quiet, under the verse of communist poet Samuil Marshak:

> Hold your eyes open,
> These days even the walls have ears
> Gossip and hearsay
> Go together with treason.

"Everyone Is Talking about It," or the Psychology of Rumor

Rumors are an informational cascade of a particular sort. What makes them interesting is that they spread so widely within a very brief time span. The distinctive characteristic of rumors is that they are known to be such. They are built on the popularity that a particular spatio-temporal configuration of information can acquire within a limited period of time. They do not necessarily propagate evaluative opinions about others. In other words, they are not merely vehicles for disseminating reputations. In this sense, they differ profoundly from gossip and hearsay, with which they are often associated. Rumor doesn't consist simply in talking about people behind their

FIGURE 1. "Ne boltai!" Nina Vatolina, 1941.
Copyright © FineArtImages/Leemage.

backs and commenting on their behavior. Rumor can consist in the spread of scandalous factual information, for instance, that in a 2005 video, Donald Trump spoke about sexually assaulting women: "Grab them by the pussy." Similarly, as the new millennium approached, the "millennium bug" rumor spread. It was not about anyone in particular. Yet it was a rumor and it was "trending." That is, it was a yet unverified piece of information whose high speed of diffusion was unrelated to its truth or probability.

The psychology of rumor in times of stress and crisis also has a long history. Rumor plays a crucial role both during wars and under dictatorships. The first significant data on this phenomenon emerged in the 1940s, initially with the publication in 1944 of research conducted by Robert Knapp (1944) and then in Gordon Allport and Joseph Portman's classic study of 1947. But why is war a propitious context for spreading rumors? According to Knapp, there are two main reasons: First, during wars, special military measures are introduced to protect the circulation of potentially strategic information, and censorship encourages the informal circulation of rumors. The second reason is the intensity of emotions during wars. When one searches for information, verified or not, out of a need for emotional solace and reassurance, one naturally latches onto rumors. Sometimes, in crisis situations, circulating information is retransmitted without any verification, simply because the "thirst" for information is so intense that one is ready to believe almost anything. Just as humor makes one laugh, according to Knapp, so rumor makes one believe. It presents itself as information that satisfies our need to believe. The pragmatics of rumor are crucial to its success. In their experiments, Allport and Portman would ask subjects to transmit information by word of mouth, as in the Chinese whispers game. They noticed that the systematic distortions of the information transmitted improved its memorability, its pertinence, and its immediacy. The experimental context of this research was the classical work of Frederic Bartlett dedicated to the constructive aspects of memory. In his book *Remembering*, published in 1932, Bartlett showed that the degradation and reconstruction of a message conveyed through Chinese whispers (or what Americans call "telephone") are a product of cognitive filters that constrain our access to our own memories. Rumors have a tendency to become conventional. As they are passed from one person to the next, they are distorted in such a way that they become increasingly standardized and memorable. This is why they can be used as *propaganda*. During wars, a highly effective instrument of persuasion is *informal propaganda*, that is, the intentional—on the part of those in power—spreading of rumors that can be easily remembered, that seem plausible, or that are salient in a certain context. Such rumors will spread rapidly even if they are false. "Successful" rumors are those that appeal to our need for wishful thinking and that confirm our deepest fears. This suggests that Spinoza was right when he argued that hope and fear are the two emotions with the greatest effect on which information we select and retain. This cocktail of credibility and strong emotion, in any case, is what creates the contagiousness of rumor in a given social context.

Just like gossip and other ways of transmitting information, rumors owe their success to their meta-representational properties, that is, to the way that opinions about the opinions of others affect the velocity of the latters' transmission. Rumors prosper precisely because they are rumors. They spread information as they spread themselves. They are collective events, the content of which does not exist independently of its diffusion. Trump's claims that his rivals were "low energy" or "crooked" spread quickly and became rumors not only because of their contents but also because of the speed with which they were spread. Trump is clearly a past master of informal propaganda. Rumors are at once *means* and *message*. Just as television stars are stars precisely because they are on television, so a bit of information will spread like wildfire precisely because it acquires the status of "rumor," carrying it into an informational avalanche that cannot be stopped. But in contrast to prejudices, which are stable components of a community's cognitive life and constitute permanent distortions of reputation, rumors have a short half-life and are quickly forgotten. Shrewd strategists of reputation know that the stains left by rumors on their image are not indelible. Whispered slurs tend to fade with time, so long as their impact does not depend on particularly significant informational content but rather on momentarily favorable conditions for absorbing the stain by a particular social tissue. Rumors, in fact, are primarily about themselves. Repeating them is just an exercise in social competence, a collective rite where words are repeated because they must be repeated, not because of their content.

But is it true that the circulation of information by rumor is bound to spread falsehoods regardless of the situation? Cass Sunstein thinks this is the case. In our society, he argues, nothing is more dangerous than rumor. For him, rumors are perverse effects of our innate cognitive tendencies. We are inclined to believe that which we already know and to accept a piece of information because others accept it, and not because it displays "better cognitive quality" than other offerings in the marketplace of ideas. This is why, in his view, an open society that facilitates the diffusion of rumors is condemned to catastrophe if we are not able to control these infections, these highly contagious viruses of information.[8]

Is he right? Is it true that a silent society, one from which the background hubbub so typical of our species had been wholly purged, would be more "rational"? I doubt it. If we analyze in detail the uses people make of rumors, we can see a large variety of cognitive strategies in which common sense and emotional reactions are combined with a measured wisdom. For instance, in situations of crisis, which are highly aus-

8. See Sunstein 2009.

picious for the diffusion of rumors, users of social networks such as Twitter that are frequently employed during emergencies do not seem to trust any information at all. Rumors are effectively retransmitted but also distrusted, rapidly corrected, and eliminated from the network after a certain number of rectifications. Users act as a kind of filter, exercising a form of *epistemic vigilance* that has nothing to do with the impossible enterprise of verifying information themselves (an "epistemological duty" dear to traditional epistemology but impracticable within the high-density informational environment in which we all now live). Vigilance is effected through various forms of selection based on microheuristics, for instance, the form of the message, its frequency, and the influence of those who retransmit it; all of this allows for a reasonable sifting of reliable from unreliable information.[9]

To sum up, if credulity is a side effect of our thirst for truth, false information does not suffice to quench that thirst. The collective process by which trustworthy information is selected out and becomes generally accepted presupposes the ingestion of large doses of what Harry Frankfurt rightly called "bullshit."

9. We conducted research at the Institut Nicod (Ecole Normale, Paris) on the use of Twitter in crisis situations. See Origgi and Bonnier 2013.

4

Assessing Uncertainty

HOW TRUSTWORTHY IS A REPUTATION?

> "He's just a man named Gatsby." "Where is he from, I mean? And what does he do?" . . . "Well, he told me once he was an Oxford man. . . . However, I don't believe it." "And you found he was an Oxford man," said Jordan helpfully. . . . "Oxford, New Mexico," snorted Tom contemptuously.
>
> —F. SCOTT FITZGERALD, *THE GREAT GATSBY*

Did Jay Gatsby really study at Oxford? And how important would an Oxford education be for such a man without a past and whose reputation for wealth and social connections was shrouded in mystery? The significance of the question becomes clear when Tom Buchanan—Daisy's upper-crust husband and heir to one of the grandest fortunes in the United States—decides to humiliate Gatsby by questioning the mysterious millionaire's curriculum vitae. He knows that this is

Gatsby's Achilles' heel. There are certain things *les nouveaux riches* cannot buy, including "good stock," breeding, and illustrious ancestors. Tom, by contrast, has been wealthy for a long time, at least by the standards of American fortunes, created mostly in the nineteenth century. He knows the rules of the social world to which he belongs and is intimately familiar with exclusive clubs for the happy few such as Oxford. So he has reason to doubt that Gatsby really studied there. And of course the report turns out to be bogus. Gatsby is no former Oxford student. He spent only a few months there as an army officer serving in World War I. Indeed, the resentment that Gatsby feels toward Tom's old-money milieu stems precisely from the humiliation he feels at being permanently excluded from it. Reputations can be deliberately polished or tarnished. But certain signals are difficult to feign. The accent of Oxford students in Gatsby's day is a good example. Their slight hesitations audible before the pronunciation of each word, their sotto voce "ums," their ways of clearing their throats before each sentence—such mannerisms were next to impossible for non-Oxonians to copy. And precisely because an Oxford education was commonly assumed to be difficult to simulate, the claim to have had one constituted a *robust signal* on which others relied when assessing the reputation of a mysterious stranger.

That an Oxford imprimatur seems to matter so much in a world such as Gatsby's and Buchanan's, where culture counts for little and where vulgar prejudice and superficial conversations reign, is also worth noting. What does this suggest about why some signals are convincing and others are not? Why do some labels bestow a kind of aura, a patina of prestige, on those who wear them, even in the eyes of those who have no comprehension of the evaluative criteria underlying them?

How can I signal the authenticity of my reputation in a way that everyone can easily recognize and believe?

This chapter focuses on the assessment and reliability of reputations. People emit signals meant to convince others of the genuineness of their reputations. Similarly, all things, objects, ideas, and indeed everything that points beyond appearances to hidden qualities, emit signals that inform us more or less credibly that these qualities really exist. In the previous chapter, I distinguished *informal* from *formal* (or objectified) reputations. Oxford belongs in that second category. Formal reputations are those that have been established through classification or notation systems called rankings. Founded in 1096, making it the second oldest university in the world, Oxford ranks second, once again, this time after Harvard, in international classifications of the best universities in the world.[1] Its reputation is ancient, worldwide, and close to unshakable. In other words it possesses one of those storied reputations that everyone trusts without quite knowing why. In fact, reputations like Oxford's are part of *common knowledge*. Everyone knows that Oxford is a prestigious university. Moreover, to return to a theme developed in chapter 3, *everyone knows that everyone knows*, so that "meta-representations" play a significant role in validating formal reputations as well as informal ones. In general, the attribution of valuable reputations and the construction of quality rankings depend on meta-representations, including our opinions about the opinions of others. Quality and value do not exist without collective coordination around, or agreement about, what everyone perceives as possessing quality and value. Various mechanisms, studied from various disciplinary perspec-

1. We will return in chapter 9 to the validity of academic classifications. Second place was attributed to Oxford in 2015 by the "prestigious" internal classification known as the Shanghai ranking: http://www.shanghairanking.com.

tives, permit large numbers of individuals to agree about *what everyone thinks*. John Maynard Keynes identified one such mechanism in the field of economics when discussing rational expectations about prices in financial markets. In *The General Theory of Employment, Interest, and Money* (1936), Keynes used the metaphor of a beauty contest to explain expectations and speculations in such markets. Several newspapers at the time ran virtual beauty pageants by publishing hundreds of photographs of attractive girls and asking the public to choose the most beautiful among them. Winning depended not on expressing one's own preferences but on guessing the likings of others. The most discriminating connoisseur of beautiful women was in the same boat as someone with zero personal appreciation of female beauty. Neither could win without guessing whom most other people would choose. The point can be generalized. The more ignorance there is in the world, the more decisive become such "opinions about opinions" in the determination of value. To understand such processes, game theory studies *coordination games*.

The effects of coordination on quality and value have also been studied in the price market. Qualitative uncertainty and informational asymmetry have become central issues in contemporary economics. Criticism of the neoclassical theory of prices as a function of supply and demand focuses on the impact of informational asymmetries on marketplace exchanges. George Akerlof, who won a Nobel Prize in economics, has shown that uncertainty about the *quality* of goods results in the self-destruction of the market.[2] A market where important

2. See Akerlof's seminal 1970 article about the market for used cars that (although it had originally been turned down by seven academic journals) earned him the Nobel Prize in 2001. The article shows how a market characterized by qualitative uncertainty, such as the one for used cars, tends to self-destruct because of the informational asym-

properties of products being bought and sold cannot be easily observed at the point of sale requires some mechanism for reassuring the buyer about the seller's reputation for fair dealing. Here again, sophisticated and unsophisticated buyers are in a similar situation. Both have to rely on indirect information about the seller's good name as a guarantee that the product being sold is what it purports to be.

Such guarantees take the form of various "seals of approval," such as brands, certifications, expert judgments, consumers' reports, and so forth, all of which serve as *judgment devices* or mechanisms for measuring, accrediting, and comparing reputations, crucial for the unobstructed functioning of the market. Rational economic agents have to rely on such mechanisms in order to reduce the *cognitive deficit* that characterizes all markets where only the seller knows what the buyer needs to know.

Sociology of Evaluation and Social Capital

A new and vast field of research in sociology, the sociology of value and evaluation, has now become a proper subdiscipline, called the Sociology of Valuation and Evaluation (SVE). It has grown rapidly in recent years and is certainly one of the most original developments in economic sociology. The goal of this field of research is to understand how value is created, how it becomes stabilized, how it compensates for informational

---

metry between sellers and buyers. The sellers know the flaws of the cars, which they hide from the buyers. The average prices, which reflect this uncertainty, are thus lower than what they should be. And the owners of used cars in good condition will not agree to sell their cars at such low prices. As a result, there will be ever more lemons in circulation, the prices will sink lower and lower, and the worst cars will push out the best ones, finally destroying the market itself.

asymmetries, and to what extent it depends on these very asymmetries.[3] In theoretical terms, SVE rejects the notion that quality and value are "data" of the economy. They are instead the outcome of a collective distribution of status. Mechanisms that differentiate between products "position" each in relation to the others. Studies of how products are evaluated again draw our attention to the relatively recent proliferation of certification mechanisms, systems of quality control, and performance evaluation. The economic ultra-liberalism of the last few decades has a hard time explaining why such purposely designed mechanisms have come to play such a critical role in mature liberal societies. Indeed, if classical economics was right, and value was simply determined by the logic of supply and demand, how would one explain pervasive uncertainties about the quality or value of items being exchanged? Why are pure economic indicators, such as price, not sufficient for choosing a product? A fundamental intuition of one of the founders of neoliberal economics, Friedrich A. Hayek, concerns precisely the *informational value* of price. In a society where information is widely dispersed and each individual has only partial access to it, *price* is a way of coordinating collective economic beliefs and behaviors. According to Hayek, in other words, price plays the role of reducing informational uncertainty and asymmetry.[4] And yet, if this is the case, why are ultra-liberal societies, where economic rationality should be triumphant, groaning under the weight of multiple and competing rating agencies and other systems of evaluation and cer-

3. See, for instance, Lamont 2012; Beckert and Musslin 2013; and Chauvin 2013.

4. This is what he writes in a famous article published in 1945: "Fundamentally, in a system in which the knowledge of the relevant facts is dispersed among many people, prices can act to coordinate the separate actions of different people in the same way as subjective values help the individual to coordinate the parts of his plan" (Hayek 1945, 526).

tification? And how to explain the growth of status anxiety in a world where access to the club of the happy few is increasingly uncertain and less and less guaranteed by the mechanisms of classical economics? These would be non-questions in a perfect world where collective coordination was ensured by the invisible hand. But the phenomena in question are there for all to see. Indeed, they represent one of the most salient characteristics of late modern societies.

In his illuminating book *Valuing the Unique: The Economics of Singularities*, economic sociologist Lucien Karpik analyzes the central question of informational economics within markets, and in particular that of *singularities*, such as cultural products whose quality defies economic quantification. According to Karpik, too, one needs to integrate a sociological analysis of judgment devices (*dispositifs*) into the study of the economy. He is referring to those mechanisms and modes of organization of knowledge that help "dissipate" the opacity of the market. Judgment devices aim at "reducing and, if possible, eliminating the cognitive deficit that characterizes consumers in the market of singularities." Judgment devices include "networks, appellations, cicerones, rankings," and what Karpik calls "confluences,"[5] that is, recommendation systems that coordinate disparate judgments. These devices transmit knowledge that has been shaped by criteria for guiding judg-

5. Karpik 2010, 44–45. Writing in the tradition of economic sociology, Karpik sees the market as depending upon judgment devices that allow consumers to evaluate the quality of singularities, that is, of goods—ever more numerous—whose quality is incommensurable within one category; for instance, Daniel Barenboim's interpretation of Bach's *Well-Tempered Clavier* is incommensurable with that of Glenn Gould; in other words, there is no objective dimension (price, weight, length, duration) on which to differentiate between the two interpretations and to guide the buyer in choosing one.

ments of quality and value. Karpik's book offers a detailed sociological analysis of the functioning of these various devices.

Karpik's *economics of singularities* is heir to two important sociological traditions. On the one hand, he is an exponent of *economic sociology*, which explains economic exchanges in terms of social relations. Of course one can trace this tradition back to Marx, but it is also associated with classical authors such as Max Weber—especially his works on the influence of religion on markets—as well as to Karl Polanyi. The latter, in his fundamental work *The Great Transformation*, proposed a *situated* account of market relations within historically specific social and institutional relations, thereby undercutting abstract concepts such as *homo economicus* and even the very concept of a *market*. More recently, a new economic sociology (or "new structuralism") has grown out of a seminal article by American sociologist Mark Granovetter, "The Strength of Weak Ties," one of the most cited articles of late twentieth-century sociology. It emphasizes the importance of *networks* for understanding the economy and in particular the notion of embeddedness. Economic relations between individuals and businesses, according to Granovetter, are always inscribed within preexisting social networks.

A rich tradition of studies on *social capital* and on *cultural capital* also plays a crucial role within the contemporary sociology of evaluation. Pierre Bourdieu introduced the notion of social capital in 1972, developing it in many subsequent publications to explain the cumulative advantages of social agents who operate within social networks. Social life is a story of accumulation, writes Bourdieu. There is no such thing as a social relation that is not embedded within a dense network of relations that precedes it. Bourdieu defines social capital as "actual or potential resources which are linked to possession of a durable network of more or less institutionalized relationships of mutual acquaintance and recognition, or in other words, to membership in a group" (1986, 251). In contrast to economic capital and to an individual's cultural capital, both of which, in large part, can be appraised objectively and in isolation, social capital depends on others. To have social ties is not an "objective" condition. It is a condition that depends on the fact that others *recognize* these ties. From this stems the importance, for Bourdieu, of the mutual recognition inherent in social capital. We have no social capital if others do not recognize it.

The notion of social capital was also taken up by James Coleman, who, in the 1980s, put forward a new synthesis between the sociological analysis of action and the economic analysis of rational choice. According to Coleman, a rational individual is not purely individualistic in his or her strategy. Social capital matters as well. Coleman defines social capital in functional terms. It can be earned and accumulated in a variety of ways that have two features in common. They all involve both participating in the social structure and facilitating individual action through this structure. Listening to "good" music, frequenting certain milieus, and playing golf are obviously very different sorts of activities. But they can all be engaged in strategically in order to accumulate social capital, that is, to attain a better position for oneself in the social structure and to facilitate this repositioning. Coleman gives the example of the diamond market in New York, which is run exclusively by members of the Orthodox Jewish community. In this case, the community provides its members with social capital that facilitates transactions, making it possible to avoid written contracts and complicated mechanisms for assuring that agreements are kept. If someone tries to steal, they will lose everything: family, friendships, respectability, reputation, and membership in the religious community. Individuals who operate within such a community therefore have a powerful reason to maintain their social capital intact. The forms of social capital at their disposal are trust, reciprocity, social norms, and the circulation of information.

Like Bourdieu, Coleman sees social capital as a *motivation for action* that should be distinguished from purely economic motivations. The behavior of social agents can be described in terms of a strategy whose aim is to maximize not only economic utility but also social utility, manifested in numerous material and immaterial advantages. Whereas Coleman studied social capital from the viewpoint of *agents*, focusing on how they accumulate such capital for strategic reasons, I want to examine social capital from the viewpoint of *observers* (or "consumers"). What interests me is how we perceive the social capital of people, things, or ideas in order then to *evaluate* them, apart from the agents' motivations and calculations. One can strategically "build" a reputation for oneself or, no less strategically, use capital inherited at birth or acquired in the circle where one is recognized. But there always remains a degree of uncertainty about how this capital is perceived and transmitted by others and how it will circulate socially. The anxiety surrounding reputation is connected to the management of this uncertainty. We can never be sure what others may do with the signals we broadcast. Network effects, for instance, are not linear. We may have a strategy for improving our standing within a social network, but there is no guarantee that our final position will correspond to our wishes. Social networks can create distortions in the ways in which social capital accumulates and is used by others. Let us now examine a few familiar examples.

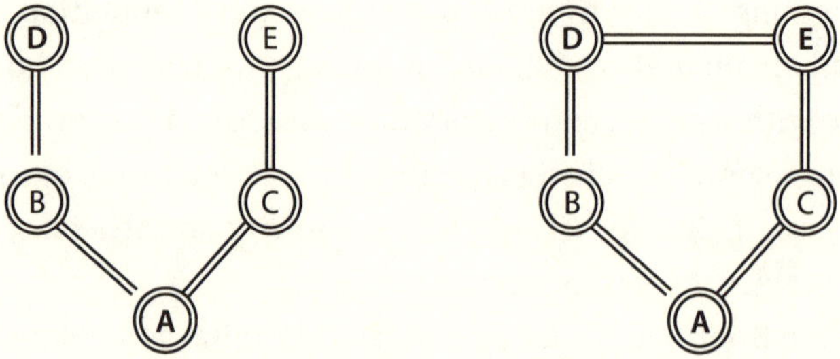

FIGURE 2. Condemnation of gossip.

One important distortion effect is due to the relation between the effectiveness of the imposition of a social norm—one of the most studied forms of social capital—and the structure of the social network. A "closed" network, as opposed to an "open" one, will make it easier to stabilize a social norm. Consider, for instance, the condemnation of gossip.

In figure 2, if A has a relation to both B and C and has behaved wrongly toward them both, and B and C are in relation to other people, D and E, who are not in relation with each other, it will be more difficult to organize a collective punishment for A, such as exclusion, negative gossip, or social norm enforcement, in order to stop A from behaving badly in the future. This is because the other members of the community are not connected with each other. If, however, D and E are in contact with each other, then social capital will be a much more effective resource for the modification of the reputation of A, because circulation of information about A will be easier.[6]

Another notorious effect of social networks, to which we will return in subsequent chapters, is the Matthew effect, studied by Robert Merton, according to which advantages within

6. See Ullmann-Margalit 1977.

a social network tend to accumulate. Most citation networks, for example, have a structure of this sort: the more cited you are, the more likely it is that you will be cited in the future. Merton took a passage from the Gospel of Matthew, hence the name "Matthew effect": "For unto every one that hath shall be given, and he shall have abundance: but from him that hath not shall be taken even that which he hath." The probability that an article that has been previously and repeatedly cited should be cited again is certainly higher than the probability that an article that has never been cited should start being cited now.

A further network effect, studied especially in labor markets for the creative professions, is due to the way relations of deference, which determine standing inside any social group, play out among the practitioners of the activity in question. "Creative" professions, such as art or scientific research, are propitious for the development of spectacular inequalities due to the distribution of relations of deference. As sociologist Pierre-Michel Menger has shown, "A research department where one world-famous researcher works will have an infinitely higher potential for development than it would have solely on the basis of the sum of individual contributions of a team of excellent researchers" (2002, 38).

Finally, the mutual influence of collective and individual reputations creates network effects of crucial importance to economics. Does belonging to a group that has a good reputation enhance one's personal reputation? In an article from 1996, Jean Tirole, who won the Nobel Prize for economics in 2015, showed that it does. Individual reputation is enhanced by belonging to a well-respected group. Such considerations evidently matter in the case, for instance, of business mergers and acquisitions. A number of experimental results, applied to various domains, such as the acquisition of new brands by a big industrial group or the award of an "appellation d'origine contrôlée" (AOC) in the case of French regional products, show the individual benefits of belonging to a group endowed with a good reputation.[7] Yet the effects of collective reputations on individual ones and vice versa remain complex. A respected group that accepts members with a lesser reputation may lose the respect it previously enjoyed. One of the typical strategies of new literary or artistic prizes whose authority their founders want to establish is, at the outset, to honor artists who already possess a reputation for excellence. In such cases, the artist's personal reputation is what establishes the reputation of the prize, rather than the other way around. The reputational dynamic between individual and collective dimensions can also bring about various and sometimes unexpected distortions of reputation, illustrated by the well-known joke of Groucho Marx: "I refuse to join any club that would have me as a member."

All this research on network effects points to an aspect of social structures analyzed by neither Bourdieu nor Coleman: their *dynamic* nature. Reputations are made or lost within dynamic processes. Social capital is therefore *uncertain capital.* We build our reputations thanks to social networks, exploiting the structure of these networks and using a variety of filters and devices that modify this structure or amplify its effects. Let us examine more closely how these filters are constructed and how they are perceived and employed in a more or less strategic fashion. My goal here is twofold. On the one hand, I would like to weave together the two sociological traditions mentioned above and that are usually considered distant from each other—classical research on social capital on the one

7. See Tirole 1996 and Gergaud et al. 2016.

hand, and the new Evaluation and Valuation Studies (EVS) on the other. From the perspective adopted in this book, one and the same fundamental question unites these two traditions. How does the "positioning" within a social network of a product or an agent in relation to other products or agents create and maintain a reputation? My view of these traditions, however, is also not uncritical. The examples of network effects described above show that the value created by the agent's positioning, however strategic it may be, remains *uncertain*, open to interpretations and vulnerable to unpredictable network effects. I therefore aim to highlight this double function of reputation. While it functions as a motivation to act strategically on the part of the agent, it also functions as a device to help observers gather information to evaluate the person using it. The intellectual acrobatics of this book consist in offering a unified account of this double function—hence my choice of an eclectic methodology that unites many different disciplines and traditions.

Reputation is the result not only of strategic positioning but also of the way in which such positioning is perceived by others. Gatsby may tell everyone, for strategic reasons, that he studied at Oxford, but how his circle then interprets this bit of information is not predetermined by any "device" designed to reduce uncertainty. Buchanan has enough information at his disposal, both about Gatsby *and* about Oxford, to recognize immediately that the signal is not at all robust. The superficial socialites around Gatsby, by contrast, will have such an indirect, vague notion of Oxford's reputation that they implicitly trust his claim. In other words, that which counts for gaining and maintaining a reputation is not only positioning within a social network but also the perception of this positioning on the part of the network's insiders and outsiders. In the next chapter, we shall examine the heuristics that influence our perceptions and lead us to classify accurately or inaccurately a person or object within a social network. Reputation can never be taken for granted and always creates uncertainty and anxiety. This is because our social position is always precarious and can never be objectively determined.

Reputational Devices

What we know about others, how we judge people and things, always depends on *traditions* that are structured by *reputational devices* more or less adequate to the transmission of these traditions. It is through these devices that we endeavor to get our bearings by interpreting various cues. Without the imprimatur of presumably knowledgeable others upon a corpus of knowledge, this corpus would remain silent, impossible to decipher. Competent epistemic subjects should be capable of integrating these signs in their search for information. In other words, we do not know the world in order to evaluate it. Rather we evaluate the world in order to know it.

The social life of people and things is inscribed within economic, social, symbolic, and hierarchical relations. These relations provide evidence of reputation that can be more or less reliable depending on the way it has been constructed. Social life is the informational trace of who we are. All our interactions generate bits of socially shared information that accumulate gradually to define how we are seen. If it is true that we need information about others to decide how to act, it is also true that others will observe our actions as pieces of information that tell them something about us. This fundamental connection between information and behavior, between *signs* and actions—analyzed in chapter 2 using the theory of signs—is crucial for the understanding of reputation. So writes Thomas Hobbes in a famous passage about honor:

> The signs by which we know our own power are those actions which proceed from the same; and the signs by which other men know it, are such actions, gesture, countenance and speech, as usually such powers produce: and the acknowledgment of power is called HONOUR; and to honour a man (inwardly in the mind) is to conceive or acknowledge, that that man hath the odds or excess of power above him that contendeth or compareth himself. . . . and according to the signs of honour and dishonour, so we estimate and make the value or WORTH of a man.[8]

Information and social ties are two sides of the same coin. This may seem to be a trivial point, but it is the basis for one of the greatest cultural revolutions of all time: the social Web and the algorithms that extract information from the collection and classification of collective behaviors, to be examined in chapter 7. This powerful link between information and reputation has not yet been studied adequately by the social sciences, which focus more on the *motivations* that drive agents to maintain a good reputation rather than on the social-cognitive uses of it by others. Without this excess of social information about what surrounds us, the world would be silent, lacking value, and unworthy of attention.

The reputational devices I analyze here focus on a variety of relations. Three main factors influence their reliability: (1) the

8. Hobbes 1640, chap. 8, #5. For an analysis of the theory of honor in Hobbes, see Carnevali 2013. Luc Boltanski and Laurent Thévenot (1991) provide an original reading of Hobbes's position regarding honor in their book on *economies of worth,* in particular with the presentation of the *city of opinion,* which corresponds, in some aspects, to the notion of reputation discussed in this chapter.

structure of relations; (2) the numerous effects and forms of judgment that can enter the structure (in the form of judgment devices, seals of approval, numerical indicators of classification, and so forth); and (3) the knowledge in possession of those who use the devices to gather information.

The Structure of Networks

Reputation obviously depends on social structure. According to economic sociology, "the informational advantage" of having strong and stable social ties with others translates into an economic advantage because we can trust those with whom we interact, reduce transaction costs, and develop a familiarity and a set of expectations that structure our actions and those of others. We become more predictable for others, just as they do for us.[9]

As we have seen, a social structure with an *open network* does not allow for the same circulation of information about the actions of others as does a closed structure. Moreover, network effects accumulate in a non-linear way. Those at the center of the network will have a higher probability of becoming even more central because their reputation, to paraphrase Hobbes, grows the more it spreads. Lastly, social networks are not homogeneous. Analyzing them shows that informal social ties tend to collect around areas of *high density*, in groups where information circulates fluently. Between such groups, it is important to add, we find gaps or "structural holes"[10] where information does not flow. Each group can be aware of the others but not of the way in which information is organized within

9. See Granovetter 1985.

10. The theory of structural holes was developed by Roland Burt (2005).

them. Of all the network effects that matter for the understanding of the dynamics of reputation, how status is distributed is one of the most important.

How Are Hierarchies Built?

Hierarchies are everywhere. They can be formal, as they are in the army, or informal, as is the case with a spontaneous classification of "who is the best" among a group of friends. A class of students is a convenient and illustrative arena for observation. Each year, during my seminar, I witness the emergence of a spontaneous classification among my students. Their mutual interactions, their participation in class, the quality of their questions and objections all allow the "best" to shine and be quickly recognized as such by the others. This informal ranking is then confirmed or falsified by the formal one, that is, by the grades I assign at the end of the semester. In my experience, it is almost always confirmed. This coincidence of informal and formal rankings can be explained by a fundamental intuition of the new structuralism in sociology. Even though a hierarchical position within the structure signals quality, the initial differences in quality contribute to the configuration of that very structure. The hierarchy is neither determined from above nor dependent solely on the performance of each single individual. It is the product of the interaction between individuals.

The sociology of status analyzes social standing as "accumulated acts of deference."[11] What makes this definition interesting is that social agents can defer to others because of attributes or qualities that are not immediately useful or important

11. See Podolny and Lynn 2009.

to those who defer. This makes the deference model of status very different from classical, strategic models of reputation. In those models, what I appreciate in the other is what satisfies my expectations of possible future interactions and exchanges. For the sociology of status, by contrast, I can defer to qualities that are of no immediate interest to me and whose existence in others is not of any palpable benefit to me. For instance, to recognize that someone in class is more intelligent than I am is of no immediate benefit to me—on the contrary, it can even harm me. And yet, I cannot help but listen more attentively to that student's questions. And I will wait in line at the end of the class to ask that student for bibliographical suggestions. Admiration for others, in most cases, is not particularly strategic.

Those to whom we routinely defer have a higher social status. Of course things are not that simple, and an agent's status is also determined by social relations, not only by performance. Status is a position that *flourishes* through a network and influences the distribution of social capital. When an agent with an elevated status becomes associated with someone with a modest status, the latter's social standing is raised but the former's is at risk of being lowered. In Jane Austen's *Pride and Prejudice,* the haughty and arrogant Darcy does not hesitate to "protect" his friend Charles Bingley by initially dissuading him from marrying the beautiful Jane Bennet because of her family's lesser social standing. Bingley's status would be reduced by an association with the Bennets. And the elopement of Lydia, one of Elizabeth and Jane's younger sisters, with the opportunist, ruthless Wickham, risks sullying forever the reputations of the older sisters and thus shattering their dream of marrying well. Lydia's reputation "besmirches" that of Elizabeth and Jane, deforming the social structure in such a way that the rich and noble Bingley and Darcy cannot restore the status of the two older sisters without first remedying Lydia's "fall." There thus exists a complex and dynamic relation between the status of agents, their intrinsic qualities, and their social capital. Darcy perceives the intrinsic qualities of Elizabeth, her intelligence, her liveliness, but also her very modest social capital. He can elevate her status by marrying her, but he would risk lowering his too much (a consideration that is still there when he first asks Elizabeth to marry him, an offer that her pride leads her to refuse). By redeeming the younger sister's tarnished reputation, he is able to restore the dignity of the discredited Bennet family while triggering the admiration of Elizabeth, who discovers his generosity and the sincerity of his feelings, and at last agrees to marry him.

Thus the dynamics of status sometimes allows us to modify our social capital thanks to our intrinsic qualities that in turn depend on our social capital. One can infer a very simple law from these models. The more social capital is uncertain and intrinsic qualities are difficult to observe, the more significant will deferential acts become. Exhibits of deference are what will enable us to attribute a value to agents. When I arrive in a new environment where I know no one, I don't yet master the criteria necessary for ascertaining the intrinsic qualities of those I meet. What will give me information about their value and allow me to attribute a status to them, to draw a *mental map* of the "good" and "bad" among them, are the observable displays of deference that insiders pay to insiders.

Inside the Device: Formal Devices

Products and ideas are subject to the same vicissitudes and uncertainties as social actors. Their value is often uncertain and, as we have seen, the market alone does not suffice to determine it, especially within the cultural sphere where we encounter the challenge of "evaluating the invaluable." In what way is Daniel Barenboim's interpretation of Bach's *Goldberg Variations* inferior or superior to that of Glenn Gould? What is the value of human life when one negotiates a hostage exchange? What is the right price a corporation should pay for having irremediably polluted the virgin lands of Alaska?[12]

Karpik's "judgment devices" help reduce uncertainty regarding quality. They provide specific information, that is, *information that already includes an evaluation.* In *Valuing the Unique,* as mentioned, Karpik analyzes systems particular to the market of singularities, a market characterized by strong informational asymmetries and by collective distributions of beliefs inscribed within *traditions,* which Karpik calls "cultural complexes." But we can extend Karpik's analysis of these devices beyond the market for cultural goods where informational asymmetry has already been thoroughly studied within the sociological literature.[13]

Without any doubt, classifications and indicators have today invaded the cognitive, social, and political spheres. Schools, hospitals, businesses, states, fortunes, financial products, Internet search results, and academic publications (which should be the ultimate encapsulation of *objective* quality) are classified, organized, valued, and set in hierarchical relations to each other, as if their intrinsic value were no longer calculable without their being compared to one another. The obsession with establishing comparative grids in the name of the *objectivity* of evaluative measures, however, risks devaluing intrinsic value in favor of comparative value.

12. Such questions are typical of the SVE.

13. See, for instance, the classical analysis of the cultural market by Hirsch 1972.

Some sociologists claim that this fixation on comparison, by now ubiquitous in all dimensions of our lives, alters substantially the relation between user and product. According to their analysis, the user's capacity to appreciate is reduced by the constant resort to comparative devices, to the detriment of appreciating the *uniqueness* of a product, an idea, or, even more disquietingly, a person.

Wherein does the ostensible *objectivity* of these classifications consist? Rankings obviously cannot claim objectivity on the basis of the factual information they provide because such pre-evaluated information is clearly not objective, depending as it does on a particular point of view and on a contestable focus on specific qualities. Their objectivity, to the extent that it exists, depends on *traditions*, on the "cultural complexes" mentioned earlier, on the rumors and word-of-mouth statements that lead everyone within a social group to believe that this hospital, say, is better than the other one, without anyone having any notion of why they believe it. The aim of such classifications is to avoid the *Oxford effect* of which Gatsby is the victim. Everyone believes that Oxford is a good university simply because, usually, people like Gatsby won't be admitted to it. In the case of Oxford, as we have seen, the weight of tradition has been maintained within contemporary rankings. But in other cases, tradition is wholly insufficient for ensuring the maintenance of quality.

Classifications are ways of creating new "traditions" in the contemporary world. In the global village, local traditions are collapsing. To non-locals they are too often simply unintelligible. This is why classifications are replacing the "common knowledge" to which people once adapted without really knowing why. We shall see a bit later how these new traditions are constructed, what are the criteria and values that they incorporate, and how they vary from one domain of knowledge to the other. The weight of a tradition shapes how reputations are attributed and values are assigned. But the reasons that lead us to trust a particular tradition may be more or less legitimate.

Variations on the Dimension of Reputation

Examining the tools that the social sciences provide for evaluating the reliability of reputations leads us to individuate a series of variables that influence the way in which a reputation is built. Informational asymmetry, the formal and informal nature of devices, the weight of authority and expertise, and the "robustness" of a reputation over time, that is, its relation to tradition, are all variables that influence how we apprehend the world through reputation.

Let us try to understand better the relationship between reputation and informational asymmetry. From what we have seen so far, we can deduce that it is a linear relationship: the stronger the informational asymmetry, the more reputation matters.[14]

By putting together the various dimensions of reputation (informational asymmetry, formalization, and the weight of authority), one can refine the argument advanced thus far. The stronger the informational asymmetry, for instance, the more reputation matters in cases such as having to choose a doctor or an expert. But in the case of art, too, and generally of taste, reputation matters greatly, even though the informational asymmetries are far less obvious there. We all have a palate to

14. A simple "law of reputation" that I have defended in, for instance, Origgi 2013a.

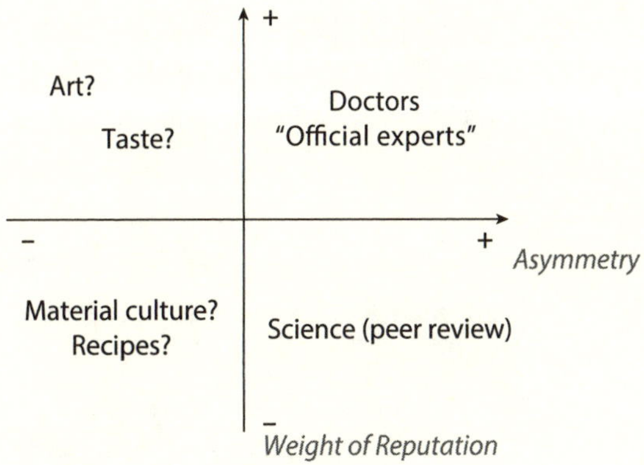

FIGURE 3. Relation between informational asymmetry and weight of reputation.

taste wine, eyes to evaluate a painting, and ears to appreciate a musical performance.

The case of science is also interesting. It certainly presents us with great informational asymmetry. But the process of evaluating scientific claims is based on a system of peer review—to be examined more closely in chapter 9—structured to be anonymous. The anonymity of the process has been increasingly questioned by sociological analyses revealing multiple distortions within the system. Yet it remains true that what establishes the quality of scientific work is not mere word-of-mouth reputation. I have tried to find areas in which both the weight of reputation and informational asymmetry are low. Food recipes seem to me an appropriate example: they are not difficult to understand and to reproduce (in other words, the informational asymmetry is low) and reputation counts for little—when I look for a recipe online, I don't care much about who wrote it. A good recipe must *work*. If a great chef offers one that is too hard to execute, no one will use it. Figure 3 sums up these variations.

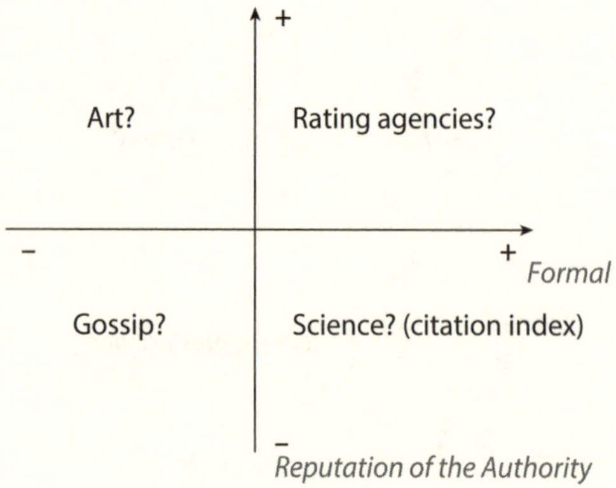

FIGURE 4. Relation between the level of formalization and the weight of authority.

One can try to vary the level of formalization of a reputation (more or less formal, according to the distinction I made earlier) and the weight of the authorities who bestow reputation. Figure 4 is the resulting diagram.

There are areas in which reputation is formal, as in the case of rating agencies, and where the influence of authority is decisive. One trusts only a very small number of such agencies, and their importance is ever increasing. This shows that the formalization of reputation does not necessarily go hand in hand with a reduction in the influence of expertise. In art, where, apart from popular devices such as www.artprice.com, reputations are much less formal, the judgment of experts weighs heavily. By contrast, in science, where reputations are nowadays formalized with the help of tools such as the *Citation Index*—to which we will also return in chapter 9—the power of authorities is ever decreasing. Lastly, gossip is a case where both variables have a low value. Both formalization and the power of authority are negligible. As we have seen in chapter 3, rumors circulate beyond the authority of their source. Any-

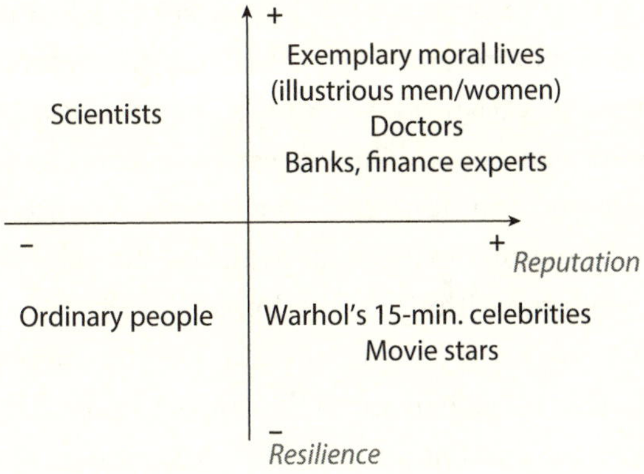

FIGURE 5. Relation between level of reputation and resilience through time.

one can add their bit to hearsay, even someone with no formal power whatsoever.

Another fascinating and mysterious dimension of reputation is time. Why are some reputations so durable, resisting all counterevidence, whereas others are so fragile that they can be destroyed by the slightest whiff of scandal? In some fields, reputations matter and are solid. Doctors and financial experts, for instance, can make many mistakes and false predictions without losing their reputations. We have seen how, in the world of research, reputation counts less, even though reputations remain persistent throughout time thanks to the Matthew effect. One case where reputation counts a great deal but does not endure for very long is celebrity. Celebrities are hyperexposed to the deference of their fans, but these acts of deference never get organized into stable networks of recognition, which is why celebrity, alas, is always fleeting.

I offer these sketches mostly as an exercise in intellectual clarification. I want to connect some of the axes along which I believe it will be fruitful to pursue future studies of reputation.

They can also provide a basis for possible experimental research. Reputation can be taken as either the independent or the dependent variable. If we study reputation as a dependent variable we can examine how it varies according to levels of informational asymmetry or formalization. Knowledge mediated by reputation obviously depends on the value that these variables assume within various domains.

In this chapter, I have roamed across the many different areas of social science research that aim to *objectify* reputation and make it measurable and reliable. I have also compared various disciplinary traditions in order to identify the rudiments of a possible theory of reputation. As one can see from the figures presented, the study of reputation has only just begun, and many pathways of research remain unexplored. A social science of reputation will have to study, under controlled conditions, many variations on the dimensions I have listed: asymmetry, authority, robustness, and temporality. One goal would be to reduce the intrinsic uncertainty that afflicts our own reputations and those we bestow on others. Understanding the mechanisms that are responsible for fluctuations of reputation could conceivably help us calm the anxiety arising from the way our own image and that of the world are regularly reflected and distorted by the ever-present social mirror.

5

The Paradox of the "Top Specialist" and the Heuristics of Reputation

> Most of us are tame enough to take bread at someone's hand. And we do thereby put ourselves in danger. So why do we do it?
>
> —ANNETTE BAIER, "TRUST"

Friends and acquaintances of mine often refer to their private physicians as the "very best specialists." One friend even announced that she had the contact information of the foremost veterinarian in town, making me cringe with guilt since I've always picked veterinarians located nearest my home. Recently, over lunch in Paris, I asked two Italian colleagues who teach in France why they preferred to go all the way back to Italy for medical care, given that the French medicine available to them rates consistently higher than Italian medicine in all international rankings. My question obviously struck them as impertinent. The conversation became uncomfortably tense. There was something obnoxious about my invoking official and "presumably objective" evaluations of European medical care in such an intimate context. I quickly realized that "objectivity" counts for little in assessing the reputation of a private physician. My "hierarchical" appeal to the superiority of French over Italian medicine had touched an exposed nerve, violating a deep emotional attachment that defies objective evaluation and is rooted in a kind of deference to authority that cannot be reduced to respect for expertise. Trying to convince my interlocutors with rational arguments had been a serious mistake. It betrayed a lack of sensitivity toward attitudes of deference that are constitutive of human identity. My friends experienced my offhand readiness to question their allegiance to a cherished doctor as highhanded and humiliating. I dropped the subject, listening with dwindling interest to shopworn praises of the famous Roman specialist in question, a family friend of the mother of one of my interlocutors.

My gaffe and the belligerent response it evoked are far from being atypical. Try citing widely respected performance evaluations when discussing personal physicians with your acquaintances. You risk seriously alienating those who, for many reasons, resent attempts to shake their unconditional loyalty toward an idolized medical practitioner. I have seen people dissolve otherwise treasured friendships rather than listen to skeptical remarks that threatened their emotional attachment to the best doctor in town.

Incidents of unquestioning devotion to renowned doctors or lawyers are so frequent, in my experience, that they should be treated not as random anecdotes but as examples of an important sociological phenomenon. I began to ask myself how it was possible that everyone could believe that they were in the care of the most professionally competent specialist. We would really be living in the best of all possible worlds if everyone could have access not only to the one they *believe* is the best but to the one who is actually the best. So how do individuals form their assessments of the quality of an expert? How do we choose doctors or lawyers? What beliefs play a role? What skills are required for selecting an expert in an appropriate way, given that the choice, when non-experts choose among experts, cannot be based on the chooser's specialized knowledge of the field? Would it be practicable, whenever we need medical treatment, to study the symptoms ourselves in order to be able to gauge the doctor's competence from a position of equality? Obviously not. So what can and should we do?

As we have seen in earlier chapters, it is doubtful that reputations develop in a linear manner. The mechanisms that allow a doctor or lawyer[1] to enjoy a reputation as the "very best specialist" are complex. They depend on structural factors that channel the way information circulates within a network and cannot be fully mastered. To the structural reasons for the contingency and fluidity of reputations, we can add a series of cognitive biases in the selection of information, as well as emotional reactions and psychological tendencies that, taken together, render an "objective" assessment of reputation all the more difficult to achieve.

Trust and Vulnerability: Why Do We Trust Others?

When we find ourselves with a doctor about to make an existential decision affecting our very survival or with an expensive lawyer to whom we have entrusted the defense of our

1. For an analysis of the "market" for lawyers where the central question posed concerns the *opacity* of the quality of service, see Karpik 1995.

dearest rights in a legal procedure whose fine points we cannot fully grasp, we are acutely *vulnerable*. To trust in others means to accept a reasonable level of vulnerability by exposing ourselves to the possibility (not the certainty) of being betrayed or cheated, or of falling into the hands of individuals whose competence we are in no position to judge. To entrust—in Latin, *confidere*—means to put something precious (such as health, money, or children) into the hands of others. It means counting on them to care for what we have entrusted to them and putting ourselves at their mercy, confiding in their benevolence. Putting ourselves in the hands of someone else in a *reasonable* way, however, requires us to know how to evaluate their *competence* in the domain in question. Trusting in their goodwill does not suffice. Competence and benevolence are the two sides of the coin of trust. And while we can get a fairly reliable sense of someone's benevolence by interacting with them personally, evaluating their professional competence is more complex and depends essentially on what we know or think we know about their reputation and the inferences we are able to draw from it. Why do we trust others? What are the reasons, the biases, and the norms that induce us to believe or disbelieve in the competence of others?

Empirical studies of trust often draw a schizophrenic picture of the agents who trust or distrust. Sometimes they are depicted as overly vigilant, strategic, and rational, and at other times as thoroughly credulous and irrational. But is it really irrational to mix rationality and emotion? Are we being unreasonable when we feel qualms about the callous doctor who examines us without a smile and who pays no attention to how we describe our condition, dismissing our reports as medically illiterate and useless chatter with no informational value? Even if he has been certified as the very best specialist according to purportedly objective criteria, a doctor's lack of rapport with patients will surely impact personal impressions of his competence.

My earlier research has led me to conclude that adopting an attitude of trust always involves a mixture of emotions, values, reasons, heuristics, and practices to which we adhere without realizing it. Although they occasionally guide us well, at other times they lead us to overestimate or underestimate the reputation of someone we are being asked to trust. The aim of this chapter is to distinguish the "good" from the "bad" uses of reputation, that is, to develop a proper epistemology of reputation. The objective is to identify a set of normative and descriptive instruments that we can use in two ways: on the one hand, to classify the heuristics we actually use, and, on the other hand, to establish some sort of criteria, along the lines of the classical epistemological tradition, to distinguish between the rules of inference that lead us to place too much or too little trust in the reputations of others and those that lead us to trust such reputations reasonably and sensibly. Traditional epistemology aims at furnishing the "rules for the direction of the mind." These rules are meant to guide thinking and organize its inferences in such a way as "to arrive at solid and true judgments about everything which comes before it," to cite René Descartes. But an epistemology for our times, such as the one I am proposing here, needs to account for other "rules of the mind," namely those that allow us to navigate a deluge of social information and to "arrive at solid and true judgments" despite the innumerable biases and distortions that affect our inferences.

Let us start, then, with a simple question, although it is one that, with a few exceptions, has been largely overlooked in the history of philosophy: Why do we trust other people? I shall distinguish seven different mechanisms, both social and cognitive, that are at the basis of our trust in others:

1. inferences regarding the reliability of the speaker
2. inferences regarding the reliability of the *content* of the information transmitted and received
3. internalized social norms of *deference* to authority
4. socially distributed reputational cues
5. robust signals
6. emotional reactions
7. moral commitments

These mechanisms do not operate in isolation from one another. Indeed, it isn't possible to distinguish any of them sharply from the rest. They overlap and combine unpredictably in the heuristics that we use to navigate the social world. Similarly, it isn't possible to distinguish clearly between those that are "reliable" and those that are not. The conditions that make them successful are complex and need to be described in detail. So let's now examine each of them in turn.

Inferences Based on the Reliability of the Speaker

The heuristics on which we routinely rely to decide whether or not to believe what we are told include multiple inferences and fleeting perceptions about the reliability of the speaker. Some signs of reliability are contextual, including, for instance, the *superior epistemic position* of a speaker in a given context. I telephone my sister in Milan to learn about local weather conditions there. She's no expert in meteorology, but the simple fact that she resides in Milan gives her decisive epistemic superiority over me in this matter, since I live in Paris and have no direct way of experiencing today's weather in Milan. Of course I could look it up on the Web, and the fact that I trust my sister more than a weather website could be based on tacit prejudices and biases that shape my thinking. I can also follow events in Syria through the tweets of a "local" observer, a blogger whose name I know and who seems to me to be well-informed. But my trust in eyewitnesses may be misplaced. My sister might glance out the window and report that the weather is good simply because she spotted a passing sunbeam, whereas if I had gone online I would have found detailed information about the storm predicted for the afternoon. Similarly, my trusted Syrian blogger may be personally biased or may be selecting information that supports his particular faction. Worse yet, he could end up not being a Syrian reporting from Syria at all. He could be a clever impostor blogging from another country, fabricating believable reports about Syria without ever leaving his bedroom.

Although the strategies I routinely employ to decide who is reliable and who is not sometimes lead me to commit serious mistakes, they remain an integral and indispensable part of my thinking. The trust they lead me to place in my interlocutors determines, at least initially, my reaction to the information these interlocutors provide. To be sure, the trust I place in others also depends on the information we have already gathered about them. *Prejudices* can play a role here, especially when such a priori prejudgments are crystallized into social stereotypes. Stereotypes are just one example among an array of possible (and more creative) ways of making inferences about the social world. We could not be rational without managing the hyperabundance of social information around us and classifying it into a series of "mental files." The process of categorizing consists essentially in making generalizations about specific cases and classifying them according to their *type* or *kind*. The problem with stereotypes is that the categories of social types into which we sort information are usually tendentious, contingent, and influenced by local cultures and traditions. A great deal of work in philosophy and cognitive sociology[2] is devoted to showing that the way in which we manage the social information around us is more complex and creative than simply adopting stereotypes widely shared within our culture. Common sense gives us the flexibility to adjust to social situations in an appropriate manner.[3] It helps us fine-tune reciprocal expectations and enrich our perception of the surrounding social world in order to "mediate between the subjectively known and the subjectively unknown," as sociologist Alfred Schütz (1964, 134) put it. These social heuristics allow us to see our interlocutor as occupying a specific social role and they guide us in attributing credibility to him or her. They allow us to map out a "social landscape" that gives us information about our interlocutors. Admittedly, our conclusions can be driven by notorious psychological biases, such as the fundamental attribution error, much studied in social psychology, according to which we have the tendency to attribute the causes of an action to a person's *character*—or to the *social type* with which we associate them—rather than to the external situation in which they find themselves and to which they must react. Some people might be inclined to believe that I am always late because I am Italian and that being late is part of the *essence* of the Italian social type, rather than inferring that I just hap-

2. For an overview of the method of cognitive sociology, see Kaufmann and Clément 2011. For the contemporary philosophical literature on stereotypes and implicit biases, see, for instance, the project *Implicit Bias and Philosophy*: www.biasproject.org.

3. The capacity to adjust to social situations, in particular to linguistic situations, has been studied by sociolinguist Aaron Cicourel (1974).

pened to be late because circumstances beyond my control prevented my arriving on time.

In order to evaluate the reliability of someone who is giving us information or advice, we credit him or her with *expertise* in a certain area. To be sure, the reputation we ascribe to someone can be influenced by many factors, including, for instance, our reliance on reputational cues that contain little informational value, as when we evaluate the competence of a doctor on the basis of his or her fashionable address or the reputation of the person who gave us the recommendation. In what follows, we shall analyze these sorts of cognitive shortcuts in greater detail. The point to stress here is that our judgments about the expertise of others, however fallible, are inferences about their reliability. Tacit and extemporaneous appraisals of this sort are ubiquitous within our epistemic practices. They create expectations regarding the credibility of someone proffering advice that affect how we construe what we are being told. In a novel by Jerzy Kosinski, *Being There*, made famous by Hal Ashby's 1979 film adaptation, the main character, Mr. Chance, played by a masterful Peter Sellers, is an old gardener who has never left his garden and who probably suffers from a mental handicap. In the film, he is a poetic and guileless figure. The owner of the garden dies and Chance finds himself wandering the streets of Washington for the first time in his life, without knowing where to go or what to do. While he watches television, fascinated, through a shop window, he is run over by a car and, after a series of fortuitous coincidences, he ends up living in the house of one of America's leading financial tycoons. He thus finds himself consorting informally with some of the most prominent men and women in the United States. One day, the president comes to visit his old friend the tycoon.

Over dinner, he asks Chance, whom he takes to be another close friend of the owner of the house, what he thinks of the recent slump on Wall Street. Chance responds, as he always does, with rhapsodic phrases about gardening: "In the garden, growth has its seasons. First comes spring and summer, but then we have fall and winter. And then we get spring and summer again. As long as the roots are not severed, all is well. And all will be well in the garden." The president broods over these sentences, attributing to them a deep meaning about the fundamental symmetry between nature and society; the next day he quotes Chance on television. The credibility that the president mistakenly attributes to Chance is of course entirely contextual. Since he is sitting at the table of his friend, the wealthy entrepreneur, he cannot be a mentally handicapped gardener. Instead, he must be a financial expert, someone with great competence and a knack for subtle analogies. It isn't the president's inference that is inappropriate, then, but rather Chance's chance presence in a situation where he does not belong. In such a context, Chance is naturally seen as a friend of friends. Through the simple effect of trust by association, he becomes an interlocutor worthy of attention.

Inferences Based on the Content of the Information

What people say and how they say it tell us something important about their credibility. This is one of the secrets of marketing: to construct messages that reassure us regarding the reliability of those who deliver them. Trust has a very rich pragmatic dimension, one that has not been sufficiently studied. Why exactly do we trust one prospective tenant on Airbnb but not another? Or why do we lend credence to a certain review on TripAdvisor? Sometimes it seems that we trust "in the dark," on the basis of a simple exchange of messages or because of a familiar writing style that reassures us. Both the content and form of a message play roles in determining our willingness to trust it. In the case of Twitter, one of the social networks where the reliability of information counts most, the linguistic coherence and structure of a tweet decisively influences its circulation. Dan Sperber's *argumentative theory* of reasoning maintains that the logical structure of an argument is an important indicator of its reliability.[4] According to this approach, we do not evaluate the content of a message solely according to factual information at our disposal. We also determine its credibility based on its structure and coherence. An argument that is logically coherent has a higher probability of being judged true than one that is poorly constructed. Of course, in this case too we run the risk of accepting information because of a selection bias. For instance, information that confirms what we already know or that is formulated in a way that resembles our habitual way of expressing ourselves is embraced more easily than discordant information expressed in an unfamiliar way. For this reason, our prospective Airbnb tenant need only be clever enough to anticipate the "right" tone to use with us to be trusted more than someone who doesn't say anything wrong but whose mode of expression is less familiar and reassuring.

Social Norms of Deference to Authority

Among the factors affecting our strategies for deciding whom and what to trust, one that is especially fundamental and deeply anchored as well as being extremely recalcitrant to

4. See Mercier and Sperber 2017.

conscious control is our tendency to defer, often tacitly and unconsciously, to norms that we have internalized over the course of a lifetime. Our mental life is populated by countless thoughts and beliefs that we only partly understand but that nevertheless structure our common sense and that we can question only with immense difficulty. Most often, these are beliefs that we adopted during a phase in our lives when deference to others was the most efficient way to learn something new, namely during childhood. Or they are beliefs we took as gospel when subjected to an authority we were in no position to dispute lest we find ourselves excluded from a group to which we belonged or which we hoped to join.

In a book about reliability and truth, historian of science Steven Shapin tells of his first experiences as a researcher in a genetics laboratory. He was entrusted with confirming the following scientific statement: "DNA contains cytosine."

> Here is what I did: I was given some pieces of rat liver which I then minced and froze in liquid nitrogen; I ground the frozen tissue and suspended it in digestion buffer; I incubated the sample at 50C for 16 hours in a tightly capped tube; [many other operations follow] I went on to hydrolize the sample and to perform a chemical test confirming the presence of nucleotide cytosine. This was DNA: I had it in my hand; I had verified the facts of its composition. (1994, 18)

Although this is a scientific experiment, the direct nature of the knowledge obtained is disputable. All the information at Shapin's disposal for carrying out this experiment and the correlation between the results obtained and the truth of the conclusions stated are based on trust in the validity of numerous laboratory practices, in teachers who trained him, and in colleagues who furnished him with the material he needed for carrying out the experiment. The *validity* of the scientific conclusion he drew could not have been established independently of the networks of trust that made asserting and defending it possible. It is worth noting that the Latin root of the word "validity" signifies power (*validus* means strong, potent, someone who has authority). One cannot learn how to navigate a field of knowledge without deferring to others, to professional practices, teachers, common sense, in short to everything that structures the epistemic landscape of that field. Common sense itself is structured by authority relations that we cannot put into question. They are at the core of our social identity. We are who we are because we defer to such authorities. In a famous article, philosopher G. E. Moore (1925) argued that statements of common sense are *true* by virtue of the evident impossibility of demonstrating their falsity. Philosophers have long discussed the status of such statements. These supposedly self-evident beliefs cannot be wholly separated from deep-seated habits of deference. I know I have a body, but if I am asked what is inside it—a heart, a liver—I will reply by deferring to the authority of others. I know I was born in Milan on a winter day. This belief too, so fundamental for my identity, is the fruit of my parents' testimony and of the fact that my father went to city hall that afternoon to declare the day and hour of my birth. In sum, authority and deference to others play a crucial role even in what we think of as "commonsense" beliefs. What I strongly believe, therefore, what I consider self-evident, is part of a *proverbial economy*, to use Steven Shapin's elegant expression.[5] Our proverbial economy is a network of

5. This how Shapin defines a proverbial economy: "a network of speech, judgment and action in which proverbial utterances are considered legitimate and valuable, in which judgment is shaped, and action prompted, by proverbs competently uttered in

actions, words, practices, conversations, and deference to shared authorities. We refer to these presuppositions as "common sense," "what everyone knows," and "the authority of our elders," and we very seldom question them because it seems wholly sensible and appropriate to trust them. Common sense, therefore, is best understood as an ineffable feeling of legitimacy whenever we put our trust in a conclusion or report that has authority in our eyes. It contains within itself beliefs that have a specific reputation: the sacrosanct reputation of tradition.

Socially Distributed Reputational Cues

During the coffee break of a conference I am attending, I enter the room where snacks are being served and the attendees are mingling and chatting informally. The conference topic is not within my area of expertise and I know few people. I try to infer who is interesting, who matters, whom to shun, and who are the leading authorities on the theme of the conference. The participants wear laminated badges inscribed with their name, title, and home institution. I try to read these nametags and to evaluate the academic status of each according to the university where they teach, or based on my having heard their name somewhere before. I can also get my bearings by observing a series of social cues. These include behavior, dress, age, and manner of introducing themselves or of presenting their papers. But what tells me the most is their attitude toward each other. Who are the central people in a conversation? Who is listened to and who is ignored? It appears that some have the ear of everyone, while others bide their time patiently before

---

pertinent ways and settings: that is to say, a cultural system in which proverbial speech has the capacity of making a difference to judgement and action" (2001, 735).

finally daring to put in their two cents' worth. We can allegedly distinguish a famous person from someone who doesn't count in the following way. When the famous person repeats the same joke for the second time in a public speech, the audience again breaks into appreciative laughter. When a person of no importance does the same, the reaction is one of embarrassed silence broken by sporadic coughing here and there. An illustrious professor at the center of a conversation may at some point encourage the circle of people besieging him or her with questions to listen to a young colleague. The small gaggle of groupies will then obediently shift their attention to the "new recruit." The famous professor's aura is thereby transferred to the junior colleague, illustrating how reputation can migrate invisibly from one person to another in an almost ghostly fashion.

Quite rapidly, the social cues I pick up during the conference intermission allow me to sketch a mental map of the coffee-break crowd. The social space around me is now clearly configured, allowing me to assign to those I observe powers and propensities that, in turn, give their statements and actions new informational value. My lasting takeaway from the conference will be the association I have inferred between ideas that were new to me and the unequal social distribution of epistemic authority that I have been able to map out during the coffee break thanks to an array of telling cues.[6]

Cues about reputation are pieces of social information present in the environment. Such cues can be picked up in an informal way, as in the case I just described—although badges on the clothes of conference-goers have a somewhat formal component—or they can be highly organized and structured to be

6. See Origgi 2013a.

more easily legible. For instance, I want to know the best wine to buy for dinner in a country whose wines I do not know. Of course, I could go to a wine bar and observe the behavior of the clients who seem the most knowledgeable. But it is more likely that I will resort to various "judgment devices" that allow me to classify information about available wines and that I trust because they belong to a sociocognitive network that I consider legitimate, including price, number of "glasses" in the *Gault & Millau* guide, Parker points, and so on. Alternatively, if I am an expert, I will rely on denomination, *cru*, and so on.

As we have seen in chapter 3, evidence of reputation spreads through communication and word of mouth. Where reputational devices (*dispositifs*) do not exist or have a low level of reliability, reputational cues are at the mercy of those who transmit them. They can be modified and manipulated. The social information we desperately try to extract from these cues is at times nothing but the reflection of biases caused by the expressed views of others. It is filtered by others and by our acts of deference before their authority. The contemptuous way an insider looks down upon a member of his own group gives me valuable information about the distribution of power within that group. Far from being neutral, that look embodies all the deference, loyalty, and commitment through which observers routinely read and decipher the world.

Robust Signals

The reputational cues I have just described are signals. They communicate the presence or absence of a certain empirically unobservable trait in an individual, idea, or object. As we have seen in chapter 2, signaling theory tries to respond to the following question: When observing specific cues of reliability in an agent whom I must decide to trust or distrust, how do I extract sufficient information from these cues to decide that the agent is as reliable as the signals imply? One problem is that signals are often indirect, filtered by the views of others and deformed by speech. Only authorities in whom we implicitly trust can turn such inherently disputable signals into something more robust. A signal thus has a twofold problem. First, how can we trust the authorities on whom we rely for sending us reliable readings of the signals emitted by the individuals, objects, or ideas we are evaluating? And second, which signals are robust and which are problematic?

How reliable is a classification, a comment on TripAdvisor, a sneering look at a woman's dress, or a disparaging remark about a bottle of wine? In chapter 2, we saw that robust signals are those that are hardest to imitate. An algorithm on the Web that classifies the best car-dealer websites is more reliable than a list drawn up by a group of experts, because the results of an algorithm are harder for interested parties to falsify. We now turn to a number of meta-signals that help us gauge the robustness or flimsiness of a reputation.

Emotional Reactions and Moral Commitments

Our "sense of others" is constructed through a mix of rationality and emotion. Taking a leap in the dark that commits us for life, in the absence of crucial information about the other, is sometimes easier than making a decision after carefully and rationally weighing the options. Trust can precede calculation of risk. The feeling of security that accompanies this kind of "motivational" trust depends on the suspension of doubt. Casting off all suspicions about the intentions of the other provides a kind of emotional solace one could describe in these terms:

"I don't know anything about you but I feel at ease and safe with you." We feel protected. We sense that the other is willing to reciprocate our trust. Hobbes, who is usually considered the originator of strategic and rational approaches to trust, recognizes this emotional dimension of trust as a passion of the soul: "TRUST is a passion proceeding from belief of him from whom we expect or hope for good, so free from doubt that upon the same we pursue no other way."[7] One could define this emotional dimension of our trust as an *optimistic* attitude regarding the benevolence and competence of others. Understanding this aspect of trust, therefore, means understanding the legitimacy of this carefree absence of doubt and the normative expectations it can create.

The psychological disposition to trust others can be determined by non-rational, emotional reactions. Well-known experiments by Janine Willis and Alexander Todorov (2006) show that we evaluate the reliability of others on the basis of blink-of-an-eye inferences based in turn on our intuitive assessment of facial expressions. These judgments are at once extemporaneous and lasting. Acquiring additional information about the persons in question won't necessarily induce us to revise our initial judgment. Trust can thus be firmly established on the basis of a first impression. The heuristics that guide us in such first-sight assessments are perceptual and based on a series of implicit biases that lead us to connect specific emotional reactions to specific facial expressions. Of course, the heuristics on which we rely to identify someone as kind do not guarantee that the person so identified will in fact be kind. More generally, the fallibility of such heuristics poses the problem of the moral commitments that arise out of rela-

7. See Hobbes 1640, chap. IX, para. 9.

tions of trust. We sometimes feel obliged to trust certain people. And, conversely, we feel that those we have trusted have moral obligations toward us. But should the fact that I am mindlessly counting on someone, driven solely by emotion, give that person a moral obligation toward me? It seems unlikely. Indeed, to expect others to honor our feelings of trust can even be a form of coercion. A mother who tells her son, "I'm sure you wouldn't marry a girl as frivolous as Anna, I trust you," puts a kind of social pressure on the young man that cannot be considered genuinely moral in nature. Morally, in fact, he is under no obligation to heed her jeering preferences. We don't owe it to others to accommodate their expectations, and this includes those expectations that result from their sincere concern for our well-being. A jilted lover's feeling of indignation will cause us annoyance or embarrassment, but not a sense that we are morally obliged to honor previous avowals of undying affection.

Virginia Woolf talks of *unreal loyalties* that ruin our lives and drive us to make imbecilic choices. We think we owe something to someone, we care about what our mother or boss thinks is right for us, and we feel guilty when our judgment deviates too greatly from that of our reference group. But there is no necessary link between our emotional commitment to a relation of trust and the moral implications of that relation. It is true that our trust is often based on emotions and commitments that we are not capable of easily putting into question, but this does not always mean that my trusting you creates moral responsibilities in you toward me.

The analysis of the heuristics, emotions, and social and cultural mechanisms that determine who and what we trust is merely a starting point for comprehending the legitimacy of our judgments. The impossibility of drawing a distinction between the epistemic, cognitive, and moral dimensions of the trust we put in others is at the heart of the question of the legitimacy of the heuristics of reputation. It is not always easy to differentiate the *normative* from the *descriptive* dimensions of the heuristics on which we commonly rely. Thus, instead of aiming to formulate a grand Theory of Reputation, it is worth beginning with a series of illustrations of *good* and *bad* practices, without attempting to fit them into some kind of comprehensive philosophical system.

The Vagaries of Reputation: Irresistible Heuristics, Inevitable Illusions

THE PARADOX OF VIOLETTA VALÉRY, OR HOW REPUTATION "FLOWS"

In the second act of Verdi's *La Traviata*, Violetta and Alfredo live together in the countryside, enjoying days of love and harmony. Taking advantage of Alfredo's momentary absence, his father, Giorgio Germont, pays a visit to Violetta. In the style of the aristocratic paterfamilias of romantic drama, he blames Violetta for conducting an immoral relationship with his son, regretting that this illicit liaison is discrediting the whole family, especially hindering the marriage of his younger daughter to a young man from a distinguished and presumably quite conservative family. Thus Germont implores Violetta to leave Alfredo in one of the most famous arias of the opera:

> God blessed me with a daughter,
> like an angel in her purity;
> if Alfredo refuses to return
> to the bosom of his family,
> the young man in love and beloved in turn,

who was soon to marry my daughter,
would reject this bond
on which our happiness depends.[8]

And Violetta responds: "Ah, I understand [Ah, comprendo]" as if the connection between her reputation and that of Alfredo's sister were self-evident. And yet this connection is illusory. It appears only because of a series of commitments to unwritten, intangible norms. Violetta is the mistress of Alfredo, not his wife. Her reputation cannot therefore seriously blemish that of his sister. What she nevertheless recognizes immediately and what, as a romantic heroine, she must accept is the social norm that condemns her. Violetta shares Germont's values and sees in her condition an obstacle to the befitting marriage of his daughter. Violetta's identity, her search for recognition in Alfredo's father's eyes, and hence her dignity and the respect of her person require her submission to norms that are contrary to her interests. Thus when she leaves Alfredo, the ill repute that had "flowed" from her to Alfredo's sister is suddenly "wiped away," as if by magic. No permanent mark remains, just some suspicions, some rumors, some gossip. But nothing has been written in indelible ink as would have happened, for instance, in the case of a crime.

8. Pura siccome un angelo

iddio mi diè una figlia;
se Alfredo nega riedere
in seno alla famiglia,
l'amato e amante giovane,
cui sposa andar dovea,
or si ricusa al vincolo
che lieti ne rendea.

La Traviata, Act 2, scene 5

In traditional societies, reputability flows through social ties. Studied closely by historians, sociologists, and anthropologists, social relations are *hierarchical*, and the status of persons is influenced by those with whom they routinely associate. If someone in a good social position associates with someone of a lower rank, the status of the former can influence that of the latter and improve it, but the reverse is also possible. The reputation of the latter can drag the reputation of the former into the gutter. Thus the uncertainty surrounding social ascent and descent generates anxiety regarding status and fear of "dangerous" social relations. An extremely lucid analysis of this phenomenon can be found in the work of Norbert Elias and John Scotson (1994). They conducted fieldwork in an English village community, focusing on the residents' apprehensions regarding newcomers who moved into the "better parts of town." The new arrivals were different from the longtime inhabitants. But the fact that they chose homes in good neighborhoods was an initial indicator of their respectability. The result was great uncertainty among the villagers and their search for other clues and cues to decide if they should or should not be seen fraternizing with the newcomers.

Two basic relations characterize our social life: *exchange* and *deference*. Exchange relations tend to be egalitarian. I exchange something, a material or immaterial good, for something more or less equivalent. Deference relations, by contrast, are intrinsically unequal and asymmetrical. One person's deference toward another does not require reciprocity. On the contrary, through such an act I signal that the status of the person to whom I defer is superior to mine. Violetta Valéry, by yielding to the pressure exerted by Alfredo's father, recognizes the social superiority of the Germont family and the risk that their status could be "diminished" by her relationship with Alfredo.

Uncertainty about social status is due to the fact that the "transfer" of status through social ties is contingent and unpredictable. If the identity of those who associate with each other is clear, then one can predict that the ones who enjoy a superior social status will lose something by associating with those of an inferior condition, while those with a lower social status will correspondingly gain. In caste-based societies, the phenomenon of "pollution" whereby those of superior social status are "contaminated" by contact with those belonging to inferior castes is well known.[9] But as soon as status and identity are uncertain, the potential risk of association becomes even higher. One doesn't know with certainty who will benefit from it and who, instead, will risk ruining their reputation.

Whenever we think about the desirability of associating with others, we have to take both relations of exchange and relations of deference into account. A relation from which we stand to gain materially might nevertheless seem, on balance, objectionable because it would lower our social status. The oscillation between relations of exchange and relations of deference was a leitmotif of European literature at the turn of the twentieth century, a period marked by a major transition of European societies from a traditional economic structure based primarily on deference and status to a modern one founded primarily on commercial exchange. In one of Thomas Mann's first novels, *Royal Highness* (1909), a prince who has inherited the throne of an imaginary small European kingdom is forced to marry a rich American in order to rescue the fi-

9. See Dumont 1966.

nances of his country, which is on the brink of bankruptcy. The prince is shy, haughty, and awkward, hide-bound by manners proper to his social class, and his frostiness and detachment are intensified by a malformed hand hidden within a white glove. During the reception at which his engagement is announced, the prince tosses inhibitions aside and starts dancing, seemingly forgetting his aristocratic status. At one point he even loses his glove, thereby revealing his secret deformity. For Mann, this loss of aristocratic self-control symbolizes the end of court society and the advent of the bourgeoisie, a social class that is typically anchored in exchange relations rather than in deference and inherited social status.

Similarly, Don Fabrizio, Prince of Salina, the protagonist of the novel *The Leopard* by Sicilian aristocrat Tomasi di Lampedusa, witnesses the fall of the Sicilian aristocracy before the rise of the new North Italian bourgeois classes during the unification of the country in 1860. This doesn't stop him from judging Angelica, the daughter of a rich Sicilian landowner and betrothed to his beloved nephew Tancredi, as a girl of "wretched origins." The transition to modernity is marvelously illustrated in the novel by the waltz that the Prince of Salina graciously grants Angelica during the Pontaleone ball in Palermo, where the young beauty is to be presented to Palermo's high society. The old and the new worlds mingle promiscuously, thereby causing the old deference relations to unravel. The ambiguity of the novel, it should be said, permits a variety of different interpretations. Does this waltz represent the end of the Salina, for example, or the rise of the new generation, incarnated in the marriage of Tancredi to Angelica?

Be this as it may, the hierarchical reading of social relations is a highly potent cognitive bias. When we calculate the risks of associating ourselves with a specific social grouping or network, we combine in a not particularly rational way considerations based on exchange and others based on status. The traditional reading of the social world, which privileges relations of deference, depends on our ability to accurately locate those we encounter in a social hierarchy. But when this becomes difficult, we are compelled to rely on cues that are not always reliable. Let's now examine some of these.

Name Your Associates and I'll Tell You Who You Are

When academics from Latin America or China travel, they often take pictures—or have pictures taken—of themselves with world-renowned professors. I've always wondered why they do it. Are they just collecting souvenirs? Or does it represent a practice that is typical of cultures where the circulation of images is a better way of communicating than verbal testimony? In the era of social networks, I have also noted, many of these images are then published on Facebook or Google +, as if to demonstrate a social link between the pictured visitor and the renowned professor. At the end of a lecture in Paris by a prestigious speaker, I took a few snapshots of her and two of her equally famous colleagues. A student who had been talking to them spontaneously stepped modestly out of the frame, obviously considering it "inappropriate" to figure in a picture with these three sacred monsters of the discipline. Generously, they called her back, inviting her to be included in a group photo, which I then sent her at her request. When she received it, she thanked me profusely, telling me that she would never have imagined being able to show her friends a picture that brought her so close to such stars.

I then attempted a rudimentary experiment in order to measure the impact of such ephemeral associations on the socially shared perception of my own reputation. During a conference in Rome marking the twentieth anniversary of the World Wide Web, I asked Tim Berners-Lee if he would pose for a selfie with me. My request annoyed his agent, who was apparently charged with defending the image of the inventor of the Web. In the agent's eyes apparently, Berners-Lee's association with someone unknown, such as me, might have detracted from his reputation! But I insisted, and, displaying the kindness of the great, Berners-Lee did me the honor of posing for a joint photo, not unlike the Prince of Salina granting a waltz to Angelica.

Back in Paris, I posted the photo on my Facebook page. Within a few hours, I had received an invitation to participate in a think tank on new technologies, three invitations to give talks, and a request for an interview in an important periodical. For those who issued these invitations, evidently, my connection with Tim Berners-Lee could not have been entirely accidental. Yes, it was true that we attended the same conference where I was one of the speakers and that, indeed, I have devoted part of my research to the study of the Web. Still, his reputation as the inventor of the Web is simply incommensurable with mine as a philosopher. Those who saw the picture I posted may have reasoned that physical proximity to the inventor of the Web is not available to everyone and that whoever is able to be photographed next to him must know him personally or belong to a social circle close to his. This is yet another illustration of how reputation "flows" from one person to another in ways that frequently escape rational evaluation. A better-known example is provided by the movie stars who put their reputation at the service of a coffee brand or a humanitarian cause, even when the connection between acting

FIGURE 6. Selfie of the author with Tim Berners-Lee. Photograph by Gloria Origgi.

renown and delicious coffee or human rights is unfathomably obscure.

Inferring the social prominence of someone after seeing them in the proximity of a famous person can at times be rational. The occasional soundness of such an inference helps explain the favorable impact of this photograph on my reputation. Yet the *heuristics of proximity* are not consistently or even usually reliable. I can find myself near an important person by sheer chance, because we are traveling on the same train or dining in the same restaurant, and in such cases the observable association is entirely contingent and transient. As a factual matter, visible proximity, be it physical or virtual, between two people who have different social statuses is systematically interpreted as giving more information than it actually does. Simply being next to each other is perceived, often quite erroneously, as a robust association that affects the reputation of both.

A good example of a relation of virtual proximity, one behind chronically manipulated distortions of scholarly and scientific reputation, is the practice of coauthoring books and articles. In an environment that feeds on reputation such as the academic one, arguments over the order of names in publications can lead to heated disputes. We know well that our prestige will be magnified by coauthoring an article or book with a famous researcher, while publication with unknowns will weaken it. This is why an infinite series of norms has been developed to establish the order of authorship (alphabetical? order of importance?). It also explains epic battles to obtain a dominant position in the list of authors as well as the practice, common in some disciplines, of including the name of the director of the laboratory in all publications, even if he or she contributed to the research only administratively and not at all by way of content. Because the director will be an older and more established researcher, the presence of his or her name will typically raise the prestige of the publication and thereby improve the reputation of the young researchers who actually did the work. Moreover, the prestige of the director will increase with each new publication, along with that of the laboratory, in a virtuous circle of cumulative advantages whose dynamics we will analyze in chapter 9, dedicated to academic prestige.

Relations of proximity are ruled by norms that need to be learned and that vary from one context to another. To be seated next to Tim Berners-Lee on a train doesn't have the same meaning as being photographed next to him or to work at his side in a research lab. A "naïve" reading of such relations is one of the main causes of distortions in the attribution of reputation. Moreover, the proximity bias is easily manipulated. This is obvious in the case of marketing campaigns that associate a perfume with a movie star. The epistemic strategy through which we can defend ourselves against our natural vulnerability to such distortions consists in asking ourselves each time if we are justified in interpreting proximity as conclusive evidence of a genuine social relation.

The Happy Few, or the Giddiness of Lists

One of the most satisfying aspects of publishing a book with a prestigious publisher is to see one's own name in the catalogue next to the great names of literature and philosophy: Naipaul, Origgi, Plato. I remember the thrill I felt when, after publishing a novel in Italy in 2008, I first saw myself listed alongside Charles Dickens, Robert Louis Stevenson, and Iris Murdoch. It felt as if I had been promoted, given the right to play in the Big Leagues, even though, of course, the proximity of my name to theirs on the same list was the result of a combination of chance and random editorial choices. It had nothing whatever to do with classification according to merit. Inclusion on a list or membership in a prestigious club gives us information about the reputation of others and says something about our own. But these appearances also create distortions that lead us to overestimate their informative value or accept an erroneous reading of their meaning.

From ancient times, exclusive clubs and lists of membership have provided grounds for assigning a status of preeminence in various contexts, above all in sports, the arts, and culture. From the Greek *agon* to artistic competitions in the Renaissance, the main techniques for the management of reputation, especially in creative contexts, have been the *tournament*, the *prize*, and the resulting *membership* of the winners in an exclusive club of the happy few. (Two examples are the winners of the gold medal in the Olympics and the winners of the Fields Medal in mathematics.) In the academic world, whose contemporary form has its origins in sixteenth- and seventeenth-century *scientific societies* and academies of scholars, membership in a scientific society remains today a sign of distinction. The very idea of *scientific truth*, developed in the seventeenth century by the British natural philosophers of the Royal Society, is hard to separate from the honor and reputation that belonging to that select society conferred on its members.[10] Membership in an exclusive club (Nobel prizes, the American Academy of Arts and Letters) signals a good reputation. We want to be part of exclusive clubs to enhance our reputation. And, if we already have a good reputation, we are likely to be recruited in order to enhance the reputation of the club. Some prizes confer prestige on their winners, while, vice versa, some authors confer prestige on the prizes they win.

Admittedly, the criteria of selection can be mysterious and the transparency of the process disputable. This is what led Jorge Luis Borges to say: "Success is a misunderstanding, maybe the worst of all." And yet the result is clear: presence on a list can launch our reputation. In a little-read book with an eloquent title, *Les cendres de la gloire ou le Prix d'un Goncourt*, Jean Carrière recollects the day of November 21, 1972, in Paris's Place Gaillon, facing the famous restaurant Drouant, where each year a small group of ten writers decides the fate of a colleague by announcing the winner of the Goncourt Prize, one of the most prestigious literary awards in France. His unexpected victory launched Carrière into the world of literary success, with over five hundred thousand copies sold in France over the next year, fourteen translations, and a total of over two million books sold worldwide. But his was to be a sadly ephemeral fame, which the author paid for with a profound depression, owing to his inability to adjust his rather modest

10. On the relation between honor and truth in the Royal Society, see Shapin 1994, in particular the second chapter.

self-image to the newly demanding reputation conferred upon him by the Goncourt. His success tormented him as if it were accusing him of being an impostor, "a crook who conceals his dirty game."[11] And yet the prize, once awarded, becomes the recipient's inescapable fate.

Rumors and criticisms have circled around the Goncourt since its inception in 1903. The failure to choose authors such as Apollinaire, Colette, and Céline—whose *Voyage to the End of the Night* was beaten in 1932 by *The Wolves* by Guy Mazeline, a novel that has vanished without a trace from the history of literature—led for years to talk of the "Goncourt scandal." The disproportionate influence of a handful of publishing houses, too, has been derided under the ironic name of Galligrasseuil, referring to the three publishers in France that normally share the prize (Gallimard, Grasset, Seuil). And yet each year the announcement at the Drouant restaurant of a prize of 10 euros (this is the nominal amount paid to the prizewinner) changes the winner's reputation and literary fate, since the prize guarantees sales of at least three hundred thousand copies.

The matter of celebrity, of how one constructs it and of its relation to reality, is a classical subject of social science.[12] It is a crucial subject, although somewhat orthogonal to the study of reputation. The fact that the inclusion of one's name on a list of the "celebrities" who populate the cultural market, such as the finalists of the Pulitzer Prize, rockets one's reputation sky-high is in large part due to the arbitrary nature of such choices. The media effects are among the consequences of being included on such lists. Here we encounter a self-fulfilling dynamic. Appearance in the media suffices to amplify the reputation of a newly anointed star. Among the many functions of

11. Carrière 1987, 22.

12. See Heinich 2012; Lilti 2014; Menger 2009; and Erner 2016.

the media in postwar American society, Robert Merton focused on the fundamental one of *status attribution*: the media confer a status on people, organizations, social movements, and institutions. The status of an individual is heightened by the attention given by the media. This does not depend entirely on the fact that ordinary people perceive the media as an authoritative source of information directed by a small group of experts who know who deserves to be talked about. The media have a self-fulfilling effect of *status legitimation*. The recognition of someone on the part of the press or television means that the gestures and opinions of that person are important enough to attract public attention. This self-fulfilling aspect is nicely illustrated by the case of "circular prestige" whereby status is transferred, as in advertisements where a well-known actor sips a brand of espresso that is even better known. Such techniques mobilize the audience's circular thoughts of the following kind: "If someone really matters, she will be at the center of media attention, and if she is at the center of media attention, then she really matters."

Merton's analysis of the media's role in status attribution dates from 1948, but it remains surprisingly enlightening, although it is less historically universal than the bias created by inclusion in clubs for the happy few that I have been stressing here. That bias creates a magnifying effect on the reputation of those who are "included" and is founded on well-known psychological mechanisms. The human mind has the tendency to attribute the general characteristics of a class to each of its individual members. That is, we are naturally inclined to adopt simplifying stereotypes and use them to get our bearings in the world. Given that cycling is one of the most popular sports in France, for instance, we may tend to attribute the characteristic "cyclist" to "Frenchmen" as such and to create a stereotype of the typical Frenchman vacationing on his bike with a baguette under his arm. When we see the name of an author on a list of "greats," similarly, we naturally ascribe to them the same attributes as those of their famous "neighbors." This effect has been thoroughly studied in social psychology. Psychologist Daniel Kahneman, who won the Nobel Prize for economics in 2002, argues that this reading of the world is due to the preference we have for causal rather than statistical explanations. The simple fact that an individual finds himself to be a member of a class—which might result from a purely statistical distribution—is interpreted as a causal relation. If he happens to be in that class it must be *because* he possesses certain qualities.[13]

No doubt, this bias constitutes a highly useful cognitive resource. It provides the basis for our intuitive capacity to infer from simple cues, such as inclusion in a class, an enormous amount of information about the individuals and objects around us. This is a very economical way to manage information that can prove particularly useful in situations where we must make a decision one way or the other but where both information and time are scarce. In this case, too, the epistemology of reputation offers a modest piece of advice: rely less on intuition and more on reflection! Formulated differently, we should always investigate the *reasons* for someone's inclusion on a list and scrutinize with a skeptical eye the *mechanisms* that underlie the process of inclusion and exclusion. This second-order information will prove precious for deciding whether we should yield to our intuitions or resist them.

Significantly, the heuristics that occasionally lead us astray when assessing someone's reputation are no different from

13. See Kahneman 2010.

those that routinely allow us to navigate the social world with confidence. As a result, we cannot hope to avoid errors of under- or overestimating reputations by abandoning such heuristics altogether. Instead, we have to train ourselves to analyze the underlying reasons and mechanisms that determine socially salient assessments of reputation in particular domains.

The list that I have presented in this chapter of the biases and heuristics that influence our assessments of reputation is obviously not exhaustive. The examples I have canvassed are meant to illustrate the role of cognitive mechanisms in the construction and distortion of reputations. These rely not only on social networks but also on the *perception* of these networks and on the thousands of modifications that our expectations, emotions, and cognitive tendencies visit upon these perceptions. In order to make our way successfully through the social world and correctly use reputation as a tool for evaluation, we have to be aware of these emotions and tendencies. That is to say, we have to exercise a form of *epistemic responsibility* in their regard. The world of reputation is configured in such a way that our perception of social relations naturally distorts our assessments. So just as traditional epistemology taught us to mistrust our senses, an epistemology of reputation instructs us to mistrust the spontaneous verdicts initially issued by our "social sense."

6

Homo Comparativus

STATUS, HONOR, AND PRESTIGE

It's not about the money. It's about the game. The game between people.

—GORDON GEKKO, *WALL STREET 2*

We must never extinguish in ourselves the thirst for immortality. Better to suffer gloriously on a great public stage than to be pin-pricked with petty torments in some obscure corner of the globe.

—HÉRAULT DE SÉCHELLES, *THÉORIE DE L'AMBITION*

What honor? What honor indeed? Such chatter! What a joke! Can honor fill your belly? No. Can honor set a broken shin? It cannot. Or mend a foot? No. Or a finger? No. Or a hair? No. Honor is not a surgeon. What is it, then? A word. What's in this word? Air, which flies away.

—GIUSEPPE VERDI, *FALSTAFF*, ACT 1, SCENE 1

In *Wall Street 2*, released two years after the 2008 financial crisis, the notorious financier Gordon Gekko, freed from prison after having served his time, reinstalls himself in a posh New York apartment. Plotting his comeback, he passes his evenings gazing spellbound at an old engraving affixed to one of the rare opaque walls in his otherwise all-glass home, whose enormous picture windows open onto a dazzling panorama of New York City, the quarry he hopes to recapture. So what exactly does Gekko see in this engraved depiction of a simple tulip bulb?

What his mind's eye beholds is one of the greatest speculative bubbles in modern history. Introduced to Holland from Turkey in the sixteenth century, tulip bulbs gave rise, in the mid-1630s, to an irrational frenzy of collective euphoria: prices spiked at such delirious heights that entire fortunes were thrown away to purchase a single bulb. At the peak of the craze, a single bulb cost the equivalent of ten times the annual income of a well-to-do family of the period. Then, as had to happen, a massive sell-off and crash ensued. In 1637 prices plummeted, and the irrationally optimistic investors who had been swept along by collective euphoria found themselves with nothing on their hands but worthless bulbous roots.

How did this happen? How did so many business-savvy investors, for the sake of a few modest tulip bulbs, end up disinheriting their descendants and coming close, as a group, to committing collective economic suicide? Mesmerized by the roller coaster of speculative euphoria implicit in the picture of the tulip on his wall, the aging Wolf of Wall Street first dismisses the idea that runaway commodity price inflation is the product of material self-interest alone: "It is not about the money," he explains.

Cool-headed, calculating, and rational, *homo economicus* would never jeopardize his own or his children's future on a whim. He is circumspect, not rash. He is methodical and coolly skeptical, not enraptured by unverifiable promises of riches to the point of ignoring all downside risks. He certainly wouldn't precipitate a global economic catastrophe in a heedless quest to maximize short-term profits.

But maniacal speculators, swept along by euphoric bubbles and panicky sell-offs, are nothing like such supposedly rational and calculating economic actors. They are gamblers, in it for the thrill. This is what Gekko is conveying when, after dismissing the thought that money is the principal driver of casino capitalism, he confesses that "it's about the game." Playing the market is a game that speculators play among themselves. Some win, some lose. Some come out on top while others fold and end up ruined and impoverished. In this game, attracting attention and being spoken about is already a kind of victory. Rivalry for material riches is less intoxicating than the race for fame and reputation. Competitors for reputation need superior social skills, not merely financial virtuosity. To best their rivals, social animals must make alliances and stabilize hierarchies. The ultimate aim in all this is "to exist," that is, to be present, to be visible, to shine brightly in the eyes of others. This reflected existence, preeminence in the public mind and especially in the opinion of market peers, is the only way human beings can avoid tumbling traceless into the abyss of nothingness after death. It is the only shred of immortality available to humankind.

This quest for an imagined and vicarious afterlife is why human beings have always played the reputation game. At stake in this game are a person's trustworthiness, believability, and social standing. This was also true in 1630s Holland: I am credible if I purchase tulip bulbs and, when I buy them, tulips become profitable investments for those who place their trust in me. People look at me, examining my credibility, and the more I become credible, the more tulip bulbs become an irresistible investment opportunity until that fatal day when the entire house of cards collapses and everyone discovers that, underneath the back-and-forth of mutually entrancing overvaluations, King Tulip has no clothes.

To discover even a minimal strand of rationality in such choices and such conduct, we need to acknowledge that reputation, too, and not material self-interest alone, is a powerful motive for human action. The crimes of Jean-Claude Romand might arguably be explained by mental illness, without seeking any further motivation for his desperate acts. But psychopathology cannot explain the cases of Gordon Gekko and the seventeenth-century purchasers of tulip bulbs, nor of Orlando Figes, who dug his reputational tomb in an effort to inflate artificially his reputation by ghostwriting the opinions of fictitious Amazon reviewers. The motivation of such individuals must be sought in their quest for reputation. Indeed, their reputation is their second ego, their social ego. Only their obsessive care for this second ego explains the often reckless decisions they make. This is what guides their actions and reactions.

In what sense can care for reputation be a motivation for action? This is the question we now need to address. To pose this question directly means surveying the social science theories capable of developing models of action that treat reputation as an independent variable, in other words as a factor that, when varied, causes subsequent actions to vary accordingly. Examples include moral theories arguing that individuals act morally not from a love of justice but with an eye to how others will judge them. Among economic theories, the most relevant are those that interpret reputation as a scarce resource and that see demand for this scarce resource as a constraint on behavior.

But before turning once more to the social sciences, we need to delve more deeply into the ontology of *homo comparativus*, the human animal whose decisions and actions hinge on relations with others and whose choices and actions are driven by a crying need for recognition and approval by others.

The Ontology of *Homo Comparativus*

Human beings are neither essentially competitive nor essentially cooperative: they are "comparative," that is to say, born and bred to draw comparisons and contrasts between themselves and others. Their actions and achievements mean nothing unless and until they are compared with the achievements and actions of others and are assessed according to some generally applicable scale of values. Value—be it moral, economic, or epistemic—is created through contextually specified differentiations. It exists by virtue of a normative contrast made manifest through comparison. Value is not inherent in things or persons themselves. Rather, like images reflected ad infinitum in two facing mirrors, value is wholly relational. It originates in the relationship between things or persons. It is the autonomous product of comparative exchange; and it has no other purpose or significance. We create value to create value. Value cannot be reduced to other preexisting factors, such as utility, scarcity, or labor as understood in economics. It is the cognitive footprint and the matrix of opinions that all human interaction engenders and that structures the perceptions we have of ourselves and others. As Karl Mannheim (1982), the founder of the sociology of culture, explained: human beings "perceive" the world *hierarchically*. We can grasp reality only on the basis of a scale of values that presupposes a hierarchically organized world. But this unavoidable perspective on the world is not solely sociocultural. It is also rooted in our physi-

FIGURE 7. Perceptual framing effects. The interior square is perceived as lighter or darker depending on the shade of the frame.

ology of perception. Our perceptual faculties are structured to detect variations in the environment. The way our organs of perception process information depends on discrepancies between qualities or attributes within any given context. Our perceptual apparatus is designed to register differences, focusing on variations, disparities, and incongruities to identify the salient characteristics of what we perceive.

A hardwired *comparative consciousness* is one of the most distinctive characteristics of human nature. It influences our perception of the world, our cognition, our emotions, and our decisions. *Homo comparativus* reads the world through an evaluative prism. Our very sense of *objectivity* presupposes a hierarchy of values. This does not mean that the world around us does not exist or that it is completely relative to our point of view. Evaluative distinctions are inscribed in the relational dimension of our world, in the plethora of social networks that knit together our reality and that permit us to extract information from the world. These networks are constitutive of the world. In that sense, there is no humanly accessible ultimate reality lying beyond or behind the experienced interconnection of events. It is thanks to these relations that we perceive the world and that information acquires salience, meaning, and value.

The impossibility of separating social passions from comparisons and rankings is by no means a new idea. Hobbes, for example, conceived the craving for *glory* as a passion quite separate and distinct from the desire for *utility*. As philosopher Barbara Carnevali, commenting on Hobbes, explains, these two passions

> are distinguished by the forms of good to which they aspire: *utility* or *glory*. One can describe these as "material passions" versus "symbolic passions." . . . The former aim at physical pleasure . . . , the second at symbolic objects which the soul enjoys in a spiritual manner. . . . This second or spiritual impulse is expressed in a perpetual desire for power after power or, more precisely, for superiority over the power of others. (2013, 52)

In *The Elements of Law, Natural and Politic*, Hobbes specifically defines the passion of *glory*—one of the three fundamental passions that agitate and inflame human rivalry—as a feeling of triumphing over others: "GLORY, or internal gloriation or triumph of the mind is that passion which proceeds from the imagination or conception of our own power, above the power of him that contends with us."[1] Glory is thus an essentially comparative passion. It consists in the pleasure of contemplating one's superiority over others, the joy of triumphing over others and relishing their defeat and subordination. A similar thought is conveyed by a phrase often attributed to Talleyrand: "When I consider myself alone, I feel chagrined; but when I compare myself with others, I rejoice."

But the significance of the irresistible drive to draw comparisons is not limited to its contribution to gratifying our self-love or flattering our narcissistic sensibilities. Comparison

1. Hobbes 1640, I, 9, §1.

has a cognitive dimension, shaping not only our moral conduct but also our approach to learning and knowledge. Without this evaluative and comparative perspective, in fact, we would be incapable of wringing information from our experience of the world.

The idea that evaluative contrasts and comparisons are indispensable not only for motivating action but also for processing information appears in a variety of forms in recent social science research. But every version of the claim stems from the same basic intuition: information is organized and experience makes sense only on the basis of a scale of relative values. Without this comparative perspective, no objectivity is possible. André Orléan, for example, has proposed a radically new framework for conceptualizing "value" in economic theory by integrating mainstream economics, increasingly isolated from neighboring disciplines by its exclusively quantitative methodology, into explanatory schemes employed in the other social sciences. Elaborating on Schumpeter's intuition that "the problem of Value must always hold the pivotal position, as the chief tool of analysis in any pure theory that works with a rational schema,"[2] Orléan rejects the idea that value derives from "utility," that is, from an independently existing and presumably measurable magnitude. Value, he argues, is first created in acts of exchange and cannot be reduced to other preexisting quantities: "Conflict over social position, no less than the urge to acquire useful goods, arises from a certain relationship to objects. More generally, value in many situations is sought after for its own sake, insofar as it represents a universal purchasing power."[3] On this premise he proposes to re-found economics,

2. Schumpeter 1954, 287.
3. Orléan 2014, loc. 71.

basing it on the concept of *relative value*, understood as the subject matter of all the social sciences. His announced purpose is "to show that market value is an autonomous phenomenon that cannot be reduced to any preexisting magnitude such as utility, labor or scarcity."[4]

We already introduced Lucien Karpik's very original sociology of markets in chapter 4. What matters for our current topic is his idea of *homo singularis*, a consumer in a market of unique products where purchasing preferences are highly individualized and idiosyncratic. Such an economic actor chooses on the basis of an *axiological rationality*, to borrow a concept from Max Weber,[5] in trying to adjust his behavior to expressed and aggregated opinions about the value of items on sale. According to Karpik, "In the market of singularities, the consumer assigns priority to quality over price" (2010, 10). He offers a sophisticated analysis of *homo singularis* as an interested and rational market actor, but one who does not behave like the conventional *homo economicus*. He participates in a complex market, pullulating with highly detailed information, where choices must be made on the basis of multiple criteria and not solely according to supply and demand. Needless to say, the singularity of a product or service that consumers consider purchasing can be perceived only on the basis of distinction and comparison. This explains the all-importance of such devices for facilitating judgment as classifications and endorsements to guide the choices of consumers.

A final example comes from sociologist Eiko Ikegami, who, in order to underline the comparative element in the construction of the "self" in Japan, reconstructs a social history of the

4. Ibid., loc. 76.

5. The Weberian term commonly translated as axiological rationality is "Wertrationalität."

Samurai to demonstrate that the specificity of Japanese civilization is not collectivism but rather a culture of comparative competition where honor and rivalrous comparisons with others play an absolutely critical role.

In sum, the thesis that man is an essentially comparative animal has been circulating among social scientists for some time. But only recently have a variety of researchers begun to transform the idea into genuine research programs that make the symbolic value of reputation pivotal to any explanation of human conduct and choice.

The Economy of Esteem

Our reputation consists in the approval or disapproval of others and the extent to which they assign value to the material or immaterial goods to which we, too, assign value. Our reputation matters to us immensely, and we constantly try to gauge its ups and downs by reading flickers of esteem or disesteem in the eyes of others.

What is esteem? In developing the rudiments of an *economy of esteem* (or *kudonomics*, from the Greek for "glory" or "acclaim"), philosopher Philip Pettit and economist Geoffrey Brennan (2004) have identified two sides of esteem: the *comparative* and the *directive*. Esteem is comparative because, most of the time, the intensity of esteem depends not on an absolute ranking but on a ranking relative to others: "x does better than y along this dimension." But esteem is also "directive" because expressing esteem for others encourages them, in numerous situations, to behave in a way that will earn our further esteem. The evaluative nature of esteem is therefore double. On the one hand, esteem is evaluative because it implies a ranking of better and worse. On the other hand, it is normative because it involves a value judgment, distinguishing actions that merit esteem from those that merit contempt or disapproval, thereby implicitly encouraging action that will predictably earn esteem rather than scorn.

Here we encounter a possible difficulty. It is well known that efforts to appear worthy of esteem, if they are intentionally and explicitly geared toward making others esteem us, can be self-defeating. According to Jon Elster, the attitude of esteem is subject to the *teleological paradox*. Actively seeking esteem, like actively seeking pleasure, can inadvertently produce the opposite of what is desired. Single-minded hedonism can lead to unhappiness because, as experience teaches, we often find pleasure only at the moment when we cease consciously seeking it. In the same way, the single-minded pursuit of esteem can easily deteriorate into ambition, self-seeking, and vanity, that is to say, into emotional proclivities that are very unlikely to earn esteem. As Elster emphasizes, "Nothing makes less of an impression than the attempt to impress others" (1983, 66). La Bruyère already formulated this paradox in the seventeenth century:

> Men wish, in their hearts, to be well thought of, and they carefully conceal this wish because they want to appear virtuous, and because to seek to derive from virtue any advantage other than virtue itself, namely esteem and praise, would mean not being virtuous but being fond of esteem and praise, in other words vain: men are very vain, and they hate nothing more than being thought so.[6]

Esteem is paid in the currency of disinterestedness. To recognize another as worthy of esteem is to suspend momentarily

6. Jean de La Bruyère, *Characters* (1688), chap. 11, "Of Man," §65.

the pursuit of one's own self-interest. Yet models of rationality typically deny that human beings can choose to put their self-interestedness aside. Every interested pursuit of disinterested behavior, we are often told, is doomed to fail. According to Pettit and Brennan, by contrast, situations exist where the demand for esteem is motivated by concern not only for oneself but also for improving coordination with others. In such cases, consciously seeking esteem is not cynical and to that extent it escapes the teleological paradox. Consider a group of individuals who have to coordinate around social norms that are not self-evident in their shared culture. For example, no one taught me that in Paris it is strictly forbidden to hang one's laundry on a clothesline out the window. When I did it, as I was used to doing in Italy, my neighbors called the police. I immediately hauled in my laundry in order not to destroy my reputation with my neighbors (and in the city of Paris) and, since then, I have carefully refrained from draping my sheets out the window to let them dry. In this case, my desire for esteem was wholly collateral or second order. It was not inscribed in the Parisian norm against publicly airing one's damp laundry. Nor was my adjustment to the expectations of my neighbors ultimately driven by my desire to win their esteem. My self-conscious "quest for esteem" simply permitted me to coordinate with the world around me by conforming my behavior to my neighbors' values. There is nothing cynical or self-defeating, I think, about seeking comity by adapting to the value hierarchies of others. Such sensitivity to the esteem and disesteem of neighbors is simply an effective psychological mechanism for coordinating social action and interaction.

In other words, the self-conscious attempt to gain the esteem of others is sometimes but not always self-defeating. A similar complexity surfaces when we try to comprehend how esteem can be *granted* voluntarily. According to Brennan and Pettit, I am naturally led, in structured social exchanges, to accord esteem to various well-specified actions while displaying contempt toward others. A certain number of "esteem services" can be conferred on others relatively easily: paying attention, for example, or commending their actions that I consider worthy of esteem and disapproving of others. In so doing, I allow a larger social circle to measure the "esteemability" of these persons. On these bases, Brennan and Pettit consider it possible to develop an "economy of esteem" based on exchanges of a scarce good regulated by supply and demand. According to their theory, rational actors seeking to acquire the rare good of esteem will specialize in domains where they can expect to obtain the greatest degree of esteem. They also aim at delivering a level of performance that they expect will maximize esteem. Brennan and Pettit's promising and original analysis nevertheless runs into a variety of problems.

First of all, in the model they propose, esteem is a *linear* quantity: the starting point of their analysis is an interaction between two people wherein "esteem for actor A is obtained from observer B by virtue of A's level of performance in some arena of action."[7] Thus B's esteem functions as an incentive of the economic type for A. A will act in a certain way in the hope and expectation that, by so doing, he will elicit B's esteem. As we have seen, however, the sources, significance, and impact of esteem cannot be captured by such a simple model. For one thing, esteem does not spread in a linear fashion: it is propagated by networks and depends on the differing levels of prestige of the authorities who accord their esteem. Linear situations, in fact, where the agent expects a palpable advantage

7. Brennan and Pettit 2004, 83.

from behaving in a way that curries esteem from his social environment, are the exception rather than the rule. Pertinent examples include cases of uncertainty about the nature of prevailing social norms. In such cases, manifestations of esteem and contempt act as *heuristics*. That is to say, they instruct us about the norms shared by a certain community. If, when visiting Singapore, I drop a wad of chewing gum on the ground, I will expose myself to corporal punishment, which, in turn, will teach me the local chewing-gum norms in an unforgettable way and will no doubt persuade me to avoid chewing gum there in the future. Nevertheless, my internalization of this norm does not make my behavior intrinsically virtuous. Indeed, I can find the anti–chewing gum norm preposterous and at the same time obey it in order to avoid coming into physically painful conflict with the local community. This is yet another instance of the "hypocritical" acceptance of norms, encountered in chapter 3's discussion of *pluralistic ignorance*, where all members of a community publicly express a certain preference believing that it is universally shared, although, in fact, no one personally entertains such a preference.[8]

Second, we never accord esteem autonomously, without regard to the way others may morally praise or condemn any particular decision to grant esteem. Indeed, most of my allocations of esteem echo authorities I believe to be "competent" at evaluating the esteem-worthiness of an action or person. In other words, esteem results from a collective evaluation, where shared norms are always subject to social pressures. There can doubtless be, as Brennan and Pettit suggest, domains where the allocation of esteem seems responsive to "universal" or non-negotiable criteria, such as respect for oth-

8. See Kuran 1997. The phenomenon of pluralistic ignorance is discussed in chapter 3.

ers, respect for the environment, or the education of children. Still, the development of an "objective" economy of esteem depends on the mutual recognition of a set of moral norms on which a preliminary agreement has already been reached. Let us therefore see if symbolic goods other than esteem, which seemingly condemns esteem-seeking agents to social conformism, can function as motivations for action.

Honor as a Motivation

In a recent book, philosopher Anthony Appiah contends that moral revolutions are best explained by the emergence of a code of honor shared among peers. Although honor is often dismissed as a premodern norm, Appiah argues that it remains an important motivation for moral action. To make his case, he focuses on three historical episodes of moral revolution: the discontinuation of dueling in Great Britain, the abandonment of foot-binding in China, and the end of the transatlantic slave trade. In all three cases, traditional moral practices were upended in a remarkably short span of time even though the rupture was neither enforced by explicit new legal prohibitions nor accompanied by a genuine shift in moral sentiments. Although every one of these practices had been criticized earlier on moral grounds, they nevertheless had survived in social habits and personal conduct. At a certain moment, however, they suddenly and completely collapsed.

What these three examples of moral revolution have in common, according to Appiah, is that each was motivated by *honor*. Drawing on the works of philosopher Stephen Darwall,[9] Appiah sketches a theory of honor that starts with the distinction between two forms of respect: respect as recognition—

9. See Darwall 2013.

when we respect others as our equals—and respect as evaluation—when we respect someone as our superior (an athlete, a hero, etc.), what Appiah calls *competitive honor* but might better be described as *deference*.

Moral revolutions occur, according to Appiah, when an implicit honor code emerges with the following dual purpose: to give honor or respect to the victims of the moral practice being overturned and to gain honor or respectability for those who boldly acknowledge the (previously denied) honor of these victims. The national honor of England, for example, became a pivotal argument in the campaign to abolish the transatlantic slave trade. British honor was contrasted with the ignominy of the rebellious American colonies where slavery was shamelessly maintained. To grant honor as a sign of respect was to gain honor by giving it:

> But systems of honor not only help us do well by others; they can help sustain us in our pursuit of our own good. . . . So, honor is no decaying vestige of a premodern order; it is, for us, what it has always been, an engine, fueled by the dialogue between our self-conceptions and the regard of others, that can drive us to take seriously our responsibilities in a world we share. A person with integrity will care that she lives up to her ideals. If she succeeds, we may owe her our respect. But caring to do right is not the same thing as caring to be worthy of respect; it is the concern for respect that connects living well with our place in a social world. (Appiah 2010, 179)

For Appiah, in other words, we are drawn toward moral action by our quest for honor and the realization that we share with others a specific honor code. Yet the link in his analysis between morality and honor remains mysterious. Only if we surreptitiously smuggle moral norms into the newly emergent honor code can we be confident that those motivated to act honorably will avoid reproducing traditional injustices, hierarchies, and amoral cultural norms. An example can help clarify the point. Wearing the veil is a morally "neutral" norm, even though it is not shared by all cultures. In France, the 2004 law that prohibited the wearing of religious symbols in public schools was widely criticized for conveying a lack of respect and recognition toward the communities that embraced that norm. But how could "honor," in such case, engender a moral revolution in either one sense (tolerance for those wearing religious symbols) or another (recognition that religious symbols convey unjust values and contradict the secularism of the republic)? How could sharing an honor code help us evaluate the norm in question? If I decide to continue to wear religious symbols because I share a moral code that prohibits me from defying the will of my family, "my honor" will dictate that I continue to wear those symbols.

What's more, Appiah does not describe in any detail the mechanisms that effect moral revolutions. A shared honor code, in his view, will facilitate a moral revolution, namely the recognition, for the first time, of a previously unrecognized class of persons. This recognition, allegedly, will simultaneously and proportionally increase the self-respect of those who take the lead in recognizing those who were previously unrecognized. But here again, the nexus between moral change and codes of honor seems purely serendipitous. I can adapt to a "wave" of normative changes out of concern for my reputation or from conformism or by imitation. In so doing, my action will contribute to a "cascade" of microtransformations that eventually culminate in a major normative shift. But that can happen even when no moral considerations are at work. In the most developed countries today, for example, we are witnessing a change of norms and habits concerning tobacco. The mixture of completely new "honor codes" displayed on cigarette packs ("smoking kills," "smoking harms the health of those around you," etc.), economic sanctions (raising the price of cigarettes), and the prohibition of smoking in public spaces is changing our relation to tobacco as well as our tolerance for smokers. I can thus decide to quit smoking because I am looking for the approval of others and because I am aware that there are fewer and fewer smokers around me as well as fewer and fewer tolerant passive smokers. This has nothing to do with sharing an honor code even if the mechanisms driving my decision to quit remain difficult to pin down.

Perhaps honor plays some role in such cases. But if it does so, we need to understand the mechanisms by which it comes into play. Reputational cascades, informational asymmetries, network effects, and the consequences of hierarchy are the principal mechanisms involved. Let us see how.

Deference, Status, Hierarchy

Honor is not a code. It is a felt relationship. It exists only in relation to others. If honor and reputation function as motives for action, the way they are structured is eminently *dynamic*, changing from interaction to interaction. In our society today, reputation has become highly fluid and context dependent. Our reputation no longer hinges, as in the past, on a fixed set of norms shared in a given social milieu. From the closed world of *fama*, honor, and the "good repute" of premodern societies, we find ourselves in the universe of infinite possibilities of interaction characteristic of modern societies. Today, as a result, the motivational force of honor and reputation depends on these new dynamics. With this in mind, we cannot hope to elucidate how honor motivates choice and conduct by simply grafting a cultural and symbolic dimension onto the rational explanation of action. Honor is not merely a matter of culture, codes, and norms, all of them locally specific and infinitely variable. The honor that matters is the product of social interactions that create and maintain hierarchical relations. This means each and every social interaction. Honor is a feeling derived from the palpable advantage of occupying a dominant position in a hierarchy. Reputation provides a long-term advantage because it accumulates over time and is propagated through social networks. As sociologist Roger Gould lucidly explains, "Dominant positions in social hierarchies of all kinds—not only hierarchies of wealth or income—carry *intrinsic* value for their occupants."[10] If we fail to understand the social dynamics that determine how social groups ascribe honor to individuals, we end up with a notion of honor—respect for a shared moral code—that does nothing to illuminate the mechanisms that distribute honor across society.

Mutual Admiration Societies

Honor and reputation emerge from the dynamics by which relative status is created and maintained in hierarchical societies. These dynamics provide the basis for our capacity to make comparative evaluations: *who is superior to whom*. The social hierarchies that emerge from such judgments are neither exclusively meritocratic (the very best tops the list) nor completely constructed, that is, imposed by institutions that define and assign social roles. Reputational hierarchies emerge grad-

10. Gould 2003, 20, my emphasis.

ually from the accumulation of a series of acts of esteem and recognition. The more gestures of recognition that an individual receives, the greater are his chances that he will receive more in the future. This is the logic of the Matthew effect, discussed in chapter 4. Already in his famous 1972 article, Merton posed the question of why hierarchies of prestige or merit, possessing a cumulative structure that privileges those on top, almost never evolve into completely asymmetrical structures of the winner-take-all variety. If, from the very outset, hierarchies have a tendency to be cumulative, shouldn't we discover, in a majority of cases, a small elite on top and a mass of nonentities below? Yet this is not what we find. Acts of *deference* that distribute honor, prestige, or reputation demand a certain degree of reciprocity. That is one of the most interesting findings of Merton's sociology of status and hierarchy. Along with Gould, sociologists Gianluca Manzo and Delia Baldassarri[11] contend that expressing deference toward a superior in a hierarchical order involves being torn between *admiration of* and *accessibility to* the person being honored. Although messages of respect, deference, and recognition tend to be directed cumulatively to a small number of individuals, inevitably multiplying subsequent expressions of the same sort, those at the top of the pyramid must from time to time return the favor—without exaggerating, of course, because the difference between a *leader* and a *follower* is signaled by the asymmetrical nature of their relationship. Yet celebrities must occasionally express admiration for their *fans*.

If someone we admire and to whom we repeatedly signal our esteem by public acts of deference never returns the favor, conveying some token of respect, we will end up forsaking him

11. See Gould 2002; Manzo and Baldassarri 2014.

or her. Even rock stars must once in a while give their devotees the impression that they love them, offering a faint whiff of top-down appreciation in exchange for the wild adulation of the crowd. Fan clubs are designed to simulate just such sops of obligatory reciprocity. The T-shirt autographed by the club's idol, the warm words addressed to an individual fan, the handshakes at the end of the concert, the shouted declarations of "I love you!" are so many techniques for consolidating the fidelity of admirers and according them a minimum of attention and consideration.

Some level of reciprocity is always required when we confer honor or reputation on others: we love to recognize those who recognize us in turn, even if we realize that the symmetry will be imperfect. Indeed, acts of deference increase asymmetries by amplifying initial differences of merit. Every time we defer to another, every time we express admiration for someone, we leave behind a trace of our evaluative assessments serving to guide others in their subsequent rankings. Such social amplification and the need for at least a weak form of reciprocity are the two principal mechanisms that explain the distribution of reputation and prestige in society. For example, in the moral revolutions described by Appiah, the harmonization of beliefs about who merits esteem between two groups that did not initially respect each other can be explained by our tendency to esteem those who esteem us. This is how we end up sharing "an honor code."

Our need to have our esteem for others reciprocated is not only a desire to be loved and recognized by others. It is also a strategy of social cognition. It represents a search for external feedback to strengthen our confidence in our evaluative choices. If those I esteem also esteem me—at least to some extent—then I am presumably on the right track when making value judgments about the social world around me. Admittedly, this self-reinforcing exchange of esteem for esteem can lead to vicious circles. Like La Fontaine's fox who convinces himself that the plump red grapes before his eyes are not yet ripe simply because he cannot reach them, we sometimes withhold or withdraw our esteem from those who fail to reciprocate. With all due respect to Groucho Marx, who spurned any club that would accept him as a member, we routinely seek to integrate ourselves into social groups that we admire and that, at the same time, treat us respectfully.

After repeatedly submitting my manuscripts to the most prestigious scientific journal in my field and being repeatedly turned down, I will undertake, at a certain point, a revaluation of values. I will begin to suspect that the journal is not as good as I once thought, eventually concluding that it is biased in its judgments and so forth. In other words, I will downgrade my respect for the journal in a kind of immune response to the lack of consideration that the journal has exhibited toward my work. Then, after fruitless attempts at being published in a top journal, I will, like other researchers, submit my article to a somewhat less prestigious journal that will, at long last, accept it. The moment I receive the acceptance letter, moreover, my relative ranking of the less prestigious journal will skyrocket. I will begin to understand how much more interesting, original, and innovative it is than the journal that rejected my work. This kind of evaluative readjustment characterizes *mutual admiration societies*,[12] that is to say, groups whose members boost

12. Henry David Thoreau coined the expression "mutual admiration societies" to describe literary circles where members praise each other reciprocally, thereby inflating everyone's reputation inside the group. The expression gained a measure of popular currency in the American song "Mutual Admiration Society," written in 1956 for the Broadway musical *Happy Hunting*.

their self-esteem by heaping on each other copious testimony of reciprocal respect.

According to Merton (1972), mutual admiration societies help maintain barriers between *insiders* and *outsiders*. For example, the authors of articles published in highly ranked academic journals have a tendency to cite each other, creating a tight-knit community of "the happy few" who signal their mutual appreciation (citation being a quintessential expression of respect) while marginalizing those to whom the gates to academic stardom are barred. This is how mutual admiration societies enforce unwritten norms of membership. To be an insider implies knowing how to draw appropriate distinctions, that is, how to be a competent judge of who should be highly regarded and who, by contrast, should be consigned to oblivion. When striving to join a group, we make an effort to imitate the judgments of, and to act like, those who are already inside the circle, praising some and dispraising others, even if we do not know exactly why. To return to the example of academic citations, most of them are echoed, as pure acts of deference, from one article to another, as if they were nothing other than signals of competence about "what someone should think of someone" in a given field. Nothing is in poorer taste than citing, as some kind of authority, an outsider to a specific community of specialists. Scholars who eccentrically display respect for an author considered unworthy of attention by insiders will not be admired for their breadth of knowledge. Instead, they risk diminishing and even destroying their own reputation.

Honoring others is always a double-edged sword. Acts of deference signal something about both those who defer and those to whom deference is paid. Thus we need some measure of social consensus about the practices and norms of according esteem if we are to strike a proper balance between our need to satisfy our personal preferences when granting respect to others and the demands of social conformity that drive us to recognize others in order to make ourselves more "acceptable" to the peer group to which we belong.

In general, changes in social behavior depend upon the emergence and diffusion of social norms. This identifies the mystery that must be solved. What rules determine when members of the audience stand up during a concert?[13] Who gets up first and why do others follow them? Where is the boundary line between the expression of personal preferences and conformity to social expectations? Where is the threshold beyond which it becomes inappropriate to remain seated while almost everyone else is standing up and enthusiastically waving their arms?

The struggle for prestige and recognition is therefore always two-sided. When we act in a way that displays our esteem for others we are establishing social hierarchies; but, in doing so, we are also changing our own social position. Can reputation, esteem, and honor function as motivations for actions? The answer is "yes," to the extent that granting and being granted a reputation are two facets of the same dynamic. It is the process by which we all seek and find our relative place in the shifting social worlds we precariously but inescapably inhabit.

13. The phenomenon of standing ovations has been studied and modeled in the literature devoted to the emergence of social norms. See Muldoon, Lisciandra, et al. 2014.

7

Information and Reputation

THE COLLECTIVE INTELLIGENCE OF THE WEB

> Civilization rests on the fact that we all benefit from knowledge we do not possess.
>
> —FRIEDRICH HAYEK, *LAW, LEGISLATION AND LIBERTY*

As should by now be clear, "reputation" is an umbrella concept covering a wide array of related but distinct phenomena: a second ego, "symbolic *grandeur*," an intentionally conveyed signal, hearsay that stabilizes or sometimes destabilizes our social identity, a motivation for action, and a powerful system for classifying information, based on the authority of others, that helps guide our judgments. We have also seen that the control we wield over our reputation is limited and precarious. We can never fully master or govern our reputation because the multiplicity of real and imaginary social "mirrors" that reflect it back and forth among themselves and then back to us distorts it, rendering it elusive, shape-shifting, and ineffable. On the other hand, we cannot live without it. Without a reputation, without this formidable system for confronting the self with its social reflection and reordering the way we see ourselves in response to the way others see us, we would be like those singers who sing off-key at a concert because the microphone's feedback loop prevents them from hearing their own voices clearly.

In the first part of this book, I concentrated on the strategic uses we make of our reputation. In what follows I would like to explore, through various case studies, how we use the reputation of both people and things to extract information from the world around us. A "cognitive" approach to reputation, focused on how we use it to understand our surroundings, was touched on briefly in chapters 4 and 5. But I now want to delve more deeply into the epistemology of reputation and detail its implications through three specific examples: reputations on the Web (this chapter), the reputation of wine (chapter 8), and academic reputation (chapter 9). Although they may at first seem miscellaneous and unrelated, the three cases have an underlying unity. Taken together, they allow us to explore the epistemological role of reputation in three pivotal areas of our cognitive life: the circulation of information, the training of taste, and the construction of knowledge. When we first come into contact with a new domain of learning, our access to facts is inevitably determined by the opinions, values, and preferences of others. As new communication technologies make it increasingly easy and tempting for any novice who so desires to venture naïvely into new domains of knowledge, this dependency on the prejudices (or prejudgments) of others should always be kept in mind.

Indeed, we are now faced with a fundamental paradigm shift in our relationship to knowledge. From the information age, we are moving toward an age of reputation in which information will have value only if it is already sifted, evaluated, and commented upon by others. Seen in this light, reputation is a central pillar of collective intelligence today. It impounds a form of knowledge on which we have to rely even though it is possessed by others. The way in which the authority of this knowledge is constructed, moreover, is what gives us the confidence to acquire it through the inevitably biased judgments of others. The case of the Web is paradigmatic. Not only does the Web represent a radical transformation in our access to knowledge, but by integrating evaluation and reputation into information-retrieval systems, using search algorithms based on the ranking of information (like PageRank), the Web has also changed the forms, object domains, disciplines, and ways in which these objects of knowledge are constructed.

With the extraordinary ability of Web 2.0 to collect and synthesize socially decentralized information in order to achieve intelligent results, the very idea of collective intelligence has entered a new phase. For much of the history of thought, such a genuinely collective intelligence was either a curiosity or a fantasy. Today it is a *fact* that is radically changing our everyday ways of thinking and decision making. It needs to be taken seriously. If collective intelligence is not yet fully operative in all of our knowledge systems, it certainly affects much of our daily lives. Google searches, Wikipedia entries, eBay transactions, social networks: none of these represents a genuine collective intelligence system, but each may well form the potential building blocks of one that could be created in the future.

A major problem with these new collectively intelligent systems is that our control over the ways of aggregating information is sometimes poor, and individual or institutional capacities for intervening in the design of the aggregation process are often very limited. I think we should take the design issue very seriously, sharpening our awareness of the biases inherent in these systems and their potential misuses. This is a general point about institutional design. No matter how many people are involved in the production of a collective outcome—a decision, an action, a cognitive achievement, and so on—the way in which their interactions are designed, what they may know and not know about each other, how they access the collective procedure, what path their actions follow, and how they merge with the actions of others affects the content of the outcome. Of course, this is well known to policymakers, constitution drafters, and all those who participate in designing democratic systems or other systems of rules that have to take multiple viewpoints into account. But the claim may appear less evident—or at least in need of a more articulate justification—when it concerns the design of knowledge and the epistemic practices on the Web. That is because the Web is usually seen as a disruptive technology whose initial effect was to explode all legitimate preexisting procedures by which knowledge was accessed, thus "empowering" its users with a new intellectual freedom, the liberty to produce, unearth, and distribute content in a totally unregulated way. Still, methods of tapping into the wisdom of crowds on the Web are various and much more clearly differentiated than is usually acknowledged. In his book *The Wisdom of Crowds*, James Surowiecki discusses different designs for capturing collective wisdom, writing that "in the end there is nothing about a *futures market* that makes it inherently smarter than, say, Google. These are all attempts to tap into the wisdom of the crowd, and that's the reason they work" (2004, 22). But sometimes the devil is in the details and the way in which the wisdom of crowds is captured makes a significant difference to its conclusions and its impact on our cognitive lives.

I will first summarize the details of some of the collective "wisdom systems" that are common on the Web. I will then provide a brief technical description of the design that underlies each. I will then argue that these systems work because of their very special way of articulating (1) individual choices and collectively filtered preferences on one hand and (2) human actions and computer processes on the other. Finally, I conclude with some epistemological remarks about the role of ranking in our epistemic practices, arguing that the success of the Web as an epistemic practice is due to its capacity to provide not so much a potentially infinite system for information storage but rather a giant network of ranking and rating systems in which information is valued only because it has been previously filtered by other people. This passion for constructing evaluative hierarchies is an all-important characteristic of collective intelligence.

Surowiecki's book contains an illuminating list of conditions that must be fulfilled before we can properly speak of a *wise crowd*. Not any and every crowd is a wise crowd. In order to avoid notorious difficulties such as group polarization, information cascades, and conformism, a group must display certain features that make it a potentially intelligent entity. Surowiecki proposes four main characteristics:

1. *Diversity of opinion* (each person should have some private information)
2. *Independence* (people's opinions are not determined by others)
3. *Decentralization* (people are able to draw on local knowledge)

4. *Aggregation* (presence of mechanisms that turn individual judgments into collective decisions).[1]

I am tempted to add a fifth condition that seems to me especially crucial in order to "accelerate" the collective filtering of information:

1. *The presence of a rating device* (each person should be able to produce a rating hierarchy, relying on past ranking systems and making—at least in some circumstances—his or her ratings available to others).

I think this last condition is particularly useful for understanding the processes of collective intelligence that the Web 2.0. has made possible, although it is not limited to that. Of course, the centrality of rating hierarchies opens the epistemological question of the cognitive value of these rankings, that is, to what extent their production and use by a group changes the ratio between truths and falsehoods produced by that group and, individually, how awareness of rankings should affect a person's beliefs. After all, rankings introduce a bias in judgment and the epistemic superiority of an admittedly biased judgment needs justification. Moreover, these rankings are the result of human activities that are collectively registered on artificial devices. Control of the heuristics and techniques that underlie this dynamics of information may be out of sight or incomprehensible for users who find themselves in the very vulnerable position of relying on external sources of information through a dynamic, machine-based channel of communication whose heuristics and biases are not under their control. Until 2002, for example, it was unknown to 60 percent of users that companies regularly paid to be included in search engines

1. Surowiecki 2004, Kindle edition, loc. 142.

and to obtain "preferred placement." In that year, the American Federal Trade Corporation issued a public recommendation asking search engine companies to disclose paid link policies and clearly mark advertisements to avoid confusing their users.[2]

The epistemic status of such collectively produced rankings, in any case, poses a series of epistemological questions:

1. Why do people trust these rankings and should they?
2. Why should we assume that the collective filtering of preferences produces wiser results on the Web?
3. What heuristics and biases in the aggregating systems on the Web should people be aware of?

These questions include a descriptive as well as a normative perspective on the social epistemology of *collective wisdom systems*. In an information-dense environment, where sources are constant competing to attract attention and the option of direct verification of the information's reliability is not available at reasonable costs, evaluation and rankings are epistemic tools and cognitive practices that provide an invaluable shortcut for gaining access to usable information. This is especially striking in contemporary, information-overloaded societies, but I think it is a permanent feature of any system for distilling information from a *corpus* of knowledge. There is no ideal knowledge that we can judge to be such without relying on the previous evaluations and adjudications made by others. And my modest epistemological prediction is that the greater our uncertainty about the content of information we receive, the greater weight we will give to the opinions of others in order

2. Princeton Survey Research Associates, "A Matter of Trust: What Users Want from Websites," Princeton (January 2002). Results of a National Survey of Internet Researchers for Consumer WebWatch, mentioned in Rogers 2004, 195.

to verify the credibility of this content. Such reliance does not necessarily make us gullible. Our *epistemic responsibility* whenever we rely on such reputational devices is to be aware of the biases that the design of each incorporates, either for technical reasons or for sociological or institutional reasons. A detailed presentation of the methods for aggregating individual choices that the Internet makes available should be thus accompanied by an analysis of the possible biases that each of these systems carries in its design.

Intelligent agents often think better in groups and sometimes think in ways that would simply be impossible for isolated individuals. The Internet is a salient example. That explains why the initial emergence of the Internet created huge expectations about a possible "overcoming" of thought processes at the individual level and the rise of new—more powerful—forms of technologically mediated intelligence. A plethora of images and metaphors of the Internet as a superintelligent agent soon invaded the literature on media studies—including the Internet as an extended mind, a distributed digital consciousness, a higher-order intelligent being, and so forth.

The collective processes that make the Internet such a powerful cognitive medium provide an example of "collective intelligence," that is, a means for aggregating individual choices and preferences. What the Internet made possible, however—and this was indeed spectacular—was a brand-new form of aggregation that simply didn't exist before its invention and worldwide diffusion. In this sense, the Internet exemplifies a novel tool for aggregating individual perspectives that can possibly serve as a basis for rethinking other institutions whose survival depends on combining in an appropriate way the dispersed pieces of knowledge independently possessed by a vast multitude of individuals.

The Internet and the Web

The salient aspect of this new form of aggregation is a special way of articulating individual choices and collectively filtered preferences through the technology of the Internet and, especially, of the World Wide Web. In this sense, it is useful to distinguish from the outset between the Internet as a networking phenomenon and the Web as a specific technology made possible by the existence of this new network. The Internet is a network whose beginnings go back to the 1960s, when American scientists at AT&T, Rand, MIT, and the Defense Communications Agency started to research alternative models for transmitting information through a network. In the classical telephone system, when you call New York from your apartment in Paris, a circuit is opened between you and the New York number—roughly a copper line that physically connects the two destinations. The new idea was to develop an alternative system—a "packet-switching" technology—by digitalizing conversations, that is, by translating waves into bits, then chopping the result into packets that could flow independently through a network while giving the impression of a real-time connection on the other end. The first decentralized network, Arpanet, started operating in the early 1970s. It was able to transfer a message by spreading its dismembered chunks through the network and then reconstructing it (or "re-membering") at the end. By the mid-1970s, email, the first important application on the network, was created. What made this net such a powerful tool was its decentralized way of growing: the Internet is a network of networks, which uses preexisting wires (like telephone networks) to make computers communicate through a number of protocols (such as TCP/IP) that are not proprietary: each new user can connect to the network by using these protocols. Every new invention of an application, a mail system, a system for video-transfers, a digital phone system, can use the same protocols. Internet protocols qualify as part of the "commons."[3] That was a boost to the growth of the network and the creativity of the applications using it. This is crucial for the wisdom of the net. Without the political decision to keep these protocols free, the net would not have grown in a decentralized manner and the collaborative knowledge practices that it has facilitated would not have been possible.

The World Wide Web, which is a much more recent invention, maintained the same philosophy of open protocols compatible with the Internet (like HTTP [hypertext transfer protocol] or HTML [hypertext markup language]). The Web is a service that operates through the Internet, a set of protocols and conventions that allows "pages" (that is, a particular format of information that makes it easy to write and read content) to be easily linked to each other by the technique of hyperlink. This is a visualization protocol that greatly simplifies the display of information. The growth of the Web is not the same thing as the growth of the Internet. The Web developed so quickly because creating a hyperlink requires no technical competence. The Web is an illustration of how an Internet application may flourish thanks to the openness of the protocols. And, truth be told, the impact of IT on collective intelligence has been due mostly to the Web.

The Web, Collective Memory, and Meta-memory

What makes the aggregation of individual preferences through the Web so special? Seen through the lens of the history of

3. On this point, see Lessig 2001.

culture, the Web is a major revolution in the storage, dissemination, and retrieval of information. The major revolutions in the history of culture have had an impact on the distribution of memory. The Web is one such revolution. Let's consider in what sense. The Web has often been compared to the invention of writing or printing. Both comparisons are valid. Introduced at the end of the fourth millennium BCE in Mesopotamia, writing is an external mnemonic device that makes possible the reorganization of intellectual life and the structuring of thoughts, neither of which is possible in oral cultures. With the introduction of writing, one part of our cognition "exits" the brain to be distributed among external supports. The visual representation of a society's knowledge makes it possible both to reorganize the knowledge in a more useful, more "logical" way by using, for example, lists, tables, or genealogical trees and to convey it from one generation to the next. What's more, the birth of "custodial" castes who oversee cultural memory, such as scribes, astrologists, and librarians, makes possible the organization of meta-memory, that is, the set of processes for accessing and recovering cultural memories.

Introduced to our culture at the end of the fifteenth century, printing redistributes cultural memory, changing the configuration of the "informational pyramid" in the diffusion of knowledge. In what sense is the Web revolution comparable to the world-changing inventions of writing and printing? In line with these two earlier revolutions, the Web increases the efficiency of recording, recovering, reproducing, and distributing cultural memory. Like writing, the Web is an external mnemonic device, although different in that it is "active" in contrast to the passive nature of the written word. Like printing, the Web is a device for redistributing cultural memory within and across a population, although again different because it crucially modifies the costs and speed of distribution. Unlike writing and printing, the Web presents a radical change in the conditions for accessing and recovering cultural memory with the introduction of new devices for managing meta-memory, that is, new processes for accessing and recovering lost or patchily recollected memories. Culture, to a large extent, consists in the conception, organization, and institutionalization of an efficient meta-memory, or a system of rules, practices, and representations that allows us to gain our bearings quickly in the sprawling wilderness of collective memory. A good part of our scholastic education consists in internalizing systems of meta-memory, classifications of style, rankings, and so forth, chosen by our particular culture. For example, it is important to know the fundamentals of rhetoric in order to rapidly "classify" a line of verse as belonging to a certain style, and hence to a certain period, so as to be able thereby to locate it precisely within, say, the corpus of Italian or French literature. Meta-memory, in other words, does not serve a merely cognitive function—to retrieve information from a literary or scientific corpus—but also a social and epistemic function, organizing this information within various systems of classifications that embody the basics of the "cultural lore" of that corpus. Retrieving information is an epistemic activity that allows us to access, through the retrieving filters, how the cultural authorities over a piece of information have classified and ranked it within that corpus. With the advent of technologies that automate the functions of accessing and recovering memory, such as search engines and knowledge-management systems, meta-memory has become part of external memory. A cognitive function, central to the cultural organization of human societies, has become automated—another "piece" of cognition thus exits our brain and is materialized through external supports. Returning to the example above, if I recall a line of poetic verse, say, "Guido, i'vorrei," but can recall neither the author nor the period and am also unable to classify the style, I can now simply enter the line of verse in the text window of a search engine and see the information instantly appear. The highly improbable combination of words in a line of verse makes possible a sufficiently relevant selection of information that yields among the first results the poem from which the line is taken (my search for this line using Google yielded 654 responses, the first ten of which contained the complete text from the poem in Dante's *Rime*).

How is this meta-memory system designed through Web technology? What is unique on the Web is that the actions of users leave a trace in the system that is immediately reusable by it, like the tracks that snails leave on the ground, which reveal to other snails the path they followed. The combination of the traces of the different patterns of use may easily be displayed in a rank ordering that informs and influences the users' future preferences and actions. The corpus of knowledge available on the Web—built and maintained by its users' individual behaviors—is automatically filtered by systems that aggregate these behaviors in a ranked order and make the latter available as filtered information to new, individual users. I will now examine two different sorts of meta-memory devices. Although both provide a selection of information that informs and influences users' behavior, these two systems are designed in different ways. The difference is noteworthy.

Collaborative Filtering: Wisdom out of Algorithms

Collaborative filtering is a way of making predictions about the preferences of users by extrapolating from the patterns of behavior exhibited by many other users. It is used mainly for commercial purposes in Web applications for e-business, although it has also been extended to other domains. One of the best-known examples of a collaborative filtering system is Amazon.com. Amazon.com is a Web application, a knowledge-management system that keeps track of users' interactions with the system and is designed to display correlations between patterns of activities in a way that informs users about other users' preferences. The best-known feature of this system is the one that associates different items up for sale: "Customers who buy X also buy Y." The originality of these systems is that the pairing between X and Y is in a sense bottom-up (although the appropriate thresholds of activities above which this correlation emerges are fixed by the information architecture of the system). The association between Surowiecki's book and Ian Ayer's *Super Crunchers* that you can find on Amazon's page for *The Wisdom of Crowds* has been generated automatically by an algorithm that aggregates user preferences and makes the correlation. This is a unique feature of these interactive systems, in which new categories are created by automatically transforming initially uncoordinated human actions into easily understandable rankings. The collective wisdom of the system is due to a division of cognitive labor between the algorithms that compose and visualize the information and the users who interact with the system. The classifications and rankings that are thereby engendered aren't based on previous cultural knowledge of habits and customs of users but on the emergence of significant patterns of aggregated preferences through individual interactions with the system. Of course, biases are possible within the system: the weights associated with each item are fixed in such a way that some items have more chances to be recommended than others. But given that the system is constantly readjusting to the repeated actions of its users, an excessively biased recommendation that couples items that users won't buy together will not be replicated often enough to stabilize within the system.

PageRank

Search engines represent another set of systems that exercise meta-memory functions through artificial devices. As we all know by experience, search engines have effected a major transformation of our epistemic practices and a profound cognitive revolution. The most remarkable innovation of these tools is due to the discovery of the structure of the Web at the beginning of this century.[4] Structured as a social network, the Web contains plentiful information about its users' preferences and habits. Second-generation search engines, such as Google, are able to exploit this structure in order to gain information about how knowledge is distributed around the world. Basically, the PageRank algorithm interprets a link that appears on page A to page B as a vote of page A for page B. But the Web is no democracy, and votes do not all possess the same weight in determining winners and losers. Votes that come from certain sites—called "hubs"—have greater weight than others and reflect, in that sense, hierarchies of reputation existing outside the Web. Roughly, a link posted on my homepage to the page of Harvard University weighs much less than a link to my page on that of Harvard University. The Web is an "aristocratic" network—to use an expression of social network theorists—that is, a network in which "the rich get richer" and the more links you accumulate the higher is the probability that you will

4. See Kleinberg 2001.

receive even more. This disparity of weights creates a "reputational landscape" that informs the result of a query. The PageRank algorithm is fed by the local knowledge and preferences of each individual user and influences them in turn by displaying a ranking of results that is naturally interpreted as a hierarchy of relevance. Note that this system is *not* a knowledge-management system: the PageRank algorithm doesn't know anything about the particular pattern of activities of each individual; it doesn't know how many times you and I go to the JSTOR website and doesn't link our navigation paths to each other. A "click" from a page to another is uninformative for PageRank, whereas a link between two pages contains a lot of information about users' knowledge that the system is able to extract.

That is why PageRank can rely on the structure of the Web as a social network, a structure revealed in 2000 by mathematician Jon Kleinberg. Today, search engines that rely on this kind of algorithm also integrate knowledge on user behavior and allow much more manipulation and biased usage.[5]

Although different in the ways described, the two systems are nevertheless comparable from the standpoint of the design of collective intelligence: neither requires any cooperation between agents in order to create a shared system of ranking. The "collaborative" aspect of the collective filtering rests more in the hands of machines than of human agents.[6] The system exploits the information that human agents either unintentionally deposit on the website by interacting with it (KM systems)

5. See Origgi and Ciranna 2017.

6. Knowledge-processing systems like Amazon.com have some collaborative filtering features that require cooperation, such as writing book reviews using the five-star rating system. These features are increasingly critical to the functioning of a collaborative filtering process.

or actively produce by creating a link from one page to another (search engines). The result is collective, but the motivation is individual.

The biases built into search engines have been a major subject of discussions, controversy, and collective fears for several years. As I mentioned earlier, the refinement of second-generation search engines such as Google allowed paid inclusions and preferred placements to be explicitly marked as such, but it took a political intervention to force the change. Also, the Matthew effect of aristocratic networks is notorious, and these tools risk giving unjustified prominence to already celebrated sites at the expense of others. Awareness of such biases should dictate a refinement of search practices as well. For example, the more improbable a string of keywords, the more relevant the filtered result. Novices and learners should be tutored in simple principles of this sort that can make them less vulnerable to built-in system biases.

Reputation Systems: How Wisdom Is Produced by Status Anxiety

The collaborative filtering of information may sometimes require greater active participation by a community than was needed in the examples cited above. In his book *Information Politics on the Web* (2004), sociologist Richard Rogers classifies Web dynamics as either "voluntaristic" or "non-voluntaristic" according to the respective role of human beings and machines in providing feedback to users. Reputation systems exemplify more "voluntaristic" Web applications than the ones discussed above. A reputation system is a special kind of collaborative filtering algorithm that determines ratings for a collection of agents based on the opinions that these agents express about each other. A reputation system collects, distributes, and aggregates feedback about its participants' past behavior.

The best-known and probably simplest reputation system with a significant impact on the Web is eBay.com, which allows commercial interactions among more than 150 million people around the world.[7] Users consist of buyers and sellers. Buyers place a bid on an item. If their bid is successful, they close the commercial transaction. Afterward, both buyers and sellers provide feedback about the quality of their transaction. The various feedbacks are then aggregated by the system into a very simple feedback profile, where positive feedbacks and negative feedbacks plus some comments are displayed to prospective users. This is how the reputation of a potential seller or buyer becomes actionable intelligence used by future buyers and sellers when deciding to pursue or reject an offered transaction. Reputation in this case has a real and measurable commercial value. In markets with decentralized and uncoordinated offers and very low information available on each offer, reputation becomes crucial information for deciding whether or not to trust the seller. Sellers on eBay are well aware of the value of their good reputation in such a special business environment where there are no face-to-face encounters between buyer and seller, no chances for the buyer to see and touch the offered item, and vagueness about the normative and legal framework of the transaction if, for example, it involves an exchange between citizens of two different countries. This explains the large number of low-cost transactions on eBay whose primary objective is to increase the percentage of the sellers' positive evaluations. The system creates a collective result by compelling cooperation, asking users to leave an

7. https://www.statista.com/statistics/242235/number-of-ebays-total-active-users/.

evaluation at the end of the transaction and sanctioning them if they don't comply. Without this active participation of its users, the system would be useless. Sellers would have no way of establishing a good reputation. Still, it is a special kind of collaborative behavior, one that requires no individual commitment to cooperation as a value. Noncooperative users are sanctioned at different levels. They can be negatively evaluated not only if the transaction isn't satisfactory but also if they do not participate in the evaluation process. Breaking the rules of eBay may lead to exclusion from the community. The design of the system's wisdom thus includes an active participation from users who fear being ostracized by the community (which would result in a loss of business opportunities). Biases are clearly possible here also. People invest in cheap transactions whose sole aim is to gain reputational points. Buyers should take this potential bias into account. It can be easily checked. If sellers offer too many suspiciously cheap items, they are probably too concerned with polishing their public image to be considered reliable.

Some reputational features are also used by noncommercial systems such as flickr.com. Flickr is a collaborative platform for sharing photos. For each picture, you can see how many users have added it among their favorite pictures and who they are.

In recent years, reputation systems have witnessed a real economic explosion: systems such as Airbnb.com, which rents apartments between individuals from all over the world, thrive through controlled management of social information generated by the reputation of the hosts.

A number of research projects have demonstrated that, in such systems, reputation functions as a kind of "money." Biologist Manfred Milinski, a pioneer in the study of the evolutionary advantages of reputation, has carried out a series of experiments showing that reputation is essential to the economic survival of these systems. The reputation gained in games of indirect reciprocity can be transmitted as social information in the form of gossip. The fascinating correlation discovered by these researchers is that the more people talk about you, the more your reputation and credibility increase. Paradoxically, the risk of the impact of negative gossip is reduced by the sheer volume of gossip.

Reputation systems differ from systems for measuring reputation by using citation analysis, such as the Science Citation Index, as we will see in greater detail in chapter 9. These systems are in one sense reputation based. They use the techniques of scientometrics to calculate the impact of a publication based on the number of times it is cited in other publications. But they don't require any active or conscious participation by the agents doing the citing in order to obtain comparative measures of reputation.

Collaborative Systems and Open Systems: Wisdom through Cooperation

Collaborative filtering on the Web may be even more voluntaristic and human based than in the examples just cited, while still necessitating Web support to achieve an intelligent outcome. Two of the most frequently discussed examples of collaborative systems that owe their success to active human cooperation in filtering and revising the information made available are the Open Source communities of software development, like the pioneer Linux and many others, and collective open-content projects such as Wikipedia. In both cases, the filtering process is humanly constructed. Code or content is made available to a community that can filter it by correcting, editing, or erasing it according to personal or shared standards of quality. I would say that these are communities of amateurs instead of experts, that is, people who love what they do and decide to share their knowledge for the sake of the community. Collective wisdom is thus created by individual human efforts that are aggregated in a common enterprise in which informal norms of cooperation are shared.

I won't discuss biases on Wikipedia: it is such a vast topic that it could be the subject of entire chapter. Let me simply mention that Larry Sanger, one of Wikipedia's founders, promoted some years ago an alternative project, citizendum.org, which adopts a policy of signed entries so that authors' identities are known. Self-promotion, ideology, and targeted attacks on reputation may of course act as biases in the selection of Wikipedia entries. But the fear that Wikipedia is a dangerous site teeming with tendentious information has been disconfirmed by facts. Thanks to its large size, Wikipedia is massively differentiated in its topics and views, and it has been shown that its reliability is no less than that of the *Encyclopedia Britannica*.[8]

Recommendation Systems: The Wisdom of Connoisseurs

Another class of systems is based on recommendations of connoisseurs in particular domains. An example of collective wisdom created from expert recommendations is TripAdvisor, which permits travelers to share reviews, tips, and advice on places, hotels, and restaurants they have visited during their travels. Expertise is here acquired by direct experience. It is

8. "Internet Encyclopaedias Go Head to Head."

not a matter of "connoisseurship" in the strict sense of the term. The tastes of the "advisors" are not more sophisticated than ours, nor are they based on expert knowledge. They are every bit like us. Their reputation is built on the site, from their choice of travel, the quality of their reports, and the small "stars" that each trip advisor can attach to each report.

Preferences are here voluntarily shared. Some recommender systems collect information from users by actively asking them to rate a number of items, or to express a preference between two items, or to create a list of items that they like. The system then compares the data to similar data collected from other users and displays a collective recommendation. This system is basically a collaborative filtering technique with a more active component: people are asked to express their preferences instead of the system's merely inferring their preferences from their behavior. This makes a huge difference. It is well known in psychology that we are not very good at introspection and sometimes we consciously express preferences that are inconsistent with our behavior. If asked, I may express a preference for classical music, but if I keep a record of how many times a week I listen to classical music compared to other kinds of music, it may become obvious that my real preferences are quite different.

Conclusions

This list of Web tools designed to produce collective wisdom illustrates the diversity of systems available for aggregating individual choices and preferences. The differences in design outlined above produce deep differences between collective IT communities. Sometimes the community is absent, as in the case of Google users, who cannot be defined as a "community" in any interesting normative sense. At other times the community is normatively demanding, as in the case of eBay, where active participation in the filtering process is needed for the survival of the community. The new collective production of knowledge that the Web—and in particular Web 2.0 and 3.0—makes possible can serve as a laboratory for designing "better" collective procedures for the production of knowledge or wise decisions only if these important differences are taken into account.

In conclusion, let me return to a more narrowly epistemological claim about the kind of knowledge engendered by these new tools. As I said at the beginning, these tools function insofar as they provide access to rankings, labeling procedures, and evaluations. Even Wikipedia, which does not display ratings, operates on the following principle. If an entry has survived on the site—that is, if it has not been erased by other hawk-eyed Wikipedians—it is worth reading. This way of measuring worthwhileness can be fairly weak, admittedly. And, as I said, discussions continue on ways to introduce more structured filtering devices on Wikipedia. But the survival of even egalitarian projects like Wikipedia depends on their capacity to incorporate rankings: the label "Wikipedia" in itself already works as a reputational cue that orients the choices of its users. Without the notoriety of the Wikipedia label, the success of the project would be much more modest.

The Web is not only a powerful reservoir of all sorts of labeled and unlabeled information. It is also a powerful reputational tool that introduces ranks, rating systems, weights, and biases into the landscape of knowledge. Even in this information-dense world, cognition without evaluation would inhabit a bleak desert landscape in which people would be paralyzed in the face of an enormous and illegible mass of information. An efficient knowledge system will inevitably grow by generating a variety of evaluative tools. That is how culture grows and how traditions gain their contours. A cultural tradition is, first of all, a labeling system distinguishing insiders from outsiders and those who innovate from those who are sunk in the magma of the past. The good news is that in the Web era such inevitable evaluations are made through new, collective tools that challenge received views and help develop and improve innovative and sometimes more democratic ways of selecting knowledge. Admittedly, this does not prevent the creation of a "canonical" corpus of knowledge. But, thankfully, these always remain tentative and revisable.

8

Experts and Connoisseurs

THE REPUTATION OF WINE

> Authority or prejudice may create a temporary fashion in favor of a bad poet or orator, but his reputation won't ever be lasting or general.
>
> —DAVID HUME, "OF THE STANDARD OF TASTE"

> It is not sufficient to exhibit to the mind a multiplicity of objects; it is farther requisite that they be exhibited with order.
>
> —MONTESQUIEU, *ESSAI SUR LE GOÛT*

Reputations on the Web develop in response to an urgent quest for information that can be assumed to be more or less correct. But what happens when the reputation in question is based not on information but on subjective value judgments, on opinions that may or may not be generally agreed upon? How is a reputation established and contested in the domain of taste and aesthetic preferences? How can we decide if the reputation of an object of taste is reliable, given the apparent lack of objective standards in matters of taste?

Relying on reputations for our understanding of the world means trusting a variety of epistemic authorities. This is especially obvious in the case of neophytes. As already mentioned, when we initially encounter a new domain of knowledge, the opinions of others, as well as their values and preferences, determine our access to facts. I turn in this chapter to reputation in the market for wine because wine, for several reasons, provides a paradigm for the role played by reputation in introducing novices to a new domain of taste. I have selected this case study, admittedly remote from my usual fields of research, for two principal reasons. On the one hand, it allows me to observe *adult novices* encountering for the first time a new cultural sphere that requires them to make value judgments. By restricting our discussion of newcomers to adults, we can avoid the kind of biases associated with deference to intellectual authority in the education of children. Adults being schooled for the first time in the world of wines find themselves facing a cultural domain strongly structured by landmarks about which they initially know nothing. I could, of course, have chosen to focus on art or music, but judgments and tastes in these fields are often shaped by school learning and, as Bourdieu has shown, by one's social milieu. Moreover, thanks to the growth of the wine market during the past twenty years, including its spread to countries lacking a traditional wine culture, the experience of novices learning to discriminate among wines is increasingly common.

The reputation of wines cannot be discussed without examining several extremely complex and interesting classification schemes. On the label of every wine bottle we can peruse the results of an intricate classification system, representing values and epistemic procedures employed to authenticate the reputation of the wine at hand. Analyzing the relationship between knowledge and social classifications in her book *How Institutions Think* (1987), anthropologist Mary Douglas alleges that the classification of wine—like every classification system—is subject to an irresistible pressure toward simplification. The more they are used by a large number of people, she contends, the less complex become the classifications being used for reasons of cognitive functionality. To support this questionable thesis, she invokes the example of the American wine classification system, developed for a market that is relatively new compared to the market in France. Unfortunately, her empirical example gainsays her theoretical claim. Precisely in the domain of wine, we are witnessing the converse. Wine classification systems are certainly changing and evolving—especially in new markets—but they are becoming more complex, not simpler. Differentiation is growing. This makes it possible to inscribe on the label of each bottle an ever-richer cluster of reputational indexes concerning the quality of the wines we buy and taste.

When opening a bottle of wine, we first have to get our bearings. We have to picture a "landscape" within which we will be able to locate ourselves in the future. It is useful in this regard to compare the old with the new systems of wine classification in France—Bordeaux and Burgundy—and in the United States. Contrary to Mary Douglas's hypothesis, it turns out, classifications in the United States, since the launching of the wine market, especially in California, have become more complex by incorporating more sophisticated reputational cues. As Lucien Karpik put it, the international sophistication of the wine market has produced a cognitive and social downgrading, or rather the emergence of a new class of relatively unsophisticated consumers. To compensate for this lack of sophistication among new wine purchasers, wine sellers have introduced a variety of value-certifying mechanisms, including wine labels, wine experts, and wine publications. The wine label is a device for encoding historical information. The authority of history speaks on the label of a great wine. Experts, for their part, legitimize a new "discourse" on wine, adding the authority of words (through their colorful characterizations of the taste of each wine) and contributing to the formulation and transmission of shared descriptions and evaluations. Finally, wine atlases, magazines, and guidebooks qualify the wine first by inclusion versus exclusion: only wines mentioned in these publications merit evaluation. Their different ways of classifying information also shape the public's relative assessment of wines. For example, the Hachette guide uses a 5-point system to evaluate 10,000 wines, while Robert Parker, the American wine-market guru, uses a 49-point system (51–100) to evaluate only 2,000 wines. Parker's system is therefore better adapted to laymen and novices, who will find under each rating a limited number of wines and can thus orient themselves more easily. But before examining these classification schemes in greater detail let me introduce the question of standards of taste.

Is Taste Subjective or Objective?

Ever since Pliny the Elder, talk about wine and its aesthetic appraisal has oscillated between accepting the subjectivity of taste and appealing to ostensibly objective systems of ranking and reputation. Book XIV of his *Historia Naturalis* is dedicated to wine, its cultivation, and its benefits. In chapter 8 of that book, Pliny acknowledges the subjective dimension of wine tasting, "Quam ob rem de principatu se quisque iudicem statuet,"[1] but only after presenting, a few lines earlier, a long and structured ranking of the best wines, based on their reputation among emperors and other distinguished personalities. Famous proverbs such as *de gustibus non est disputandum* or *chacun son goût* are often cited alongside remarks on the need for "standards" or rules of taste to help structure our sense of discrimination. Even Parker, the internationally acclaimed "taste pundit" whose rating system has revolutionized the wine market, claims that subjective taste is the ultimate judge. As he writes in his subscribers-only website of wine rating (robertparker.com): "There can never be any substitute for your own palate nor any better education than tasting the wine yourself." Or consider the following declaration appearing in one of the most authoritative books on wine ever published, Hugh Johnson's *World Atlas of Wine*: "The best judge of the right styles of wine for your palate is you. There are no absolutes of right and wrong in wine appreciation."[2] Yet this book is an extended tribute to the reputation-validating and rating systems of the various regions in which wine is produced all over the world. Wine taste is the paradigmatic case of subjective experience. It is highly variable, not only from one person to the next but also for the same individual from one occasion to another. It is ineffable and incommunicable and depends upon a unique combination of external and internal conditions. Yet the world of wine is a domain in which experts have a major role in defining

1. Pliny, *His. Nat.*, XIV, 8: "Who can entertain a doubt that some kinds of wine are more agreeable to the palate than others, or that even out of the very same vat there are occasionally produced wines that are by no means of equal goodness, the one being much superior to the other, whether it is that it is owing to the cask, or to some other fortuitous circumstance? Let each person, therefore, *constitute himself his own judge as to which kind it is that occupies the pre-eminence.*"

2. Johnson and Robinson 2014, 49 (5th ed.).

the very experience of taste. This should come as no surprise. Wine is an aesthetic experience and, as such, needs evaluative criteria.

Hume's famous essay *Of the Standard of Taste* argues that we need a principle, a rule, that allows us to discriminate between good and bad taste. He finds the standard he seeks in the "joint verdict of true judges," explaining his thought as follows:

> Strong sense, united to delicate sentiment, improved by practice, perfected by comparison, and cleared of all prejudice, can alone entitle critics to this valuable character; and the joint verdict of such, wherever they are to be found, is the true standard of taste and beauty. (1985, 23)

For Hume, a true judge is a connoisseur, that is, a person well acquainted with an aesthetic domain and competent to transmit to others his or her seasoned judgment on the matter.

Connoisseurship is an elusive concept that vaguely refers to a special kind of expertise. If most of us are able to recognize a connoisseur in an aesthetic domain, like fine arts or interior decoration, it would be hard to say precisely what defines him or her as such. Is a connoisseur just someone who has good taste or does she or he have some sort of objective expertise in a domain? The tension between subjective experience and objective expertise is especially vivid in the world of wine because, on the one hand, taste, like smell, is considered a lower sense, whose relation to aesthetic judgment is less clear-cut than that of sight and hearing, and, on the other hand, knowledge of wine is not a well-defined epistemic field, so connoisseurs in the world of wine are often considered as no more than snobs who bluff and pretend to an expertise that hasn't any serious objective grounds.

What is wine connoisseurship about? In trying to define it, Italian gastronomist Carlo Petrini, founder of the Slow Food movement, plays with the common etymology of the two Italian words *sapore* (taste) and *sapere* (knowledge), both deriving from a Latin root meaning simultaneously "having taste" and "knowing." Taste requires knowledge to become good taste, that is, to belong to the licit sensory pleasures that a particular society considers legitimate. Yet the word "gastronomy" entered the European lexicon only recently in the 1801 poem by Joseph Berchoux, *La gastronomie, ou L'homme des champs à table* as a kind of joke, an oxymoron in which two markedly contradictory terms are joined to convey the idea of an impossible "science of the stomach," alluding humorously to the word "astronomy."

Sensory pleasures such as food and wine have lately been admitted among the proper pleasures of our society. Alcohol consumption is still forbidden by some religions and in many countries; and food restrictions and proscriptions are found in every culture. Perhaps talking about wine and food has become so sophisticated in order to put some distance between aesthetic taste and the lower origins of the pleasures of palate. But I do not aim here to provide a sociological account of wine talk and its place in the mechanisms of social recognition and social distinction. This is an interesting topic in itself and one that has been explored at length in sociology, especially in Pierre Bourdieu's seminal work (1984) on the social critique of taste. I want instead to approach the question from the point of view of social epistemology, trying to understand how various knowledge structures—such as classifications, ranking systems, and reputational systems—guide us in acquiring a capacity for discrimination in a particular *epistemic domain.* Taste, as Kant says (1798/2006), is an acquired disposition to discriminate and appraise. I shall consider wine taste in this sense as an interesting example of a more general epistemic process of appraisal that underlies our acquisition of expertise in many different fields of knowledge and practice. Wine seems of special epistemological interest because it is an epistemic domain that we enter as adults and sometimes without much cultural background shaping our taste and judgment. Usually we do not undergo any institutional education in wine tasting even in places, like southern Europe, where one is very likely to be exposed to wine talk and appraisal from childhood. We deliberatively decide to learn about wine, defer to experts, and acquire their manners and expertise. Thus, trying to elucidate what sorts of epistemic strategies are at stake in the case of acquiring a taste for wine seems at first glance easier than in other domains where the ability to discriminate can be affected by age, school learning, and institutionally structured educational curricula. My general point will be that acquiring expertise in wine is not radically different from acquiring epistemic competence in other domains of knowledge. Acquiring taste as a discriminatory ability, a "sense of quality" that allows us to sort items of cultural knowledge, is a process that has not been well investigated in epistemology and cognitive science but that plays a crucial role in knowledge acquisition. We need experts, tags, labels, and rating systems in order to acquire a capacity for discrimination, to understand the style of thought that is proper to a particular epistemic domain. I use the expression "epistemic domain" in a rather intuitive way, referring to any structured field of knowledge in which some principled discriminatory criteria for what counts as knowledge within it exist and can be learned. In this sense, the expression "epistemic domain" is equivalent to Foucault's expression "body of knowledge."[3] Without the mastery of some credible procedures for sorting information and enabling us to navigate through bodies of knowledge we would face the impossible task of Bouvard and Pécuchet, the two heroes of Flaubert who decide to retire and riffle through every known discipline without, in the end, being able to learn anything.

Let me state my point in this way. The first step toward mastering a body of knowledge involves learning who other people trust as masters of that knowledge. Assessing an expert's or a label's reputation is a way of orienting our trust in a new domain of knowledge so as to defer appropriately to the expertise of others (the expert or the labeling institution) in the early learning phase when making autonomous judgments is not yet possible. This is a controversial epistemological point and needs further elaboration. According to the classical view, a crucial requirement of any epistemology—whose aim is to tell us how we ought to arrive at our beliefs—is to ensure the autonomy of our processes of knowledge acquisition. Various criteria, rules, and principles on how to employ and apply our minds have been put forward throughout the history of philosophy as guarantees for preserving the autonomy and freedom of thought necessary for the acquisition of knowledge. In this book, I defend a quite different idea, namely that deferring to indirect criteria to evaluate information—such as the reputation or trustworthiness of our interlocutors—is a fundamental epistemic strategy that has to be taken into account in any serious study of the processes of knowledge acquisition.

3. Michel Foucault (1970) uses the expression "body of knowledge" to refer to any structured domain of cultural knowledge that distinguishes itself by its systematic criteria of classification and its internal procedures of representing and sorting information. In this sense, Western music, astronomy, and gastronomy are all bodies of knowledge.

Formulated differently, we do not acquire information in order to assess other people's reputation; we assess their reputation in order to acquire information. Adopting this approach gives rise to a number of epistemological questions:

- By what processes are systems of reputations and ranking constructed in a given domain?
- How are different processes used to obtain information about that domain?
- How do people use these systems to orient their discrimination?
- What is the role of experts' trustworthiness in maintaining or challenging these systems?

In order to elucidate these questions I will analyze three examples that illustrate the complex relations between the institutional systems of classifications, the trustworthiness of experts, and the acquisition of taste in the domain of wine: the French appellation systems, the Californian systems, and the rise of the credibility of taste pundit Robert Parker and his influence on the wine market.

Classification and Reputation: The French versus the Californian Appellation Systems

In *How Institutions Think*, Douglas compares two systems of wine classification: the famous 1855 classification of Bordeaux wines in France and the more recent classification system of Californian wines. Her aim is to demonstrate how institutional and public pressure affects our ways of acquiring categories in a domain of knowledge. After a detailed description of the two different labeling systems—the Bordeaux regional-based system versus the Californian grape-based system—she concludes that the Californian labeling system marked a transition in our thinking about wine from the old and complex French regional-based system, whose way of condensing information "can only be unpacked by a connoisseur," to the new, more pragmatic, and market-oriented grape-based system: "This is how the names get changed and how the people and the things are re-jigged to fit the new categories. . . . They make new kinds of institutions, and the institutions make new labels, and the new labels make new kinds of people" (1987, 108). According to Douglas, this difference between the two classificatory styles expresses a conceptual shift in our way of thinking about wine. Yet her prediction of a transition from the French classification system to the Californian classification system has not been borne out: Hugh Johnson's *World Atlas of Wine*, which she dismisses as irrelevant to understanding the contemporary wine market, has now published its seventh edition and is still the best-selling book in the world of wine. It is true that the two systems are very different, and it is definitely worth exploring in greater detail how these variations impact our discernment. But the resilience of the regional-based French classifications systems suggests that the distinct role of these labeling systems exists not just to provide us with the categories that enable us to classify reality. These labeling systems are resilient as long as they are also reputational systems, that is, as long as the label informs us how to appraise the value of the items in question. From this perspective, the Californian appellation system is not a rationalization of the French system toward a more pragmatic or market-oriented wine categorization. It simply establishes a separate network of deferential relations that consumers use in order to orient their choices. But let us have a closer look at these two systems of classification.

Quality and Reputation: The Bourgogne and Bordeaux Classification Systems

French appellation systems are quite idiosyncratic and vary from one region to another. The two most famous areas of French wine production, Bourgogne and Bordeaux, have completely separate classification systems: the Bourgogne is based on a complex system of quality of land, while the Bordeaux is based on the châteaux system.

The Bourgogne classification system was systematized and unified in 1906 by the Institut National des Appellations d'Origine (INAO), building on previous local classification systems. It divides lands according to their position and soil composition into small vineyards that form the various appellations: Chablis, Meursault, Beaune, Côtes de Nuits, Vosne Romanée, and so forth. It further sorts the vineyards into four quality classes: Grands Crus (a rank earned by only thirty-two small vineyards or *climats*, which produce the best wines in Bourgogne: Musigny, Chambertin, Montrachet, Chambertin Clos de Bese, Romanee Conti, etc.); Premiers Crus (about six hundred vineyards that are usually indicated on the bottle by the name of the village plus the name of the vineyard: Gevrey-Chambertin, Clos St. Jacques, Chambolles-Musigny Les Amoureuses); the appellation *communale*, which allows a wine to be called by the name of the village in which the vineyard is situated (like Meursault or Pommard, but also Gevrey-Chambertin, Chambolle-Musigny, Puligny-Montrachet—all village wines unless from a specific *climat*); and finally, a generic appellation Bourgogne blanc et rouge reserved for less well-situated vineyards or for grapes taken from many, sometimes—in the case of good producers—quite good vineyards. This classification is a reputational system that establishes, in a fairly robust way, quality standards on a double level: first, by dividing up the whole region into small plots of land and attributing appellations to them; and second, by imposing on this fragmentation a four-level ranking system of vineyard quality. A connoisseur's eye will thus read on a bottle's label detailed information about the wine's reputation according to the quality of the vineyard in which it is produced. Bordeaux wines are classified according to a variety of local ranking systems, the best known of which is that of the châteaux in the Medoc region (with the exception of the Chateau Haut-Brion in Graves) that was established in 1855, in response to Napoleon III's request to rank Medoc wines for the Parisian Exposition Universelle, a selective showcase of French elite culture. The ranking was established by wine industry brokers according to the château's reputation and its trading prices over the previous hundred years. The Grand Crus were already produced differently from ordinary Bordeaux wines, typically from older wine stocks that often reached more than fifty years of age, thus raising the reputation of the château proprietors who could afford to keep large stocks for so long. The château's reputation, calculated in terms of prices, was the key ingredient in establishing the 1855 ranking system, a very different criterion than that of the land quality used in the Bourgogne system. A château is a controlled vineyard that has winemaking and storage facilities on the property. Its reputation therefore depends not only on the vineyard's position and soil quality but also on the savoir faire and past performances of the proprietors. As Hugh Johnson explains in his *World Atlas*, a *Maître de Chai* is a central figure of the château, one whose craft is supposed to be inherited from father and grandfather. The 1855 classification included sixty châteaux from Medoc and one from Graves, ranked as first, second, third, fourth, and fifth "growths" (*crus*). Only four châteaux were ranked among the Premiers Crus: Lafite, Margaux, Latour, and Haut-Brion (a fifth Premier Cru, Mouton-Rothschild, was added almost a hundred years later).

By giving a primary role to the reputation of the châteaux, the Bordeaux reputational system provides consumers with quite different cues. Winemakers' mastery and their credibility over the years are the relevant cues for assessing whom to trust among producers in this highly fragmented market. An experimental study in economics on quality expectations, reputation, and prices in the Bordeaux wine market, designed to contrast its land-marked reputational system with the Bordeaux system of châteaux, shows that the price premium associated with a better reputation exceeds by twenty times the price associated with current quality.[4] In a highly fragmented market, where information gathering about individual producers is very costly, the epistemic role of a château's reputation is decisive for orienting the preferences of buyers.

Deference Relations: The California 1978 Appellation System

The California appellation system was established in 1978 by the Bureau of Alcohol, Tobacco and Firearms (ATF) with the aim of improving the reputation of American wines (California produces more than 90 percent of the wine made in United States) by allowing a wine to be named after a "politically designated" region.

In 1980, "American Viticultural Areas" (AVA) were created, that is, delineated winegrowing regions that have distinctive

4. Landon and Smith 1998.

geographical features, such as Napa Valley, Sonoma Valley, or Anderson Valley. A winemaker who uses one of these legal appellations doesn't need to produce wine inside the designated area: it suffices that at least 85 percent of the grapes present in the wine should come from it. The AVA system doesn't fix which variety of grape or yield should grow in a particular area and in which percentage. A wine produced with 85 percent Napa Valley Chardonnay grape will deserve to be a Chardonnay with the Napa Valley appellation. A Californian winery has much more freedom than a French one in choosing its appellations. Many producers still ignore the AVA classifications and prefer to stick to the simpler labeling used before 1980, that is, naming the winery plus the grape variant. Others are not only committed to the AVA systems but have also started to inscribe on their labels the name of locally renowned vineyards now associated with a specific grape variety, such as Zinfandel in Dry-Creek Valley and Pinot Noir in the cooler hills of Carneros. Differentiation of areas and vineyards is still ongoing, producing a very different picture from that drawn by Mary Douglas, who, as mentioned, predicted an inevitable simplification of American wine classification systems toward a grape-based labeling. In fact, as the reputation of Californian wines grows, the more fine-grained and stratified the California classification system becomes, thus incorporating information that can be decrypted only by an expert. The relative freedom of labeling adapted by Californian winemakers doesn't simplify the classification system. It leads rather to the establishment of a complex network of deferential relations among appellations and wineries, as has been shown by economist Joël M. Podolny (2005). If a winery in one region puts the name of another region on its labels in order to indicate a better quality of grapes coming from that region, this is interpreted as an act of deference toward that region and will contribute to its overall reputation and to the impact of the appellation on the price of the relevant wines. As Podolny shows, half of the bottles that bear the name "Napa Valley" on their labels are not produced within Napa Valley. This is a clear act of deference and acknowledgment of the superiority of the grapes coming from this particular AVA. An example of a strategy used to influence status perception through affiliation with an appellation is the recent association of the Gallo winery, the largest producer of wine in the United States whose reputation is associated with cheap and mediocre wines, with the appellation Sonoma Valley, an obvious attempt to change its reputation and improve the public perception of its wine. The use of the label "Gallo of Sonoma" is an act of deference of the Gallo vineyards toward the Sonoma region, thus signaling a more careful selection of the provenance of its grapes. This act of deference has a double effect. On the one hand, it makes transparent to consumers the relationship between the two entities, that is, the fact that Gallo buys grapes from Sonoma Valley. On the other hand, it contributes to stabilizing a distinct identity of the label "Gallo of Sonoma," which will orient consumers' choices. Podolny's case study of the reputational network created by Californian wineries' affiliations shows how this network retroactively recasts past evaluations of a wine's quality, an important parameter for fixing prices in a market. That is, the reputation that a particular winery, far from being determined by its past, instead influences how its past is evaluated.

So here we have a third kind of reputational system, in which people rely on "who is associated with whom" in order to get information about a particular wine, given that it would be too costly and cumbersome to obtain this information from direct inspection of the wine's quality.

These three examples show how different reputational systems provide consumers with evaluation heuristics rooted in the biases of different approaches: the Bourgogne system provides cues about the quality of the vineyards, the Bordeaux system about the mastery of the châteaux, and the California system about the social network of status relations. These different types of cues incorporate evaluations that are used by consumers to gather information that would be very costly to obtain otherwise. The "normative landscape" encoded in this ranking system orients the novice in his or her first steps within the new domain of knowledge of wine.

Credibility, Trust, and Moral Qualities: The Rise of Robert Parker's Trustworthiness

As Steven Shapin has pointed out (2005), it is remarkable that the world's most famous taste pundit during the last few decades, Robert Parker, comes from the United States. A former lawyer, born in Baltimore in 1947, Parker began writing wine reports around 1975 and has since become one of the most respected critics throughout the world. By 1998, his publication, *The Wine Advocate*, had more than 45,000 subscribers. His rise coincides with the rise of American wine and its now worldwide reputation. Parker's best-known revolution is his rating system based on a 100-point scale, a much more flexible system than the usual 20-point scales: 96–100 points correspond to an extraordinary wine, 90–95 to an outstanding wine, 80–89 to a barely above-average to very good wine, 70–79 an average wine, and so forth. Almost every wine shop in the United States displays the Parker points below the prices of wines to provide some guidance to their customers. How did Robert Parker succeed in imposing himself as the world's most authoritative connoisseur in the domain of wine expertise? Why do people everywhere trust his judgments? His fame was originally based on his appraisal of the 1982 vintage of Bordeaux, which "British experts" described as overripe and not worth buying for the long term. His positive evaluation was eventually endorsed by the rest of the world. Yet his rise was not without controversy. In 2004, or so the story goes, he was heavily criticized by one of Britain's leading wine critics, Jancis Robinson, for having awarded a 95–100 rating to a 2003 vintage Chateau Pavie, a "ridiculous wine" according to Robinson and one whose appreciators deserved a "brain and palate transplant."[5] Still, despite such attempts to question his reputation, Parker is internationally considered a man of exquisite and precise taste, a "true judge," in Hume's words, whose infallible taste buds dictate the laws of oenological excellence. Experts in the wine industry play a key role in balancing the effects of reputation as we have seen earlier in this chapter: blind tasting is a way of ensuring a criterion of quality independent of the classifications detailed above. When different blind evaluations converge, we can conclude that we now possess an objective measure of the "perceived" quality of a wine (as opposed to its "expected quality," that is, its reputation). Professional blind tastings are performed under controlled conditions by panels of experts. But Parker has never agreed to be part of these panels. He presents himself as an independent critic and has not been formally trained in wine. He started his bimonthly publication as a vocation, abandoning his legal career against the advice of friends and relatives. So, again, why is Parker trusted? Why, given that he doesn't appeal to any professional expertise or rigorous standard of

5. Cited by Eric Asimov in a 2006 *New York Times* article on Robert Parker: http://www.nytimes.com/2006/03/22/dining/decanting-robert-parker.html.

evaluation, should we admit the superiority of his personal tasting facilities: exceptional palate, taste buds, and memory that are never mistaken? Against this superhuman view of a "million-dollar nose," which can be used as a litmus test to determine the quality of a wine, I would rather explore an alternative explanation. Parker is identified as a modern incarnation of a gentleman or a man of honor, and for this reason he is considered trustworthy, a friend of the ordinary consumer, not siding with the experts and the elite. The socio-epistemological role of the moral qualities of gentlemanly status and honor in the truthfulness of evaluations has been superbly addressed by Shapin in his work on truth and credibility in the emergence of modern science. He explores "the connections between the identity of individuals making claims and the credibility of what they claim" (1994, 126) and the way in which judgments of the truth or falsity of knowledge claims incorporate assessments of the source of knowledge during the emergence of experimental science in the seventeenth century. A similar connection between the acceptance of normative standards and the display of moral qualities, such as integrity and freedom of action, can also be discerned in assessments of the credibility of a taste expert such as Robert Parker. Parker is supposedly incorruptible: *The Wine Advocate*'s subtitle is: *The Independent Consumer's Bimonthly Guide to Fine Wine*. He sees himself as a self-appointed consumer's advocate, a crusader whose mission is to free the world of wine from hypocrisy and bad faith. His publication doesn't accept advertising. He does not accept gifts from wine producers or invitations to vineyards, does not speculate on the wine market, and prefers to taste alone at home, without the pressure of social occasions. His detachment is a guarantee of trustworthiness. He also shows a total disregard for the lore of wine hierarchies. He is not a snob as he suggests that his British competitors, overly sensitive to the lineages of wines, are. As his admirers claim, he brings a democratic breeze into the wine industry by detaching the evaluation of wines from the reputation of their location and history. His simple and synthetic reports lack the verbosity of those issued by other critics and are easy to understand. Integrity, democracy, and intelligibility are constituents of Parker's self-professed identity, and it is on the basis of such appraisals of his identity that consumers decide to trust him. While convergence of content and other indirect epistemic criteria usually play a role in assessing the credibility of reports, Parker's case is somewhat different. It is the display of his moral qualities that reinforces his authority. The relation between an expert's trustworthiness and historically determined reputational systems is thus quite complex. Experts are not simply tools or instruments that allow the consumer to assess the real quality of the wine by proxy or to decipher unintelligible information from a wine label. Rather, experts participate in the maintenance and the transformations of the reputational systems by counterbalancing their role, challenging their hierarchies or reinforcing them. Novices who approach a complex and traditional corpus of knowledge such as wine expertise are confronted with a normative landscape, rich in cues that they use to orient their sense of discrimination.

The lore of tradition is structured by the classifications, ranks, and reputational systems that teach us what is canonical for any given corpus of knowledge. We learn these maps quickly by using heuristics that allow us rapidly to associate values with items. But we are not blindly deferential to this lore. To the extent that we acquire an autonomous capacity for discrimination, we challenge and revise it by relying on our own experience and on that of experts we consider trustworthy in that domain. A socio-epistemological investigation into the different heuristics we construct and use to structure a body of knowledge is a worthy project, even in cultural domains where facts of the matter are difficult to pin down. The ability to discriminate among wines is not a "science," of course. But this does not imply that our acquisition of the ability to discriminate is deprived of any objective value.[6] Although a science of wine is still beyond our ken, the sketch of an epistemology of wine that I have just outlined is an attempt to describe how people do and should structure their knowledge, which heuristics they employ, and which experts they trust in navigating a historically embedded and epistemologically entangled corpus of knowledge such as wine expertise. Gaston Bachelard used to say that science has not had the philosophy it deserves. In the case of wine, it would be perhaps more appropriate to say that philosophy has not had the science it deserves.

6. On this point, see Hughson and Boakes 2002.

9

Academic Reputation, or Voluntary Epistemic Servitude

> Where is the wisdom we have lost in knowledge?
> Where is the knowledge we have lost in information?
>
> —T. S. ELIOT, "CHORUSES FROM 'THE ROCK'"

> No one who speaks of the greatest and most important thing in the world means anything that really exists.
>
> —ROBERT MUSIL, *THE MAN WITHOUT QUALITIES*

One evening, as recounted in David Lodge's novel *Changing Places*, the members of a university literature department play a game called Humiliation. All the professors in turn must name a book they haven't read, gaining a point for every colleague present who has, on the contrary, actually read the book in question. Naturally, in a literature department where every faculty member is presumed to be an accomplished scholar, the participants begin by citing rare and little-known books. This is how they avoid having to confess any embarrassing lacuna in their literary erudition. In taking this evasive tack, however, they earn no points in the game because there is little likelihood that the others will have read such recherché works either. One participant, whose desire for triumphing over the others overcomes his concern to protect his reputation, finally cracks, confessing scandalously: "Hamlet!" He wins the game, to be sure, but his scholarly reputation is in tatters. The next morning, he is peremptorily summoned by the chairman of the department.

If there is an institution that feeds on reputation, it is the academy. Prestige, notoriety, standing, and reputation reign supreme within its halls. Professors and scholars are not only more motivated by symbolic rewards than by economic interest. They also spend a great deal of time designing institutions whose primary purpose is the creation, maintenance, and evaluation of each other's reputation and eminence. Such rankings are sometimes even treated as if they were the most dependable hallmarks of the Truth itself.

A classical subject of the sociology of knowledge,[1] academic reputation has been deeply affected, in recent years, by extensive recourse to citation indexes, by globalization, and by radical reforms in the management of science undertaken at the behest of certain nations. These changes have created new biases that condition the way reputations are constructed. The entanglement of diverse rating and ranking systems, as well as the norms and practices governing their use, "constructs" the objectivity of academic reputations in a way that blends old practices and new dynamics with sometimes unpredictable

1. See Merton 1942/1973; Bourdieu 1984; and Elias, Martins, and Whitley 1982.

results. In this chapter, I will try to show how the very idea of an academic reputation changed radically after these new systems for calibrating reputations came into their own.

The most characteristic feature of the contemporary "science market" is the stratification of different reputational logics that are structured around three profoundly distinct economies: (1) an economy of esteem and prestige that dominates the competitive sport of scientific research; (2) an economy of money that controls new markets for scientific publishing and university education; and (3) an economy of fame (prizes, recognition, national acclaim) that characterizes the system of public incentives for research and the governance of research institutions at both national and global levels. (A parallel global marketplace for fame can be found in the participation of national teams in the Olympic Games.) In science and academic research, to stick to our topic, the third "economy" results in the increased importance ascribed to relative positioning in international scientific rankings, in the frequency of rhetorical appeals to excellence and productivity, and in the proliferation of national academic evaluation agencies (such as HCERES in France, ANVUR in Italy, ANECA in Spain, and QAA in England).[2] As the three systems interact, in any case, they create new reputational logics that have profoundly transformed the profession of scientific and scholarly research.

According to a recent estimate of global scientific output, more than fifty million articles have appeared in peer-reviewed journals. This figure, moreover, continues to swell.[3] The aver-

2. For a list of European evaluation agencies that adhere to the quality standards set in the Treaty of Bologna, see www.eqar.eu/.

3. See Jinha 2010.

age annual increase in the number of new articles published between 1995 and 2007 was 2.5 percent. In 2006 alone, more than one million articles appeared in 23,750 scientific journals. The dizzying expansion of this body of knowledge has been precipitated by a series of major technological and social transformations, including:

- changes in research involving written contributions, owing to recent revolutions in information technology;
- changes in the interconnectivity of scientific literature, owing to the collaborative work typical of big science;
- network dynamics created by the introduction of new bibliometric indicators, such as the citation index and the impact factor, to which we shall return;
- the imposition by governments and agencies that fund research of new forms of quality control, including the introduction of an audit culture into national academic systems; and
- the advent of a new industrial-production model for scientific publishing, and the emergence of a competitive-market culture in the university, which can be summarized by the notorious warning: "publish or perish."

These new dynamics have transformed scientific life and refashioned the way knowledge is produced. Science today bears a greater resemblance to entrepreneurial activity than to the disinterested contemplation that has, at least ideally, characterized it since its origins. Merton, one of the founding fathers of the sociology of science, described research as a distinct sphere of human activity, governed by norms of its own that are radically different from those governing other activities such as buying and selling in an economic marketplace. He employed the acronym CUDOS to describe the idiosyncratic norms of science: communalism, universalism, disinterestedness, and organized skepticism.[4] The acronym naturally evokes the Greek term *kudos*, meaning "glory" or "renown," mentioned in chapter 6 when we discussed "kudonomics" or the "economy of esteem" studied by Pettit and Brennan. The publish-or-perish slogan itself originally emerged as a social norm governing the acquisition of non-material prestige. But it has by now evolved into a quantitative measure of output on the model of industrial production.

Striking today is the growing gap between the traditional norms that once governed science as an organized research activity and the new rules generated by state-of-the-art techniques for the mass production of knowledge. These new technological capacities have colonized the older distinctive system of traditional norms, creating a paradoxical situation in which scientific research with the characteristics of an economic marketplace can exploit a "labor force" that is still motivated primarily by non-material prestige and reputation. This awkward mélange has had a number of consciously planned as well as unforeseen effects on the production and dissemination of scientific knowledge that need to be examined more closely. For example, the deeply rooted belief that the canonical format for the communication of knowledge is the "article" published in a scientific journal has nothing to do with its being the most efficient means toward that end, especially given the flagrant distortions in the way scientific credit for each publication is ascribed. But this stubbornly held convic-

4. See Merton 1942/1973.

tion does reveal a perverse strain in the system worth exploring in greater detail.[5]

Reputation and Interest: The Entanglement of Two Knowledge Economies

Why do we—researchers and university professors—insist on publishing academic articles in peer-reviewed scientific journals? Several possible responses are offered by researchers themselves, of which—if I can trust my own experience—the most recurrent are the following:

- published articles are the best way to inform the research community of the advances we are making in our field;
- they represent the standard format for the communication of scientific findings, the most concise way for a new scientific idea to be expressed and evaluated; and they embody a whole series of social norms endorsed by the scholarly community, some dating from the first scientific publication of this type, the *Philosophical Transactions of the Royal Society* (1665);
- only this type of publication ensures and protects the researchers' prestige and reputation; and
- research articles are a sort of slow-motion "conversation": I write an article, I submit it to a journal that sends it out to be reviewed by peers, I receive the comments, I improve my article, I resubmit, and so forth.

5. See Origgi 2010; Casati, Origgi, and Simon 2011.

I have heard such justifications hundreds of times, because all those involved in scholarly research feel the need to justify, to themselves and others, a career devoted to publishing articles read on average by 1.5 people—articles that are often difficult to locate, even for colleagues, and for which, on principle, no compensation is paid.

Let's begin with the first response. I now have more than four thousand messages in my email inbox. I participate in online conferences and forums that apprise me of new developments in my research areas well before articles about them can appear in academic journals. (In the humanities and social sciences, the interlude between submission and publication is more than one year.) The question therefore arises: Is publishing in a prestigious journal really the most effective means for communicating advances in knowledge? Of course not. If I continue to insist on publishing in such venues it is obviously because of incentives that have little or nothing to do with communicating the findings of my research.

The second response is undoubtedly true. The research article is the traditional format par excellence of scientific communication, a format that has exhibited a formidable longevity in the history of science. Beginning with the 1665 publication of the first scientific journal, the *Philosophical Transactions of the Royal Society*, the scientific article established new rules of the game for *philosophia naturalis*, that is, for modern science. These rules have remained substantially unchanged up to the present day. The agreed-upon format for publishing scientific research embodies a whole series of standards of truth and honesty, a new "code of honor" deemed to express the relation of the modern researcher to both nature and the scientific community. These new norms are based on experimentation, disinterestedness, and the sharing of scientific results in the public domain.[6] It was at the Royal Society and in the presence of luminaries such as Robert Boyle, John Walkins, Robert Hooke, and, later, Isaac Newton that a certain new conception of intellectual property took shape. This conception continues to provide the justification for scientific authority today. First of all, the scientific community is a community of peers. Participants find themselves among the happy few who are well-informed about current scientific controversies. They discuss newly fielded hypotheses that will become scientific truths once endorsed by a sufficient number of colleagues. Second, scientific truths can never become privately owned intellectual property. No scientists worthy of the name can acquire personal ownership of what they discover (which would hypothetically include the right to keep it hidden) because such discoveries concern nature; and nature is a common preserve belonging jointly to all mankind. Scientists can therefore draw only indirect benefits from their discoveries, notably prestige and recognition as well as the right to exploit their findings commercially through officially awarded patents. The history of scientific authority is therefore, from the beginning, distinct from the history of intellectual property. The copyright laws that emerged in England and France at the beginning of the eighteenth century were designed to foster intellectual creativity but do not cover purely scientific authors. The "gentleman scientist" is a disinterested being who investigates the truth for the common good and makes his results available to others by publishing them in the bulletins of scholarly associations such as the Royal Society. Robert Boyle even argued for the anonymous publication of results, to emphasize the disinterestedness of scientific research.

6. See Biagioli and Galison 2003.

Although the eighteenth-century scientist's commitment to fair play is hard to detect in the bloodbath of "publish or perish" permeating science today, the fundamental rules of scientific publishing have remained substantially unchanged. A journal is considered "scientific" only if it is administered by a committee of peers. These peers guide the process for filtering knowledge through the famous peer-review system that should be considered the gold standard of truth in contemporary science. What is true is what is judged by peers to be publishable. No economic benefits accrue to publishing one's work in this type of journal. The benefits can only be indirect: reputation, prizes, and patents. Thus, while it is true that the scientific article remains the standard format for the publication of research findings, the reason for this holdover from the past has more to do with the scientific code of honor than with the efficient communication of knowledge.

The third response, which sees the publication of scientific articles as the most reliable way of gaining a reputation and receiving credit for one's work, is perfectly predictable. Although rating and ranking systems designed to provide "objective" metrics of scientific output have recently come into vogue in the administration of knowledge, scientific reputations do not depend entirely on such systems. There is no one-to-one correlation between the prestige researchers enjoy among their peers and their prestige measured by scientometrics. A number of studies show that maximum dissemination in peer-reviewed journals influences one's remuneration and career but not necessarily one's reputation for high-quality work.[7] Moreover, the shaping of reputations on the Web has reached a point where publications in blogs or forums unscreened by

7. Hamermesh and Pfann 2009.

peer review can nevertheless decisively influence a researcher's reputation. An article published in a reputable journal is now far from being the only way to acquire a scholarly or scientific reputation. In reality, it never was. But today it remains a valuable "bargaining chip" in the pursuit of reputation owing to the sui generis dynamics of contemporary scientific research.

The fourth response is even easier to criticize. If research is indeed a "conversation," then articles published in peer-reviewed journals do more to hinder than to facilitate it. In accredited journals, as everyone knows, we find only articles that experts in the field have already read and commented upon and discussed at length in seminars, conferences, international colloquia, and email exchanges. The interval between submission and publication, as mentioned, can be painfully long, sometimes up to eighteen months depending on the discipline. (The "slowest" fields in this regard are the social sciences and economics, and the "fastest" are chemistry and physics, with an average delay of nine months before publication.)[8] No scientific community conducts "conversations" with yearlong gaps in the debate. Scientific journals, as a consequence, are wholly inefficient vehicles for facilitating back-and-forth, mutually correcting deliberation among researchers in a field.

In short, the justifications commonly invoked to explain to ourselves and others why we doggedly insist on publishing in peer-reviewed journals are facially implausible.

So why do we continue to play this strange publishing game for specialists? We do so because the research article has become the standard unit of measurement in science. It is the

8. Bjork and Solomon 2014.

canonical format in which scientific content can circulate, not among scientists themselves (as we have seen, they have many other pathways for disseminating and questioning results) but in the citation and impact measuring systems at the core of the new knowledge market. The construction of academic reputations depends essentially on "the scientific article" as the standard unit of measurement by which the new scientometrics gauges scientific reputations and assigns scientific credit. This otherwise outdated publication format, in which traditional standards for gaining a reputation and receiving credit are vestigially embedded, is kept alive by its structural role in the dynamics of citation systems. This is how traditional reputational norms, once they come into contact with new systems for measuring reputations, come to partake in a "perverse" dynamic whose results are largely uncontrollable.

Measurable Impact as an Objectification of Reputation

One of the major innovations in the contemporary production of knowledge has been the quantification of scientific reputations by systems for calculating the "impact factor" of a researcher, journal, or institution. What does it mean to acquire scientific prestige and to be given credit for scientific achievements? Modern scientometrics offers an unambiguous answer to this question: to have a reputation is to have a measurable impact on the research of others, that is, to be quoted many times in their publications. If a colleague appreciates one of my articles, he quotes it in his, which increases my reputation. Conversely, if I write hundreds of articles that nobody quotes, my impact is zero and my reputation languishes. One's impact factor is very easy to calculate. It was introduced in the 1960s following the publication by Eugene Garfield in 1958 of the Science Citation Index (SCI). Garfield proposed this new scientometric tool to help "navigate" the immense and interconnected scientific literature developing in the wake of World War II, thanks to Big Science, that is, to the increasingly collaborative and institutionalized nature of scientific research. But the SCI did not originally have an evaluative purpose. It was meant to serve as a resource that academic institutions could purchase, a kind of directory of scientific journals, detailing the interconnections between their publications. An expert in scientometrics, Garfield began by extracting comparative performance indicators from various journals. The impact factor (IF) was one of these indicators. The IF of a journal for the year 2010 is a ratio between the number of citations published in 2010 to articles published by that journal in 2009 and 2008 and the total number of articles the journal published in 2009 and 2008. The IFs calculated and published by Clarivate Analytics, formerly a part of Thomson Reuters, are used to measure the average citation rate of articles published in a journal over the course of two years. Each year, they publish the *Journal Citation Report*, which the academic community views as an important verdict on the quality of journals. Initially released together with the SCI, the *Journal Citation Report* is now an independent tool that publishes a series of impact indicators, including not only the impact factor but also the "immediacy index," which divides the number of citations that articles in a journal receive in a given year by the number of articles published in the same year, and the "cited half-life" or the number of years it takes for the rate by which an article is cited to decline by 50 percent.

Such quantifications of scientific reputation, while not improving the quality of research, have measurably increased the volume of scientific output because the impact measures used by science rating systems serve as incentives to productivity. Although the scientific community understands best the many biases that distort attributions of impact,[9] we find ourselves today trapped in a system that fails to engage in constructive self-criticism and that turns scientists into willing collaborators in a system organized according to a commercial logic. Indeed, researchers now engage in a kind of voluntary servitude, magnanimously providing the content of articles which, after being tossed into the scientometrics hopper, ultimately increase the value of productivity indicators in a marketplace that resembles a new "science of scientific work"[10] more than it resembles "science" conceived as a calling devoted to the advancement of knowledge. We work, in short, to accumulate reputations in the service of a system that accumulates profits.

Another important aspect of these altered dynamics relates to the sui generis interpretation of copyright as a system for ascribing credit and gaining reputation rather than for protecting property rights. The old norm that regulated the law on scientific discoveries distinguished them clearly from patentable inventions and decreed them unprotected by a right of property by virtue of the metaphysical intuition that nature

9. Speaking of well-known biases, we know that the value of IF, which is the most widely used metric, is affected by sociological factors, such as the discipline or type of publication (letter, full article, review) and the average number of authors per article, as well as statistical factors such as the size of the journal and the period of the time during which the journal's impact is measured used in establishing the measurement. In addition, journals in narrow disciplinary areas tend to have a higher impact factor. The number of authors is also important. (This is particularly true in the hard sciences. The average in the social sciences is two authors whereas in physics the average is four.) A shorter article, such as a letter or a review, has a higher immediacy factor and a shorter half-life (see Christenson and Sigelman 1985).

10. The expression comes from Winkler, Glänzel, et al. in their contribution to Menger and Mairesse 2015.

cannot be privately possessed. But this traditional norm has now become, quite perversely, a way of exploiting the work of researchers by rewarding them solely with non-material accolades while allowing scientific publishers to exploit their work commercially. At the same time, authors are encouraged to accumulate scientific credit according to a logic of self-interest—a logic thoroughly at odds with the traditional norms of science—and to maximize their reputational "profit margin" according to a competitive model typical of market activities. Once again, traditional norms are distorted by the competitive dynamics of the knowledge production system, producing unexpected effects, such as, in this case, internecine disputes over how credit is to be allocated, influenced by the order of names in the list of coresearchers, the presence of a greater or lesser number of "authors," and other criteria for attributing "paternity" to an article. In effect, each discipline applies different criteria for "sharing" scientific credit. In several of the hard sciences, for example, it is normal, and even obligatory, to include the laboratory director in the list of an article's coauthors, with his or her name placed first or last according to discipline, a practice unknown in the human sciences. Moreover, the weight ascribed to the order of names attached to a published piece of research varies greatly. Sometimes names are listed alphabetically, while at other times the ordering reflects a true estimate of the level of contribution of each author, or merely the relative seniority of researchers, or the power relations prevailing inside the lab.[11] These logics promiscuously mix the new market spirit (competition and accumulation) and the old norms of science (reputation and intellectual authority), with the curious result that researchers

11. See Migheli and Ramello 2014; and Casati, Origgi, and Simon 2011.

strive to acquire an eminently symbolic good, reputation, whose correlation with economic benefits remains totally unclear and uncertain.

Scientific publishers, on the other hand, monetize the scientific work whose copyright they control, just like any other publishing industry. No exception, reflecting the traditional distinction between scientific and literary authors, is made for science. Because of the traditional norm decreeing nature to be the common property of mankind, scientific authors cannot profit directly from their own discoveries. But scientific publishers, unhampered by such quaint inhibitions, step into the breach to profit handsomely from scientific discoveries not their own. The scientific publishing industry, moreover, is structured as an oligopoly dominated by a few very large publishing houses: Springer-Kluwer, Elsevier, and Wiley-Blackwell.[12] The operating margins for this type of industry are much greater than in other sectors especially because the "workers" (all of us who write scientific articles) are not remunerated.[13] In effect, the particular way in which copyright is structured in this sector pushes scientific publishing toward a concentration of production in the hands of a small group of actors, increasing the already outsized domination of large publishers over small ones. Academic competition is no longer just a contest between researchers: it is above all a struggle for market share among major publishers who offer "packages" of journals to libraries and research institutions. These so-called Big Deals[14] consume much of the scarce funding available to universities for the purchase of books and transform their li-

12. These three, taken together, control 42 percent of the market. The rest of the market is distributed among small publishers, each controlling only 3 percent of scientific and scholarly journals. See McGuigan and Russell 2008.

13. See Deutsche Bank 2015.

14. See Edlin and Rubinfeld 2004; and Origgi and Ramello 2015.

braries into retailers for the profit-oriented system of scientific publications. Instead of a truly competitive market, in which libraries could choose titles on a unit-by-unit basis according to their quality, Big Deals force research institutions to make bundled purchases that reduce choice. Publishers, for their part, use the reputation of a few titles with a very high impact factor to induce university and research libraries to purchase a whole catalogue or package of journals. That is how they have managed to jack up the budgets of universities and libraries devoted to journals, budgets, which, between 1986 and 2011 in the United States, increased by 402 percent.[15]

Another consequence of the new uses of science is the evolution of the role played by peer review in citation systems. Peer review is a distinctive feature of modern science. Merton defined its role as follows: "The referee system in science involves the systematic use of judges to assess the acceptability of manuscripts submitted for publication. The referee is thus an example of status judges who are charged with evaluating the quality of role-performances in a social system" (1973, 460).

This judicial or evaluator role exists in other spheres too, in arts and in sports, for instance. But in the case of science, the judge exercises a particular function, that of defining scientific authenticity or certifying the truth of science. Whatever its limits, the referee system is now universally considered an essential element in the definition of science. As physicist John Ziman put it in his book devoted to the problems of mass production in science: "An article in a reputable journal does not merely represent the opinions of its author; it bears the imprimatur of scientific authenticity, as given to it by the editor and the referees he may have consulted. The

15. These data are provided by the Association for Research Libraries: http://www.arl.org/storage/documents/monograph-serial-costs.pdf.

referee is the lynchpin about which the whole business of Science is pivoted" (1966, 148).

The peer-review system has long made research into a distinctive production system where the judgment of peers, rather than market demand, determines value. There are other areas where judges and experts play a crucial role—in wine, as we have seen, and in sport—but "experts" are not exactly peers. They are not—at least not any longer—producers of the same products or performers of the same performances that they are asked to judge. Consequently, the authority of their judgment does not hinge on their belonging to the same circle as those they evaluate, whereas such shared membership is crucial in the case of science. This is why science is so deeply and naturally linked to the ethos of the academic profession, an ethos that distinguishes it sharply from professions with a commercial purpose. This detachment from the profit motive is an essential condition for the autonomy of science and the freedom of inquiry. It also protects the implicit contract between science and the state, guaranteeing the high quality of scientific publications and therefore the state's continued commitment to investing in research.

Peer review, introduced in 1752 by the Royal Society to guarantee the quality of its publications in the *Philosophical Transactions*, functions today more or less as it did back then. At that time, an article was addressed to a group of the society's members who would issue a judgment, rejecting the article or accepting it as an original and advanced contribution to knowledge. Some historians, such as Mario Biagioli (2002), while admitting that the origins of this system are uncertain, suggest that it could have developed out of the eighteenth-century practice of censoring books, which was subsequently adjusted and applied to scientific journals.

Today, the role played by peer review is being overshadowed by the preponderant weight ascribed to impact factors and citation indexes. Peer review nevertheless remains fundamental as a hurdle that must be overcome to have one's work appear in scientific publications. Its residual function is to guarantee the "scientificity" of publications, thereby justifying the lack of monetary compensation for the authors. Only peer-reviewed journals fail to remunerate authors. (And note that referees, too, go unpaid.) Peer review therefore remains a barrier to the transformation of scientific copyright along commercial lines, but it plays a decreasingly important role as a gateway to reputation and prestige. Karpik distinguishes between a "citation" model and a "committee" model in the science selection process, emphasizing that the former has become especially influential in the allocation of research funds as well as in promotion decisions. The opinions of peers and experts, their reputation and their authority, are increasingly put into question by the quantitative force of impact, measured, as we have seen, by the number of citations.

In short, research now finds itself in a paradoxical situation. It is enslaved by a system it has helped create and from which researchers have a hard time achieving any critical distance. What we have is a system that exploits the old game of personal competition for reputation among researchers—based on acknowledgment and emulation by peers—and from which profits are drawn neither by researchers nor by universities but mostly by the scientific publishing industry that operates according to the logic of market competition. This outcome shows that reputational strategies and motivations cannot easily be converted into economic strategies and motivations without completely distorting the system of interactions they are supposed to steer.

Consider, for example, "emulation," defined by the *OED* as the "endeavour to equal or surpass others in any achievement or quality; also, the desire or ambition to equal or excel." Every successful master-pupil relationship is buoyed up by this ambition or hope. The intrinsic virtues and proven accomplishments of our teachers lead us to acknowledge their intellectual authority. But our admiration for their writings and discoveries also stimulates our desire to surpass them. This is how knowledge advances. Emulation, or the desire to excel high performers in the eyes of society, is one of the most ancient principles upon which education is founded. One already finds it, for example, in Herodotus when he emphasizes the importance of accolades in the Olympic Games. Emulation is seen as a virtuous motivation linked to prestige and reputation. We want to do better than our masters in order to deserve the laurels of preeminence (degrees, diplomas, prizes, congratulations of the jury, and so forth) as defined by the milieu in which we wish to be recognized.

Maintaining the tricky balance between outperforming all scientific predecessors and acquiring a positive reputation among the members of the existing scientific community is a challenge familiar to these circles. We must move beyond what has been previously accomplished, but not so far beyond as to discourage recognition by peers or to snap our connection to the cultural tradition that our work seeks to extend. Too much innovation and we run the risk of not being recognized or, worse, being ostracized as a threat to our tradition. Efforts to avoid this risk, unfortunately, often result in "academicism," producing justified criticisms of the conformist effects of emulation.[16] It remains true, in any case, that emulation is also

16. The value of emulation in education is a classic theme of pedagogy. See Cogswell 1836.

and correctly considered a "virtue" of systems based on a logic of prestige. The commercial systems of contemporary science, however, have replaced emulation with rivalry.[17] Rivalry is defined in dictionaries as "the competition of persons who make a claim to the same thing." It is therefore an essentially competitive passion aimed at achieving a result and, in doing so, surpassing a rival. But this style or form of competition is in no way motivated by admiration for that rival. A rival, as opposed to a master we hope to emulate, is an individual who is in our way, someone to fight, humble, and defeat. Gaining academic distinction comes at the price of besting such competitors, leaving them in the dust. Hence the tendency of these new systems to foster ethically dubious practices, such as salami slicing, meaning the practice of dividing articles into shorter subsections that can be published separately, thereby artificially inflating the number of one's publications. Other practices with a similar aim include self-plagiarism and the use of positions of authority (for example, as a referee for journal articles) to compel others to cite one's own works.[18]

In short, the dynamics generated by these new systems "impose" a competitive-commercial and profit-seeking logic onto scientific researchers who are, by profession, oriented toward the pursuit of non-material benefits such as admiration by peers. The distinction between emulation and rivalry as motivating passions for researchers illustrates this awkward superimposition. The result is unconvincing and distorts research practices as well as the way researchers justify their own work. Everyone recognizes the senselessness of much scientific productivity today, which often has no cognizable aim other than keeping the knowledge-production system in

17. On this point, see Karpik 2011.

18. See Casati, Origgi, and Simon 2011.

motion. Nevertheless, it is very difficult to escape from the viselike grip of this logic. It imposes itself, as market systems do, with an intrinsic necessity difficult to resist. What makes scientific production distinct is that it has no consumers in the ordinary sense, nor does the logic of supply and demand apply, apart from the jockeying for profitable precedence among scientific publishing houses. Scientific researchers are at the same time producers, consumers, and judges of the system of knowledge. The logic that governs their activity is not the logic of the market but the logic of the happy few, which has always irritated society's power wielders because it is inherently unpredictable and potentially disobedient. The powerful have always aspired to control the production and acquisition of knowledge. This aspiration is embodied today in the new market spirit dominating late liberal societies with all the perverse consequences that we have seen. The most pernicious result is that a logic of material interest has now been foisted on the scientific community, supplanting the traditional logic of esteem and reputation. As we have seen throughout this book, the fluctuating boundary between these material and nonmaterial motivations disorients scientific researchers, rendering them incapable of clearly explaining their own actions and, in the end, making them less rational than they would be if their second ego, the one whose fulfillment depends on recognition by knowledgeable others, was allowed to assume the precedence it once had.

To conclude our discussion of the vagaries of the system of contemporary research, let us consider briefly the third "economy of prestige" at work in this field: the economy of preeminence that characterizes national and international competitions among research institutions. This economy, too, has been profoundly altered by the emergence of new reputational systems for classifying institutions and by the introduction of an auditing culture into research institutions and universities. The effects have been perverse, as usual; but in this case it has not been wholly unexpected.

The New "Sovietology" of Research Management

When the Soviet Union collapsed in 1990–91, Sovietologists questioned the future of their profession. Ron Amman, executive director of the Economic and Social Research Council in Great Britain from 1994 to 2002, was therefore surprised to discover that his knowledge of the Soviet system was so easily transferable to the new managerial culture in scientific research that had grown dominant in Britain since the early 1980s:

> It gradually dawned upon me that the careful study of Soviet central planning which had absorbed my attention for over twenty years, far from being a waste of time, had instead provided me with unique qualifications—not so much in technical expertise but certainly in understanding. The growing managerial pressures in the public sector in Britain, which caused dismay and incomprehension to many colleagues, were instantaneously recognizable to an old Soviet hand. (2003, 287)

Amman studied the number of administrative levels in the higher education system in Great Britain and compared it to the number of levels present in the machine-tool industry in the Soviet Union, revealing suggestive parallels between the two bureaucratic structures: "Within such a planning system the volume of transactions was so huge and the interdependent relationships were so complex that real control was quite impossible" (2003, 289). In effect, all actors in the system were obliged to succeed in accomplishing their tasks and producing their "deliverables" on schedule, creating an incentive to falsify routine productivity reports in order to satisfy on paper the performance measures imposed by the system. The origin of the British system dates back to 1979 and to Thatcher's policy of reducing public spending by "strengthening the market" and thus introducing a quasi-market culture into higher education. But in publicly funded education and research there is no real market because the state provides the money and there are no consumers in the ordinary economic sense. In Britain, those who were supposed to assess the quality of the "product" were very often less competent than the producers, namely, the professors and researchers. The consequence was an oppressive colonization of academic culture by the culture of auditing. This development was politically motivated, according to Amman, and was aimed at undermining the autonomy of research institutes and universities.

Here again, as Menger and Mairesse (2015) have shown, "performance culture" has had a perverse impact on the relation between the evaluation of research and the evaluation of teaching. Research is a competitive activity while teaching is only modestly so, if at all. Today, international systems for rating and ranking universities, such as the famous Shanghai Ranking,[19] give greater weight to research than to teaching because the former's added value is easier to calculate using

19. Established in 2003 by Shanghai's Jiao Tong University, the Annual Ranking of World Universities (ARWU) is published annually and has earned an international reputation. It covers universities that have at least one Nobel Prize winner or a Fields

standard economic indicators. This explains the numerous incentives created by university administrators to encourage the "production" of research by professors whose main job is to teach (that is, to transfer knowledge to the next generation). These inducements to engage in research at all costs have resulted in a proliferation of mediocre publications that inflate production statistics in order to satisfy the indicators. This disastrous British situation, which should have served as a negative example for other European countries, was instead taken as a model and generated, during the 2000s, a national and European Union bureaucracy that administers research in the manner of the "Parallel Campaign" described by Robert Musil in *The Man without Qualities*, a great project whose goal and content are difficult to determine:

> Diotima began by calling the Parallel Campaign a unique, never-to-recur opportunity to bring into existence what must be regarded as the greatest and most important thing in the world. "We must and will bring to life a truly great idea. We have the opportunity, and we must not fail to use it." "Do you have something specific in mind," Ulrich asked naively. No, Diotima did not have anything specific in mind. How could she? No one who speaks of the greatest and most important thing in the world means anything that really exists. What peculiar property of the world would it be equivalent to? It all amounts to one thing being greater and more important, or more beautiful and sadder, than another; in other words, the existence of a hierarchy of values

---

Medal winner on their faculties and a considerable number of publications in *Nature* and *Science*.

> and the comparative mode, which surely implies an end point and a superlative. (1996, 95)

Playing for prestige according to the new rules of academic competition is not unlike playing the game of humiliation with which this chapter began. In our eagerness to win contemporary ranking competitions, we end up destroying the "immortal part of us," namely our reputations as scientists and scholars devoted to the pursuit of knowledge for knowledge's own sake.

10

Reputation in Democracies

INSTRUCTIONS FOR USE

> A thing is a thing, not what is said of that thing.
>
> —ALEJANDRO G. IÑÁRRITU, *BIRDMAN OR (THE UNEXPECTED VIRTUE OF IGNORANCE)*

In the Academy Award–winning film *Birdman*, an apocryphal quotation from Susan Sontag is taped to the dressing-room mirror of Riggan Thomson, a Hollywood actor once famous for his performances, two decades earlier, in the title role of a series of films dedicated to the superhero Birdman. The quote reads, cryptically: "A thing is a thing, not what is said of that thing." As the film opens, Thomson is trying to relaunch his career, this time as a stage actor on Broadway. He wants to rediscover an authenticity that he feels he lost when basking self-indulgently in the fanfare he enjoyed as a Hollywood superhero. But his Birdman alter ego, like a voice from the past, continues to torment him. It urges him to drop his highbrow Broadway ambitions and reassume the larger-than-life personality that the mega-public for superheroes once projected upon him. The siren song of his inner Birdman is calling him back toward a self that was constructed entirely by the gaze of admiring moviegoers. At first, Riggan resists and fights back. He redoubles his commitment to staging a theatrical adaptation of Raymond Carver's *What We Talk About When We Talk About Love*. But in the end he yields. The implication of the film seems to be that there is no true self and no inauthentic self. We are what others say we are. We are nothing more. No profound identity lurks beyond or beneath our social image. There is no intimate and hidden part of us that is solely our own, unshared by others. There is no real ego to be espied on the far side of the thousand social mirrors that refract our image. We do not exist independently of what others say and think about us.

Riggan Thomson's conscience is a cartoon version of Hegelian "spirit." His ego is nothing other than his insatiable craving to be recognized, his desire to be noticed and attended to by others. And does not Raymond Carver's story have a similar implication? After all, what does Carver himself speak about when he speaks about love? Isn't he, too, preoccupied with the way life is lived in and through the eyes of others? In the story that lends its title to Carver's short-story collection, Terri's former and abusive boyfriend, Ed, discovers that she does not love him anymore. And isn't his subsequent suicide an act of love? For Carver apparently yes, because without Terri's love, Ed simply does not exist.

The protagonist of *Birdman* is torn and disoriented. Reflected images of his former superhero self ricochet endlessly around him in a cacophony of forms of recognition that mingle success, glory, art, popularity, and finally love. The dizzying truth that agitates and perturbs his mind is that the apocryphal quote fastened to his dressing-room mirror is entirely false and that, to the contrary, his seductive Birdman doppelgänger is essentially right: *a thing is nothing but what is said about that thing.*

The theme of *Birdman* has been the theme of this book as well: what people say about us and, indeed, about everything that exists provides the only available window through which we can come to know ourselves and recognize the world. The reason is simple: to exist means to be assigned a value in a *ranking*, in a system that makes comparisons possible. To be is to be comparable.

This "metaphysics of morals" has significant epistemological and political implications. Let's begin with epistemology. As we have already seen, the claim that *to be is to be compared* overturns the classical conception of knowledge according to which awareness of an object of knowledge precedes its evaluation. What I have been arguing, on the contrary, is that we evaluate in order to know, meaning we have to locate the objects of our knowledge in an evaluative system so that we can compare them with each other. This perspective does not require us to sink into radical relativism according to which, since everything is "constructed," no objectivity is possible. Even if the world as we know it were entirely constructed, in any case, certain ways of constructing it would be more legitimate than others and would contribute more than others to improving our intellectual and moral life. While depending on various systems for classifying and assessing information that help us make sense of what surrounds us, for example, we can still distinguish good and bad uses of reputation as a source of knowledge or reason for belief.

The systemic biases and cognitive deficits detailed in chapters 4 and 5 show that distinguishing between good and bad uses of reputation requires a certain *epistemic responsibility*. If I trust a doctor simply because his office is located in a prestigious part of town, I am obviously using a defective reputational heuristic that has little chance of providing me with an objective evaluation of the doctor in question. If I pay attention to other clues (for example, the doctor's collegial network and medical-school diplomas, the hospital where the doctor has admitting privileges, and possibly the doctor's medical publications), then I can arrive at a more accurate, albeit more indirect, estimate of his or her professional competence. Judicious use of evidence depends not only on the secondhand information available to me but also on my epistemic responsibility, that is, on a cognitively vigilant attitude toward my sources of information and the reasons that lead me to trust them.

Most of the information available to us is indirect and dependent on the assessments of others. But this does not necessarily make us gullible or easy to manipulate, contrary to the mildly paranoid thesis advanced by those—from Cass Sunstein in his essay *Infotopia* to French sociologist Gérald Bronner in *La démocratie des crédules*—who have written about the social acquisition of knowledge in contemporary societies. Rather than turning us into dupes, the synergy among new collective mechanisms for the acquisition and filtering of information has made us into more sophisticated cognitive creatures than in the past. It is simply that we now exercise different cognitive skills. Our social cognition—our grasp of who is trustworthy or which informants are reliable—is today much more important than our individual mastery of the kinds of inference that can now perhaps be better carried out by calculating machines! Epistemic responsibility for culling "good" information from the mass of information available falls on both the informant and the recipient of the information. Those who receive information cannot be passive and unthinking, incapable of criticizing their own cognitive biases, like children willing to believe whatever they hear. Of course, informants should behave honestly and conscientiously when conveying information. But the world being imperfect, those who receive information from informants of uncertain integrity must always stay alert to the possibility of disinformation. If I trust a Web page without even checking what URL it came from, I'm not behaving like a responsible consumer of information. If I implicitly trust a scientific result because it is published in a classified digital document on the Web with a DOI (Digital Object Identifier) number attached, without knowing anything about how and why DOI numbers are assigned to documents (numbers that, in reality, can be easily acquired by any institution and that have nothing to do with the scientific prestige of the publication, making them similar to the ISBN of a book), in this case, too, I have not made a responsible use of my epistemic capacities. If I believe that the best university in the world is the one that is at the top of an international ranking whose standards of excellence and whose selection procedures are totally opaque to me, I am again behaving in an epistemically irresponsible way. There is, in general, no reason to accept uncritically the verdicts of rating agencies, including those that rank academic institutions, any more than we should blindly trust the information-filtering algorithms that play an increasingly prominent role in our cognitive lives. Evaluation systems and information-filtering mechanisms are never wholly neutral and can always be criticized through a second-order analysis of the way in which they were constructed. Epistemic responsibility means refusing to defer uncritically to imposed value hierarchies and mental schemes.

In this sense, most political and institutional decisions today are made in an irresponsible manner because based on the uncritical acceptance of (potentially spurious) indicators announcing that the reputation of a certain person or organization, for instance, is merited, even when no one has bothered to examine how such a conclusion was reached. This becomes particularly evident when we examine the impact of specific reputational signals and their power of seduction. Not even the most cynical editors and literary critics will remain indifferent to the new winner of the National Book Award or the Prix Goncourt, even if they are perfectly aware of the less than transparent procedures by which such prizes are bestowed. It is as if a blind faith in the serendipity of events, an epistemic fatalism tinged with unjustified optimism, tacitly structures the way we decide which information is reliable. A combination of circumstances, often utterly fortuitous, can cause a person or object that interests us to be highly ranked in a public and semi-official way. And once this ranking becomes common knowledge, that person or object will never again look the same in our eyes. They will have received a reputational bonus from the simple fact of having been placed high on an important list, whatever undisclosed considerations actually brought them there. This indirect effect of ranking can be illustrated by the snob who loves hobnobbing in venues frequented by the fashionably rich because, even though gate-crashing will not make him any more prosperous, merely being in attendance gives him a feeling of belonging to the happy few.

The problem, as we have seen, is that our intuitive judgments about the value of reputational cues, though perhaps harmless in the case of snobs, become dangerous when they affect political life and public choices. This is not to say that naive and ill-informed uses of reputational indicia by institutions are always malevolent. (Explanatory approaches that savor of paranoia should be avoided.) Often they are simply the result of ignorance. On the other hand, the ignorance of rulers might reasonably be judged a form of professional malpractice. In any case, as Harry Frankfurt argued in his little essay *On Bullshit* (2006), incompetence can sometimes be a worse sin than dishonesty, because the incompetent cannot even assume responsibility for their own socially damaging transgressions.

Inhabitants of a society that lives on reputation, on information gleaned from rankings, need to develop skills to navigate a deluge of value-laden information. We should not accept uncritically the result of any ranking without first examining how it was made and who made it. Today, for example, new academic assessment metrics have been introduced in almost every country and, together with international metrics such as the SCI and other similar algorithms, they allow non-scientists and non-academics to evaluate the scientific work of academics. A critical approach toward these indexes, aimed at combatting their misuse, has developed only recently and in the rather specialized field of the sociology of science, producing some serious critical literature that has, however, done little to inhibit the ill-informed appeals to such metrics. Evaluating a scientific researcher by measuring that researcher's "output," when we know that in many cases he or she produces only to satisfy standard measurement criteria (a bit like Keynes's proposal to have workers dig holes so that they can subsequently fill them in), should not affect something as serious as determining the worth of a researcher's contribution to science.

We still lack appropriate and effective methods for navigating among epistemic hierarchies and guarding against an obtuse and potentially authoritarian manipulation of ranking methods that affect and can sometimes unfairly solidify reputations. Throughout the long history of philosophy, traditional epistemology has dealt with direct knowledge of the world, namely perception and inference. But the epistemology that interests us today, focused on *indirect* knowledge of the world, has a very short history. As a consequence, what are often presented as ways to render evaluation objective, namely ranking systems and metrics of popularity and prestige, are based on prescientific intuitions and subjective anxieties about social status strongly influenced by traditional prejudices associated with the perception of hierarchy. This brings us, by way of conclusion, to the good and bad uses of reputation as a source of recognition and social identity, in other words, to the ethical and political dimensions of our subject.

Honor, Hierarchies, and Democracy

In the social sciences, starting with Durkheim and Weber, it was commonplace to analyze the evolution of Western society as a transition from highly stratified and patriarchal societies (systems in which social hierarchies were associated with political rulers and dynasties) to a society ruled by bureaucracy, an acephalous system of rational management in which, as Weber says, "in this respect the most irresistible force is rational discipline, which eradicates not only personal charisma but also stratification by status groups, or at least transforms them in a rationalizing direction."[1] If archaic societies were typi-

1. "Mit der Rationalisierung der politischen und ökonomischen Bedarfsdeckung geht das Umsichgreifen der Disziplinierung als einer universellen Erscheinung unaufhaltsam vor sich und schränkt die Bedeutung des Charisma und des individuelle differenzierten Handelns zunehmend ein" (Weber 1922, 655). For the English, see Weber 1978, 1149.

cally based on particularisms, such as kinship, personal loyalty, and hierarchies imposed arbitrarily from above, modernization involves an irresistible process of rationalization, universalization, depersonalization, and increasing egalitarianism.

Modernity, or rather late modernity, is often associated in the social sciences with the rationalization of honor and prestige relations through the replacement of "status" by "contract" as the main organizing principle of society. The bureaucratization of the world, according to this view, goes hand in hand with its disenchantment. Interpersonal relationships are no longer founded on the status or honor attributed to individuals on the basis of ascription and lineage but rather on the basis of the bureaucratic office that an individual occupies, an office allegedly defined and assigned in an impersonal manner without regard to the family background or bloodline of the officeholder. The social status of individuals in modern society is said to depend on the place they have obtained in a hierarchy, not on their family's reputation. So if modern bureaucracies have rationalized social status, they have certainly not eliminated it. The organizations that populate contemporary societies locate individuals in hierarchies and thereby reproduce earlier symbolic struggles to attain higher status. Universities issue certificates, diplomas, and awards in order to erect hierarchies of merit among students. We know that people employed by an organization for a long and uninterrupted stretch of years acquire *seniority*, a status that gives them privileges that newcomers do not share.

Understanding the resiliently hierarchical patterning of late modern societies means identifying a link or continuity between archaic and modern social orders. Liberal democracy and the market economy, based as they are on perceived self-interest rather than communal bonds, have not eliminated the hierarchical structures shaping social ties in a society. Admittedly, modern organizations justify hierarchies as a condition for effectiveness. Yet, as sociologist Roger Gould has demonstrated, this explanation "presupposes that people have an interest in occupying superior roles and a certain disposition to accept subordinate positions" (2003, 21). Otherwise hierarchies based on effectiveness would be unsustainable. True, we can imagine incentive systems that do not depend essentially on relations between superiors and inferiors. But the fact that such hierarchies are ubiquitous even in market democracies indicates the importance of such comparative relations of superiority and inferiority in our society as well.

One might argue that the presence of hierarchies within societies today represents only an efficacious use by modern organizations of vestigial habits surviving from traditional society. It is perfectly rational for a complex bureaucratic system to exploit traditional springs of action, such as deference to authority and the desire to command, to run parts of a modern polity, including the army, the school system, universities, and public administration, where personal success is rewarded more by social prestige than by material benefits. But we can also explain the ubiquity of hierarchies in ostensibly "egalitarian" modern societies in a different way, by invoking the structure of individual relations. Gould, a leading scholar of the origins of hierarchy, argues that as social relationships grow more complex, struggles for positions of status and preeminence also multiply. That is why hierarchies emerge or reemerge even when a central institution attempts to suppress them. The competition for visibility, for positioning, is therefore a natural social proclivity. No process of social evolution can eliminate it entirely. In a hyperconnected world like ours, social networks proliferate and thereby increase opportunities for individuals to compare themselves with each other; the vertical polarity between "high" and "low" resurfaces in a seemingly irrepressible way.

So what can we do to resist this spontaneous tendency toward a stratification of social relationships seemingly generated by the very nature of social interaction? Among other things, we should begin to develop, in the social sciences, theories that take as their unit of analysis not the rational self-interested actor, still dominant in economics and the neoclassical theory of rational choice, but a much more complex and dramatic personality, a reputational actor who is eminently social and whose rationality cannot be explained without taking symbolic motivations into account. The problem with the rationally calculating and self-interested agents assumed by classical theories is less their egoism than their radical insulation from others, their insensitivity to what others think of them, and how such opinions condition them. To act rationally means, among other things, anticipating the likely impact of our actions on the social network that recognizes us and that helps stabilize our identity, a network that our every action necessarily perturbs and modifies. Individuals act to project a social image that helps give them a recognizable identity. This projection occurs through interaction with others, creating relationships of trust on one hand and of domination/subordination on the other and thereby ceaselessly distributing and redistributing social status. If we do not take these consequences of our actions into account, if we limit ourselves to an individualistic and self-interested theory of behavior, not only will we run the risk of no longer understanding the true springs of human action, but we will also be tempted to structure institutions around incentives and sanctions that ignore what motivates people to act, assuming the existence of an abstract subject that does not match who human beings really are. Just as in the case of epistemology, where the social dimension of evaluation (ontologically) precedes the individual acquisition of knowledge, so in politics and morality, social interaction precedes individual action. Our future understanding of social action will depend essentially on how well our future social science theories manage to grasp the nature of *homo comparativus*.

Identity Amplified on the Web

Our lives today are thoroughly interwoven with social networks. A second aspect of this new "lifeworld" (*Lebenswelt*) is the permanent generation of "avatars" of our social image: personal Web pages, Facebook profiles, the various public traces of ourselves that we continually generate. Our social information accompanies us everywhere and renders us both stronger and more fragile. It makes us stronger because it allows us to "manage" our identity in a way that would be impossible in societies where social information is managed exclusively from above. On the other hand we all know the extent to which such traces escape our personal control. They are manipulated and refract, rather than reflect, our image into myriad fragments in which we do not always recognize ourselves.

The reasons others talk about us are seldom the reasons we want them to talk about us. The fraught relation between our aspirational or idealized self-image and the way others, speaking among themselves, actually depict and evaluate our character and behavior has been one of the persistent themes of this book. The gap may be large and personally frustrating or small and personally gratifying. To improve our understanding of this tense and fertile relation, I have tried to theorize afresh the process by which human identities are constructed, including the way we project images of ourselves as unique individuals (following modernity's stress on individualism in law, art, marriage, religion, science, education, sport, and so forth), as opposed to passive acquiescence in the inauthentic roles supposedly "ascribed" by preindustrial or traditional social orders.

The human subject in the Internet age is neither authentic nor phony. Indeed, the distinction between authenticity (complete freedom from the opinions of others) and bad faith (renouncing inner freedom and succumbing to social pressures) is much too sharply drawn. The human being today is an intensely social subject, a cognitive being who constructs itself through the continuous internalization of feedback received from observers whose reflected judgments the targeted subject then seeks ceaselessly to influence and embellish. In other words, the human subject has a double nature, and that is why it cannot simplify itself, or become "one," without dissolving itself entirely. If we nevertheless wished to attribute some meaning to the concept of "authenticity," we might define it as the encounter, rare and perfect, between the image we want to give of ourselves and the way we are seen by others, as in the famous Gatsby's smile discussed in chapter 4. In such cases, our social ego, our reputation, allows us to feel that we are what we would like to be when others wholeheartedly accept our idealized self-image.

But notice: we become authentic not by turning our backs on society in a gesture of total (or "inner") freedom but, on the contrary, precisely thanks to the gaze of others. Reputation is not a mere shadow cast by our character on the wall. Such a trite image denies any constitutive role of reputation in the development of character. Exposing the inadequacy of this cavalierly dismissive attitude toward reputation has been one of the central purposes of this book. Our dynamically shape-shifting reputation is an integral and dynamic ingredient in the development of human personality. Our ego is double and its double nature is what motivates us. Without consciousness of the interdependence between me and my image in the eyes of others, between my actions and my reputation, I cannot understand either who I am or why I act.

REFERENCES

Akerlof, G. A. 1970. "The Market for 'Lemons': Quality Uncertainty and the Market Mechanism." *Quarterly Journal of Economics* 84, no. 3: 488–500.

Alexander, R. D. 1986. "Ostracism and Indirect Reciprocity: The Reproductive Significance of Humour." *Ethology and Sociobiology* 7:253–70.

———. 1987. *The Biology of Moral Systems*. New York: De Gruyter.

Allen, E., and B. Beckwith. 1975. "Against Sociobiology." *New York Review of Books*, November 13. http://www.nybooks.com/articles/archives/1975/nov/13/against-sociobiology/.

Allport, G., and J. Portman. 1947. *The Psychology of Rumors*. Cambridge, MA: Harvard University Press.

Amman, R. 2003. "A Sovietological View of Modern Britain." *Political Quarterly* 74, no. 4: 287–301.

Appadurai, A. 1986. *The Social Life of Things*. Cambridge: Cambridge University Press.

Appiah, A. 2010. *The Honor Code: How Moral Revolutions Happen*. New York: W. W. Norton.

Axelrod, R. 1984. *The Evolution of Cooperation*. New York: Basic Books.

Baier, A. 1991. "Trust." The Tanner Lectures. Princeton University, March 6–8.

Balzac, H. de. 1999. *Béatrix*. Trans. K. P. Wormeley. Project Gutenberg Etext.

———. 2004. *Lost Illusions*. Trans. H. Hunt. New York: Penguin.

Bartlett, F. 1932. *Remembering: A Study in Experimental and Social Psychology*. Cambridge: Cambridge University Press.

Baumard, N., and D. Sperber. 2013. "Morale et réputation dans une perspective évolutionniste." In Origgi 2013b, 11–28.

Beckert, J., and P. Aspers, eds. 2011. *The Worth of Goods*. New York: Oxford University Press.

Beckert, J., and C. Musselin. 2013. *Constructing Quality*. New York: Oxford University Press.

Benjamin, W. 1968. *Illuminations*. Trans. H. Zohn. New York: Schocken.

Besnier, N. 2009. *Gossip and the Everyday Production of Politics*. Honolulu: University of Hawaii Press.

Biagioli, M. 2002. "From Book Censorship to Academic Peer Review." *Emergences* 12, no. 1: 1–45.

Biagioli, M., and P. Galison. 2003. *Scientific Authorship: Credit and Intellectual Property in Science.* London: Routledge.

Bjork, B. C., and D. Solomon. 2014. "The Publishing Delay in Scholarly Peer-Reviewed Journals." http://openaccesspublishing.org/oa11/article.pdf.

Blumenthal, S. 2017. "The First Family." *London Review of Books* 39, no. 4.

Boltanski, L., and L. Thévenot. 1991. *De la justification.* Paris: Gallimard.

Bourdieu, P. 1979. *La Distinction.* Paris: Minuit. English translation. 1984. *Distinction.* London: Routledge.

———. 1980. "Le capital social: Notes provisoires." *Actes de la recherche en sciences sociales*, no. 31 (January): 2–3.

———. 1984. *Homo academicus.* Paris: Minuit, 1984.

———. 1986. "The Forms of Capital." In *Handbook of Theory and Research for the Sociology of Education*, ed. J. Richardson, 241–58. Westport, CT: Greenwood.

Brennan, G., and P. Pettit. 2004. *The Economy of Esteem: An Essay on Civil and Political Society.* New York: Oxford University Press.

Bronner, G. 2013. *La démocratie des crédules.* Paris: Presses Universitaires de France.

Burt, R. S. 2005. *Brokerage and Closure: An Introduction to Social Capital.* New York: Oxford University Press.

Carnevali, B. 2003. "'Glory': La lutte pour la réputation dans le modèle hobbesien." *Communications* 93:49–67.

———. 2006. "Aura et Ambiance: Léon Daudet tra Proust e Benjamin." *Rivista di Estetica* 46, no. 33: 117–41.

———. 2012. *Romantisme et reconnaissance.* Geneva: Droz.

———. 2013. *Le apparenze sociali.* Bologna: Il Mulino.

Carrère, E. 2000. *L'Adversaire.* Paris: P.O.L. English translation by L. Coverdale. 2001. *The Adversary: A True Story of Monstrous Deception.* New York: Bloomsbury.

Carrière, J. 1987. *Les cendres de la gloire ou le prix d'un Goncourt.* Paris: Editions Robert Laffont.

Casati, R., G. Origgi, and J. Simon. 2011. "Micro-credits in Scientific Publishing." *Journal of Documentation* 67, no. 6: 958–74.

Charcot, J.-M. 1892–93. *Clinique des maladies du système nerveux.* Ed. G. Guinon. Paris: Bureau du Progrès Medical.

Chauvin, P. M. 2013. "La sociologie des réputations." *Communications* 93:131–46.

Christenson, J. A., and L. Sigelman. 1985. "Accrediting Knowledge: Journal Stature and Citation Impact in Social Science." *Social Science Quarterly* 66:964–75.

Cialdini, R. 1984. *Influence: The Psychology of Persuasion.* New York: Harper and Collins.

Cicourel, A. 1974. *Cognitive Sociology: Language and Meaning in Social Interaction.* New York: Free Press.

Clément, F. 2012. Preface to *Anatomie de la rumeur* by C. Sunstein. Geneva: Markus Haller.

Cogswell, J. 1836. "Principle of Emulation." *North American Review* 93, no. 43: 496–515.

Cohen, D., R. E. Nisbett, B. Bowdle, and N. Schwarz. 1996. "Insult, Aggression, and the Southern Culture of Honor: An 'Experimental Ethnography.'" *Journal of Personality and Social Psychology* 70, no. 5: 945–60.

Coleman, J. 1988. "Social Capital in the Creation of Human Capital." *American Journal of Sociology* 94:95–120.

Cooley, C. H. 1902. *Human Nature and the Social Order*. New York: Charles Scribner's Sons.

Darnton, R. 2010. *The Devil in the Holy Water, or the Art of Slander from Louis XIV to Napoleon*. Philadelphia: University of Pennsylvania Press.

Darwall, S. 2004. "Respect and the Second Person Standpoint." *Proceedings and Addresses of the American Philosophical Association* 78:43–60.

———. 2013. *Honor, History and Relationship*. New York: Oxford University Press.

De Beauvoir, S. 2009. *The Second Sex*. New York: Vintage.

Deutsche Bank. 2015. "Reed Elsevier: Moving the Supertanker." *Company Focus: Global Equity Research Report*. January.

Douglas, M. 1987. *How Institutions Think*. London: Routledge and Kegan Paul.

Duerr, P. 1998. *Nudité et pudeur: Le mythe de la civilization*. Paris: Editions de la Maison des Sciences de l'Homme.

Dumont, L. 1966. *Homo Hierarchicus*. Paris: Gallimard.

Dunbar, R. 1996. *Grooming, Gossip and the Evolution of Language*. London: Faber and Faber.

Edlin, A. S., and D. L. Rubinfeld. 2004. "Exclusion or Efficient Pricing? The 'Big Deal' Bundling of Academic Journals." *Antitrust Law Journal* 72:128–59.

Elias, N. 1983. *The Court Society*. New York: Pantheon Books. English translation of the German original: *Die höfische Gesellschaft*. Berlin: Hermann Luchterhand Verlag, 1969.

———. 1994. *The Civilizing Process*. London: Blackwell. Partial translation of *Über den Prozeß der Zivilisation*. Basel: Verlag Haus zum Falken, 1939.

Elias, N., H. Martins, and R. Whitley, eds. 1982. *Scientific Establishments and Hierarchies: Sociology of the Sciences*. Vol. 6. Dordrecht: Reidel Publishing Company.

Elias, N., and J. L. Scotson. 1994. *The Established and the Outsider*. New York: Sage.

Eliot, T. S. 1934/1963. "Choruses from 'The Rock.'" In *Collected Poems, 1909–1962*. Boston: Houghton Mifflin Harcourt.

Elster, J. 1983. *Sour Grapes*. Cambridge: Cambridge University Press.

———. 1999. *The Alchemies of the Mind*. New York: Cambridge University Press.

———. 2009. *Le désintéressement*. Paris: Seuil.

———. 2013. "Réputation et caractère." In Origgi 2013b, 29–48.

Erner, G. 2016. *La souverainété du people*. Paris: Gallimard.

Fenster, T. S., and D. L. Smail, eds. 2003. *Fama: The Politics of Reputation in Medieval Europe*. Ithaca: Cornell University Press.

Figes, O. 1996. *A People's Tragedy: The Russian Revolution, 1891–1924*. New York: Penguin.

———. 2012. *Just Send Me Word*. New York: Metropolitan Books.

Fitzgerald, F. S. *The Great Gatsby*. New York: Scribner, 2004.

Foucault, M. 1970. *The Order of Things*. New York: Pantheon Books.

———. 1977. "Nietzsche, Genealogy, History." In *Language, Counter-memory, Practice: Selected Essays and Interviews*, ed. D. Bouchard, 139–64. Ithaca: Cornell University Press.

Frank, R. 1988. *Passions within Reason: The Strategic Role of Emotions*. New York: W. W. Norton.

Frankfurt, H. 2006. *De l'art de dire des conneries*. Paris: Editions 10/18.

Gambetta, D. 2009. "Signaling." In *The Oxford Handbook of Analytical Sociology*, 168–94. Oxford: Oxford University Press.

Gergaud, O., F. Livat, B. Rickard, and F. Warzynski. 2016. "The Costs and Benefits of Collective Reputation: Who Gains and Who Loses from Generic Promotion Programs?" Working Papers 231135. American Association of Wine Economists.

Gigerenzer, G., R. Hertwig, and T. Pachur, eds. 2011. *Heuristics: The Foundations of Adaptive Behavior*. New York: Oxford University Press.

Glucksman, M. 1963. "Gossip and Scandal." *Current Anthropology* 4, no. 3: 308–16.

Goffman, E. 1956. *The Presentation of Self in Everyday Life*. New York: Random House.

———. 1967. *Interaction Rituals: Essays in Face to Face Behaviour*. New York: Aldine.

Gould, R. 2002. "The Origins of Status Hierarchies: A Formal Theory and an Empirical Test." *American Journal of Sociology* 107, no. 5: 1143–78.

———. 2003. *Collision of Wills*. Chicago: University of Chicago Press.

Gould, S., and R. Lewontin. 1979. "The Spandrels of San Marco and the Panglossian Paradigm: A Critique of the Adaptationist Program." *Proceedings of the Royal Society of London* 205, no. 1161: 581–98.

Granovetter, M. S. 1973. "The Strength of Weak Ties." *American Journal of Sociology* 6:1360–80.

———. 1985. "Economic Action and Social Structure: The Problem of Embeddedness." *American Journal of Sociology* 91, no. 3: 481–510.

Grice, P. 1957. "Meaning." *Philosophical Review* 66, no. 3: 377–88.

Gruenewald, T., et al. 2004. "Acute Threat to the Social Self: Shame, Social Self-esteem, and Cortisol Activity." *Psychosomatic Medicine* 66:915–24.

Haldane, W. D. 1955. "Population Genetics." *New Biology* 18:34–51.

Haley, K., and D. Fessler. 2006. "Nobody's Watching? Subtle Cues Affect Generosity in an Anonymous Economic Game." *Evolution and Human Behavior* 26, no. 3: 245–56.

Hamermesh, D. S., and G. A. Pfann. 2009. "Markets for Reputation: Evidence on Quality and Quantity in Academe." NBER Working Paper 15527. Cambridge, MA: National Bureau of Economic Research.

Hamilton, W. D. 1963. "The Evolution of Altruistic Behavior." *American Naturalist* 97, no. 896: 354–56.

Hayek, F. A. 1945. "The Use of Knowledge in Society." *American Economic Review* 35, no. 4: 519–30.

———. 1978. *Law, Legislation and Liberty*. Vol. 1. Chicago: University of Chicago Press.

Heinich, N. 2012. *De la visibilité*. Paris: Gallimard.

Henrich, J., R. Boyd, et al. 2004. *Foundations of Human Sociality: Economic Experiments and Ethnographic Evidence from Fifteen Small-Scale Societies*. Oxford: Oxford University Press.

Henrich, J., and F. Gil-White. 2001. "The Evolution of Prestige." *Evolution and Human Behavior* 22:165–96.

Hirsch, P. M. 1972. "Processing Fads and Fashions: An Organization-Set Analysis of Cultural Industry Systems." *American Journal of Sociology* 77, no. 4: 639–59.

Hobbes, T. 1640. *The Elements of Law, Natural and Politic*. http://www.constitution.org/th/elements.htm.

Hughson, A. L., and R. A. Boakes. 2002. "The Knowing Nose: The Role of Knowledge in Wine Expertise." *Food Quality and Preference* 13, no. 7–8: 463–72.

Hume, D. 1985. "Of the Standard of Taste." In *Essays Moral, Political and Literary*. Indianapolis: Liberty Classics.

Ikegami, E. 1995. *The Taming of the Samurai: Honorific Individualism and the Making of Modern Japan*. Cambridge, MA: Harvard University Press.

"Internet Encyclopaedias Go Head to Head." 2005. *Nature* 438 (December 15).

Jinha, A. E. 2010. "Article 50 Millions: An Estimate of the Numbers of Scholarly Articles in Existence." *Learned Publishing* 23:258–63.

Johnson, H., and J. Robinson. 2014. *World Atlas of Wine*. 7th ed. London: Mitchell Beazley.

Kahneman, D. 2010. *Thinking, Fast and Slow*. New York: Random House.

Kant, I. 1798/2006. *Anthropology from a Pragmatic Point of View*. Ed. R. B. Louden. Cambridge: Cambridge University Press.

Karpik, L. 1995. *Les avocats entre l'Etat, le public et le marché: XIIIème–XXème siècle*. Paris: Gallimard.

———. 2010. *Valuing the Unique: The Economics of Singularities*. Princeton: Princeton University Press.

———. 2011. "What Is the Price of a Scientific Paper?" In *The Worth of Goods*, ed. J. Beckert, P. Aspers. New York: Oxford University Press.

Katz, D., and F. H. Allport. 1931. *Students' Attitude*. Syracuse, NY: Craftsmann.

Kaufmann, L., and F. Clément, eds. 2011. *La sociologie cognitive*. Paris: Maison des Sciences de l'Homme.

Keynes, J. M. 1936. *The General Theory of Employment, Interest and Money*. London: Macmillan.

Kleinberg, J. 2001. "The Structure of the Web." *Science* 294, no. 5528: 1849–50.

Knapp, R. H. 1944. "A Psychology of Rumor." *Public Opinion Quarterly* 8, no. 1: 22–37.

Kuran, T. 1997. *Private Truths, Public Lies*. Cambridge, MA: Harvard University Press.

Kurzban, R. 2001. "The Social Psychophysics of Cooperation: Nonverbal Communication in a Public Goods Game." *Journal of Nonverbal Behavior* 25, no. 4: 241–59.

Laclos, P. C. de. 1995. *Les Liaisons dangereuses*. Trans. D. Parmée. Oxford: Oxford University Press.

Lamont, M. 2012. "Toward a Comparative Sociology of Valuation and Evaluation." *Annual Review of Sociology* 38, no. 21: 201–21.

Landon, S., and C. E. Smith. 1998. "Quality Expectations, Reputation and Price." *Southern Economic Journal* 64, no. 3: 628–47.

Lazarsfeld, P., and R. Merton. 1948. "Mass Communication, Popular Taste and Organized Social Action." In *The Communication of Ideas*, ed. L. Bryson. New York: Harper and Brothers.

Leary, M. 2005. "Sociometer Theory and the Pursuit of Relational Value: Getting to the Root of Self-esteem." *European Review of Social Psychology*, no. 16: 75–111.

Lessig, L. 2001. *The Future of Ideas: The Fate of the Commons in a Connected World.* New York: Random House.

Lewis, M., and D. Ramsay. 2002. "Cortisol Response to Embarrassment and Shame." *Child Development* 73:1034–45.

Lilti, A. 2014. *Figures publiques.* Paris: Fayard.

Mannheim, K. 1982. *Structures of Thinking.* London: Routledge and Kegan Paul.

Manzo, G., and D. Baldassarri. 2014. "Heuristics, Interactions, and Status Hierarchies: An Agent-Based Model of Deference Exchange." *Sociological Methods and Research*, pp. 1–59.

McGuigan, G., and R. D. Russell. 2008. "The Business of Academic Publishing: A Strategic Analysis of the Academic Journal Publishing Industry and Its Impact on the Future of Scholarly Publishing." *Electronic Journal of Academic and Special Librarianship* 9, no. 3.

Menger, P.-M. 2002. *Portrait de l'artiste en travailleur.* Paris: Seuil.

———. 2009. *Le travail créateur: S'accomplir dans l'incertain.* Paris: Gallimard-Seuil Hautes-Etudes.

Menger, P.-M., and J. Mairesse, eds. 2015. Introduction to the special issue: "Compétition, productivité, incitations et carrières dans l'enseignement supérieur et la recherche." *Revue Economique* 66, no. 1: 5–12.

Mercier, H., and D. Sperber. 2017. *The Enigma of Reason.* Cambridge, MA: Harvard University Press.

Merton, R. 1942/1973. "The Normative Structure of Science." In R. Merton, *The Sociology of Science*, ed. N. W. Stoler. Chicago: University of Chicago Press.

———. 1968. "The Matthew Effect in Science." *Science* 159:56–63.

———. 1972. "Insiders and Outsiders: A Chapter in the Sociology of Knowledge." *American Journal of Sociology* 78:9–47.

———. 1973. "Institutionalized Patterns of Evaluation in Science." In *The Sociology of Science.* Chicago: University of Chicago Press.

Migheli, M., and G. Ramello. 2014. "Open Access Journals and Academics' Behavior." *ICER Working Papers*, International Centre for Economic Research.

Milinski, M. 2016. "Reputation, a Universal Currency for Human Social Interactions." *Philosophical Transactions of the Royal Society.* B 371: 20150100.

Miller, G. D. 2012. *The Shadow of the Past.* Ithaca: Cornell University Press.

Monod, J. C. 2012. *Qu'est-ce qu'un chef en démocratie?* Paris: Seuil.

Montesquieu, C.-L. de Secondat. 1967. *Essai sur le goût.* Paris: Droz.

Moore, G. E. 1925. "A Defense of Common Sense." In *Contemporary British Philosophy*, 2nd ser., ed. J. H. Muirhead, 192–233. London: George Allen and Unwin.

Muldoon, R., C. Lisciandra, et al. 2014. "On the Emergence of Descriptive Norms." *Politics, Philosophy, and Economics* 13, no. 1: 3–22.

Musil, R. 1996. *The Man without Qualities*. Vol. 1. New York: Vintage.

Nisbett, R. E., and D. Cohen. 1996. *Culture of Honor: The Psychology of Violence in the South*. Boulder, CO: Westview Press.

Nowak, M. A., and K. Sigmund. 2005. "Evolution of Indirect Reciprocity." *Nature* 437:1291–98.

Origgi, G. 2010. "Epistemic Vigilance and Epistemic Responsibility in the Liquid World of Scientific Publications." *Social Epistemology* 24, no. 3: 149–59.

———. 2013a. "Un certain regard: Pour une épistémologie de la réputation." In Origgi 2013b, 101–20.

———, ed. 2013b. *La Réputation*, special issue of the journal *Communications* 93. Paris: Seuil.

Origgi, G., and P. Bonnier. 2013. "Trust, Networks and Democracy in the Age of the Social Web." *Proceedings of the ACM Web Science Conference*. May 2–4, Paris. http://www.websci13.org/program/.

Origgi, G., and S. Ciranna. 2017. "Epistemic Injustice: The Case of Digital Environments." In *The Routledge Handbook of Epistemic Injustice*, ed. J. Kidd, J. Medina, et al., ch. 29. New York: Routledge.

Origgi, G., and G. Ramello, eds. 2015. *Current Dynamics of Scholarly Publishing*, special issue of *Evaluation Review* 39, no. 1.

Orléan, A. 2014. *The Empire of Value*. Cambridge, MA: MIT Press.

Park, R. E. 1950. *Race and Culture*. Glencoe, IL: The Free Press.

Pasquino, P. 2007. "Eléazar ou le martyre juif." Paper presented at the workshop Réputation, Rome, Fondazione Olivetti, April.

Podolny, J. 2005. *Status Signals*. Princeton: Princeton University Press.

Podolny, J., and F. Lynn. 2009. "Status." In *Oxford Handbook of Analytical Sociology*, ed. P. Haedström and P. Bearman, 544–65. Oxford: Oxford University Press.

Proust, M. 2003–4. *In Search of Lost Time*. Gen. ed. C. Prendergast. Trans. L. Davis, M. Treharne, J. Grieve, J. Sturrock, C. Clark, P. Collier, and I. Patterson. 6 vols. London: Allen Lane. Based on the French La Pléiade edition (1987–89), except *The Fugitive*, which is based on the 1954 definitive French edition. Vols. 1–4: New York: Viking. Kindle ed.: M. Proust, *In Search of Lost Time*, trans. C. K. Scott Moncrieff and T. Kilmartin and rev. D. J. Enright. New York: Vintage.

Quine, W. V. O. 1960. *Word and Object*. Cambridge, MA: Harvard University Press.

Richerson, P. J., and R. Boyd. 2005. *Not by Genes Alone*. Chicago: University of Chicago Press.

Rochat, P. 2009. *Others in Mind: Social Origins of Self-Consciousness*. New York: Cambridge University Press.

Rochefoucauld, F. de La. 1678/2006. *Maximes et réflexions diverses*. Trans. J. Heard, *Maxims of Le Duc de la Rochefoucauld*. New York: Dover.

Rogers, R. 2004. *Information Politics on the Web*. Cambridge, MA: MIT Press.

Rooks, G., F. Tazelaar, and C. Snijders. 2010. "Gossip and Reputation in Business Networks." *European Sociological Review* 27, no. 1: 90–106.

Rousseau, J.-J. 2012. "Discourse on the Origins of Inequality." Part 2. In *The Major Political Writings of Jean-Jacques Rousseau: The Two "Discourses" and the "Social Contract."* Chicago: University of Chicago Press.

Santayana, G. 1922. *Soliloquies in England and Later Soliloquies*. New York: Scribner's.

Schumpeter, J. 1954. *History of Economic Analysis*. London: Allen and Unwin.

Schütz, A. 1964. *Collected Papers*. Vol. 2. Ed. A. Brodersen. The Hague: Martinus Nijhoff.

Séchelles, H. de. 1927. *Théorie de l'ambition*. Paris: Stendhal et compagnie.

Shapin, S. 1994. *A Social History of Truth*. Chicago: University of Chicago Press.

———. 2001. "Proverbial Economies: How an Understanding of Some Linguistic and Social Features of Common Sense Can Throw Light on More Prestigious Bodies of Knowledge, Science for Example." *Social Studies of Science* 31, no. 5: 731–69.

———. 2005. "Hedonistic Fruits Bombs." *London Review of Books* 27, no. 3.

Smith, A. *The Theory of Moral Sentiments*. 1759/1976. The Glasgow Edition of the Works and Correspondence of Adam Smith, vol. 1, ed. D. D. Raphael and A. L. Macfie. Oxford: Oxford University Press.

Sommerfeld, R. D., H. J. Krambeck, and M. Milinksi. 2008. "Multiple Gossip Statements and Their Effect on Reputation and Trustworthiness." *Proceedings of the Royal Society, Series B, Biological Sciences* 275, no. 1650: 2529–36.

Sperber, D. 1996. *Explaining Culture: A Naturalistic Approach*. London: Basil Blackwell.

———, ed. 2000. *Metarepresentations*. New York: Oxford University Press.

Sperber, D., and H. Mercier. 2017. *The Enigma of Reason*. Cambridge, MA: Harvard University Press.

Sunstein, C. 2009. *On Rumours*. Princeton: Princeton University Press.

Surowiecki, J. 2004. *The Wisdom of Crowds*. New York: Random House.

Tannen, D. 1990. *You Just Don't Understand*. New York: William Morrow.

Tirole, J. 1996. "A Theory of Collective Reputations." *Review of Economic Studies* 63, no. 1: 1–22.

Trivers, R. 1971. "The Evolution of Reciprocal Altruism." *Quarterly Review of Biology* 46:35–57.

Ullmann-Margalit, E. 1977. *The Emergence of Norms*. Oxford: Clarendon Press.

Veblen, T. 1899. *The Theory of the Leisure Class*. New York: Macmillan.

Weber, M. 1922. *Wirtschaft und Gesellschaft*. English translation. 1978. *Economy and Society*, ed. G. Roth and C. Wittich. Berkeley: University of California Press.

Willis, J., and A. Todorov. 2006. "First Impressions: Making Up Your Mind after a 100-ms Exposure to a Face." *Psychological Science* 17:592–98.

Wilson, E. O. 1975. *Sociobiology*. Cambridge, MA: Harvard University Press.

Ziman, J. M. 1966. *Public Knowledge: The Social Dimension of Science*. Cambridge: Cambridge University Press.

INDEX

A NOTE ON THE TYPE

This book has been composed in Adobe Text and Gotham. Adobe Text, designed by Robert Slimbach for Adobe, bridges the gap between fifteenth- and sixteenth-century calligraphic and eighteenth-century Modern styles. Gotham, inspired by New York street signs, was designed by Tobias Frere-Jones for Hoefler & Co.